TEACHING YOUR OWN PRESCHOOL CHILDREN

Kay Kuzma

TEACHING YOUR OWN PRESCHOOL CHILDREN

A DOUBLEDAY-GALILEE ORIGINAL

DOUBLEDAY & COMPANY, INC.
GARDEN CITY, NEW YORK, 1980

47,862

Drawings, based on the author's sketches, by Marta Cone

ISBN: 0-385-15822-x
Library of Congress Catalog Card Number 79-8733

Dedicated to my children, the students,
   Kimberly (which is long for "Kim"),
   Karlene (which is long for "Kari"),
   Kevin (which is just right)—
      for teaching me more than I taught them,
and to my husband, the principal,
   Jan,
      for his love and leadership.

Contents

Introduction

This is my diary/planbook of the plans, activities, and experiences Jan, my husband, and I had with our own children, Kim, Kari, and Kevin, during the school year when the children were five, four, and two years of age.

Teaching one's own child is a job for which few parents are formally prepared. But this does not negate the importance of the task. Actively teaching a child is something that must be done if the child is to achieve his potential adequately.

The rate at which young children learn is truly phenomenal. During the first six years the brain's development is most rapid and the rate of learning is greater than it will ever be again in the child's life. Language develops from coos and cries into the formation of complicated sentence structures and an understanding and production of over a thousand vocabulary words. From the simple uncontrolled flailing of arms and legs the child learns to grasp, crawl, walk, run, jump, and in many instances to swim, roller skate, and balance a two-wheeler. While we might interpret a responsive smile at about six weeks of age as the first sign of the child's social development, by six years he has established relationships not only with his family, but also with his own set of friends and acquaintances. The foundation for his personality development has been firmly laid, and barring significant changes that might occur in his life, he will probably be as an adult very much like the person he is as he enters that first-grade classroom.

Knowing all this, what is a parent's responsibility in guiding, teaching, and molding a young child who is rapidly developing in so many ways?

Every parent is a teacher, whether he or she chooses to be or not. The fact is, children learn both the positive and the negative from the adults they live with! But the quality of what the child learns will be in direct proportion to the quality of the teaching he receives. In most cases quality education in the home will not occur unless parents choose to offer the child the learning opportunities he needs to maximize his development.

By the time children are two, three, or four years of age, many parents choose to supplement their home teaching program with a nursery-school experience. I did too. All of my children have attended and thoroughly enjoyed nursery school with a wide variety of teachers, playmates, and fascinating materials and equipment. But one year my children begged, "Mommy, you teach us." I accepted their challenging request and became what I call a teacher-mother.

I discovered that being a teacher-mother was somewhat different than just being a mother or just being a teacher of other people's children. Although my goal was a 9–11 A.M. program, I soon found that preschool stretched into every part of the day—and sometimes the night. My home preschool curriculum was much broader than I had when I taught in the classroom. It now had to encompass everything from academics to character development. And my ultimate objective was far different. Not only was I preparing my children for meeting educational challenges successfully, but also I was preparing them to meet life's challenges successfully. I was not just responsible for supplementing a child's home experiences, I also had to build a total program that would hopefully maximize each of my own children's full developmental potential—without relying on someone else to fill in the gaps. Although I continued to plan learning activities to meet specific objectives, I became more and more attuned to taking advantage of the teachable moment—whether or not it came between 9:00 A.M. and 11:00 A.M. The biggest change was in my attitude. Where before I was committed to being a good mother, that job now took on new meaning as I became committed also to the task of teaching.

In a way, this book is a how-to book for other parents who want to provide a preschool experience for their children at home. Yet it is much more. It is an intimate journal of our family's life.

Many of the comments and incidents are very personal. I have tried not to edit out all of the bad, which might give the impression of an ideal family. Every family has both positive and negative experiences. Our family is no exception. However, in this book I have emphasized the positive experiences. Where we have failed, Jan and I are thankful we have the assurance that Christ can help us to overcome our mistakes and to continue growing and learning together as a family.

Jan's and my philosophy of child rearing (teaching) is our own. We haven't borrowed it in total from our parents or from child-rearing experts. Rather, we have remembered, listened, and read; we have sifted, sorted, and shared until we have developed a system that works for us. If I were to summarize our philosophy in a few words, I would say that we believe in having a good time together now as we train for the future. Our goal is to spend quality time together as a family so each individual can develop his potential within a warm, loving, and stimulating environment. We want to teach our children well.

I give special thanks to Ethel Young. Her friendship and professional guidance have brought satisfaction and enrichment to my life. I spent a week with Ethel at a General Conference Early Childhood Education workshop the summer before I began this book. As we talked and studied together, the first thoughts of becoming my children's teacher were sown.

To Pat Phillips a special thanks for critiquing and typing the manuscript for this book. And to Roland Phillips a special thanks for carrying the manuscript back and forth so many times without the loss of a page.

To Linda Larsen, the children's librarian at the Redland's A. K. Smiley Library, for her help through the years.

To Esther Glaser, who taught me and encouraged me to write.

To Jan, my husband and principal, who shares joyfully the responsibilities of teaching and caring for our children, I give public thanks. His concern is for our welfare, and he knows the children will be happy when I'm happy. His constant encouragement and high esteem for my motherly as well as for my professional activities lead me to sacrifice my own selfish desires in order to fulfill his trust.

I thank my parents, Willard and Irene Humpal, for giving me a beautiful home education. Their high expectations for me and their genuine pleasure in all of my accomplishments have always inspired me to do my best.

Finally and foremost, I give God the glory. For I know, "With men it is impossible, but not with God. For with God all things are possible." (Mk. 10:27)

SEPTEMBER — the door
We must open to explore
Preschool together

Tuesday, September 3 / The First Day

It's 7:30 A.M., the day after Labor Day. This is the day I promised my children we would start preschool together. I made the promise in one of those daydreaming moments at our vacation beach when I imagined I could do anything.

The children pressed me, "Mommy, when are you going to start preschool with us?"

Without thinking I replied, "After Labor Day."

"When is after Labor Day?"

"In September after our vacation."

"Right after our vacation?"

"Yes, right after our vacation," I agreed.

"Yippee, the day after Labor Day, the day after Labor Day," they all chanted.

I started today with my traditional "Things to Do" list.

Things to Do

unpack	write to relatives
can peaches	groceries
clean kitchen	call office
vacuum	water strawberries
dust	preschool
wash	

I was at the bottom of my list before I realized that today is the day after Labor Day, which means "preschool." I must remember tomorrow to put preschool at the top. After all, teaching my three little ones is the most important job I have. Everything else can wait, but their minds and bodies are growing quickly. They won't wait for me to finish all of the other items on my list.

One day at the beach I had worked out the teaching system I was going to use in our home preschool. I had decided that each day I would write different learning activities on three-by-five cards. The children could then choose which activity they wanted to do. When they had completed an activity they could keep the card in a box. It was a good idea, and I will plan to do it in the future, but I don't have time for that today.

Kim and Kari just walked into the study, where I am writing. With sleepy eyes and blankets in hand they announce, "Mommy, Kevin is awake."

I must go.

Later:

Before I knew it, nine o'clock had come. I realized that if I procrastinated any longer, the day would soon be over. I must start preschool, ready or not. So I informed the children that when they heard me playing the piano, they were to come running. That was to be the signal that preschool was beginning. It was then that Kim saved the day. "Oh goody," she said. "I want to bake a cake; learn to read; play a game; and . . ."

I immediately sat down with a blank piece of paper and as Kim mentioned an activity, I carefully printed it on the paper so that she could see it. This was her list:

Kim's "Things to Do" List

1. bake a cake	6. read story books
2. learn to read	7. play outside
3. play a game	8. cut and paste paper
4. play with felt pieces	9. pick up pretty rocks
5. draw	10. make sand bowls

The activities she selected were not exactly ones I would have chosen, remembering the peaches that needed to be canned and the long "Things to Do" list. But here was a start.

I then asked Kari what she wanted to learn. Being just fifteen months younger than Kim, it is easier for her just to copy what her sister says than to think of something herself. "What does Kim want to learn?" she asked.

"That's not fair," I countered. "This is your special list, because you are a special person who has good ideas of your own. What do *you* want to do?"

She thought of a few activities and then Kim decided that she wanted to do the same things. So as their "Things to Do" lists grew, they became more similar—while my day got shorter.

Kari's "Things to Do" List

1. learn ABCs
2. learn about money
3. pick pretty roses
4. bake a cake
5. play with felt pieces
6. cut and paste paper
7. pick up pretty rocks

When I asked Kevin what he wanted to do, he replied, "I no, no, no," which is his way of saying, "I don't know."

I tacked the children's lists on my kitchen bulletin board, which was already filled with their drawings and photographs, lists of activities, and special lectures for Jan and me to attend—if we aren't too busy or too tired—and my special "Lucy" poster, which expresses my daily wish: "I don't want any DOWNS, I just want UPS and UPS and UPS."

The "Things to Do" lists took care of my four- and five-year-olds, but what should I plan for Kevin? What do you plan for a two-year-old who won't interfere with the older children's activities?

In less than three minutes I prepared the environment. For Kevin, I put three puzzles and a book in one corner of the living room; for the girls I placed a cake mix, measuring cup, and bowls on the kitchen table, a matching game (match a word with an activity) on the coffee table, the felt pieces (animals, birds, and people) and the flannel board in one corner, and finally I placed a scale beside a bowl of grapefruit. I added the last activity as a surprise. I had picked up the old scale at a garage sale just before we left on our summer vacation, and hadn't had time to show the children how it worked.

After everything was ready I took a deep breath as if I were preparing for thirty children (how do teachers handle that many?) and sat down at the piano. I opened the hymnal to a familiar song and started playing "Praise Ye the Father." I love the hymn. It is so simple and majestic. And above everything else I want my children always to remember to praise God. The words seemed so appropriate:

> Praise ye the Father
> For His loving kindness.
> Tenderly cares He
> For His erring children . . .
>
> Anon

When I started playing, my three rambunctious children came running to begin their long-awaited adventure with their teacher-mother. I gathered them in my arms and suggested we could learn this hymn. The girls sat on the bench on each side of me, and Kevin sat on my lap.

Kevin "helped" me play the piano while the girls enthusiastically sang, even though they were not familiar with the words. I tried to explain the words, but received the impression that they were far more interested in the experience than in trying to understand. The children seemed to have confidence that I knew exactly what and how to teach them. I wish I were as confident. After a short prayer asking God's guidance for all of us, I explained to the children what I had prepared for preschool.

"Each one of you can choose a place to work," I spoke as if I were in charge of a classroom full of activity centers. "In the kitchen is a cake mix." (I had to settle for a mix since I didn't have any eggs.) "On the coffee table is a game. The felts are over near the couch. The scale is on the table. The puzzles and book are for Kevin. Where would you like to begin working?"

The cake won by a unanimous decision as everyone ran to the kitchen. You would have thought my children were suffering from "baking deprivation" to see them scramble for the closest chair and start to rip the box open. Yet almost daily they help me cook or bake something. The attraction must have been the tiny cake pans I had also found at the garage sale. After they mixed the cake, greased the pans, and poured the batter, I helped them carefully set all of the dials on the oven. Then we went into the living room to wait. Twenty minutes later the buzzer rang. There was a mad scramble as we ran to open the oven door. Where were the cakes?

After a quick glance around the messed-up kitchen, we found them still on the table where we left them. In my overconcern to make this cake-baking lesson as academic as possible, teaching about such things as 350 degrees, and how to read on the box the time for baking, and then finding that exact number on the timer, I had forgotten the essential thing: to put the cake in the oven! And so after a good laugh, we began again.

Kevin had escaped about halfway through the cake-baking lesson, and I now found his trail. His first stop must have been the grapefruit, because the bowl was empty and there were a dozen grapefruit in various places on the floor, as if the living room were a bowling alley.

I decided to look for Kevin after I helped the girls get started with something else. I'm convinced the best teacher-to-child ratio is one to one or one to two. The third child is almost impossible to keep track of, especially if the children are different ages and have different needs and interests.

The scale was a good experience for the girls. There were so many number concepts to talk about. For example: What do four grapefruit weigh? How many grapefruit does it take to make the scale reach six pounds? Find two grapefruit that weigh the same. On the first day with the scale, we even got into ounces. Now how do you go about explaining ounces to a four-year-old? I tried. "An ounce is one of the lines after the big line with a number that shows a pound. There are sixteen ounces in a pound, so there are sixteen little ounce lines after the big pound line, because each line shows where an ounce is." I just held my breath, hoping that neither child would count those tiny ounce lines and discover in reality there were only fifteen, the sixteenth tiny line, showing another full pound, indicated by a big line. Why didn't someone ever teach me how to explain ounces to a child? Well, the girls listened politely, trusting fully that I knew what I was talking about.

The game I put out for Kim was too hard. It was one of those eighty-nine-cent games you get at a department-store sale. Some matching games that match jobs with workers, or animals with houses, are appropriate for preschoolers. But the object of this was to match the printed name of an activity with the picture of the activity. After Kim started working on it I realized a child had to know how to read to do it correctly. But Kim was determined to try. She seemed to feel that if I put the game out for her she must be able to do it. She had done matching games since she was two years old and so was wiser than I at first had thought. After sorting through the cards, she put all the cards with blue backgrounds together, then the pink ones, white ones, and yellow ones. There were four cards in each color group. She then asked me what three of the four words said and she matched them to the activity with no difficulty by assuming the fourth word matched the card that was left.

Where was Kevin? I finally found him in the bedroom making his boats go "brrrrrr." I dragged him out to educate him about puzzles. He could care less. After a few attempts at the puzzles, he discovered pieces could be thrown just as easily as grapefruit. I decided boats were not such a bad preschool activity.

Then the felts. Although this appeared on both girls' lists, I really put these out for a selfish reason. Apparently the last time the felt pieces were used was on one of those rush days. In order to get the room straightened up quickly, they had gotten scrambled as they were put away. Now they needed sorting. I figured sorting was an academic occupation, so why not make it useful as well? Kari cheerfully sorted out the felt birds while Kim finished the job, putting the felt animals, people, houses, furnishings, and trees all in separate plastic bags.

At eleven o'clock we sat at the piano again, sang some old favorites like "Jingle Bells," and it was over.

It was Kim who announced "clean-up time," one of the good things she remembered from her more formal preschool days. It was no sooner said than carried out without so much as a word from me. Before I knew it, I was peeling peaches, wondering how I was going to get lunch made and get everyone to the swimming pool before it closed at one o'clock.

Wednesday, September 4 / Meet the Principal

As I gather up the licked-clean spoons and the pudding pan I say, "Now quickly, let's get that family room cleaned up before your daddy gets home."

I give the orders like a drill sergeant and they scurry about trying to finish their tasks while I kneel down on the floor to unscramble a puzzle.

Then I hear the familiar, "Hello, everybody! I'm home!"

"Daddy's home! Daddy's home! Daddy's home!" the children chant. Their tasks are forgotten as they run to his open arms.

"Hi, darlin'," I call. I rush to put the last few pieces of a puzzle together and hurriedly pick up the closest toys. I glance around the room. I might as well give up. I'll never get this mess straightened up before I'm found. Principals always have a way of dropping in on a classroom at the most inopportune moment.

"What did you do all day?" I hear him ask the children.

"Nothing," they reply, "just played."

As Jan carries our three students into the family room he reaches down and greets me with a kiss. "And what did you do today?" he cheerfully and innocently asks.

"Oh nothing," I say with my arms loaded with toys, "just played!"

We laugh but the children are quick to defend me. "No, she didn't. She made pudding for supper!"

"Ya, and we got to lick out the spoons."

"I got pan," Kevin shouted.

And so begins the report to the principal of our preschool day.

I have written quite a lot about myself (the teacher) and the children (the students), but I haven't said very much about Jan (the principal). Our relationship is such that he does not view himself as a principal in this preschool adventure, as much as a co-teacher. It is just that his work schedule is more demanding than mine, and since we all depend upon his paycheck for our sustenance, he is unable to spend the number of hours that I do with the children. But being a concerned father, he makes up in quality what is lacking in quantity of time with the children.

The children may have fun with me, but they have a ball with their daddy. The principal's office is never off limits to them, whether it is at work or at home. When he is in his home office (my study) writing checks or letters, the children are often right beside him writing their checks or letters. Weekly and sometimes daily they also visit his office at work. Jan not only teaches statistics at the university, but he is also an administrator. So he is often available at his office. The children love to surprise him by unexpectedly dropping by. I'm sure our visits really have ceased to surprise him because I think the children are his only visitors who don't always knock first! And the way they go down the hall, I think he would have to be concentrating really deeply on a problem not to hear them coming. But he acts surprised and they enjoy it.

This morning I left the children for a *few* minutes in Jan's office at work while I ran down to my office to pick up my mail and left some work for the secretary. When I returned the children were all busy writing on paper, cutting, stapling, or drawing on his chalkboard. He never seems embarrassed when his superiors, colleagues, or employees come to his office and find the children there. The children always have the feeling that their daddy is proud to have them around and that they belong there because it is their daddy's office.

As the principal, Jan may delegate most of the teaching responsibility to me, but he has strong feelings about what the children should be learning, and I appreciate his leadership. Even though his area of expertise is not child development or early-childhood education, as is mine, he has probably read almost as much in the area as I have, and is always coming up with new ideas about how we should be working with the children and what we should be teaching them.

His primary concern is that the children not only develop essential skills to do well in school, but also that they develop good characters. So it was not surprising to me when he suggested that we should really be systematically working on helping them develop important character traits like integrity, honesty, industry, and persistence.

I know that these traits are primarily taught by parental example. That is one reason I'm glad the children and I have the principal we have. He is a good example for all of us.

Thursday, September 5 / The Home-preschool Environment

After the students, a teacher, and a principal, what else is required before operating a home preschool? I think the following are essential:

1. A *"used" house.* "Used" is the best word that I know to describe the perfect home for preschoolers. It is certainly not the spic-and-span, spotless showpiece that I once dreamed I would live in with my Prince Charming. After the children are tucked in bed for the night and I get my second wind, I restore our home to a semiperfect state, and each week on Friday as the sun goes down the house glistens. But in between, our house looks used. It's lived in, worked in, and played in.

2. A *designated work-play area.* My children don't need to play in the whole house. They much prefer a special corner that is theirs, to constant restrictions wherever they roam. Our bedroom is off limits for child play. The living room is partially restricted. It can be shut off from the rest of the house, and I like to keep it ready for guests, but there are some things in the living room that the children enjoy, such as the piano, and the Christmas tree during the Christmas season. I discourage playing there when they can play elsewhere just as easily. If our house were arranged differently I would also restrict them to one bathroom so I could count on one always being clean and the toilet flushed, just in case guests arrive unexpectedly. Other than this the house is for the children.

Our main work-play area centers around the family room and kitchen, which has a direct access to a bathroom and the backyard. The floor is not carpeted. When the children are building intricate block structures that need a firm foundation or are painting, I am very glad for smooth vinyl flooring. The family-room furniture is sturdy and comfortable. It is the kind of furniture that shoes can touch, and even nicks and scratches can be accepted with only a hearty sigh and not a heart attack. The essential furniture in the family room is the three bean-bag chairs and the child-size table and chairs. I often wish I had room for two tables so one could be for art work and the other for the children's games or other activities. But the floor is a good substitute.

3. *Easily accessible storage areas.* The storage area for books and toys is on low, open shelves in the children's bedrooms. I try not to keep all of their toys down at the same time, since they like change and too many toys are only confusing to a child. I have found that if I put a few toys up in the cupboard and bring them down periodically they are almost like new toys again. The girls organize their own shelves. I help Kevin keep his in order. I am trying to teach him that he must take one toy down at a time and then put it back before taking another one.

I'm against toy boxes. They help make the room look orderly, but every time I look inside a toy box the toys are anything but orderly. The sought-after toy always manages to be at the bottom of the box, which means emptying the entire contents before the toy can be retrieved.

Since I value independence in my children I feel it is important to have their clothes hung low enough so that they can dress themselves and hang them up by themselves.

4. *A bulletin board.* Preschool children, as well as older children, enjoy displaying their creative work, and I need a bulletin board to help me keep organized. My kitchen bulletin board (four feet by eight feet) is always crammed full, and my refrigerator door is usually decorated with pictures held up by little magnets. Each of the children's bedrooms has a bulletin board, but I find that they are not used as much. It is more fun displaying a work of art where everyone can see it.

5. *Toys.* Toys are the tools of childhood. Perhaps the best "toys" are household items, like a mop or broom that can be used by the child when doing practical duties, but there are some other toys that I wouldn't want to try to do without. Here is my list of essential toys.

a. Outdoor toys: The outside toys that I value are the traditional toys I had when I was a child, such as a swing set-climbing gym (which can be as simple as a good, sturdy tree for climbing with a tire swing attached to a rope), a sandbox, a tricycle (or bicycle), roller skates, jump rope, and plain old dirt (with a shovel and bucket) and water. An extra bonus in our yard is the two-story playhouse. Our children love it, but if it weren't for their grandpa they would be playing house with large packing boxes and blankets.

b. Puzzles: For preschoolers, I prefer the expensive wooden puzzles. When pieces get lost I make my own by placing clear polyethylene wrap over the hole where the missing piece belongs and forcing wood putty into the hole. I flatten the top out with a knife and let it dry. I don't always get it painted exactly the right color, but at least it fits the hole. My children have a few very easy puzzles (four or five pieces), which Kevin is just beginning to master. Then they have some easy puzzles of ten to twelve pieces (for three-year-olds). The puzzles from eighteen to twenty-eight pieces are more difficult, and Kari has just recently been able to master these. Kim is ready for something new and finds that the cardboard puzzles that have sixty-three large interlocking pieces are a challenge to her.

c. Concept games: There are so many of these games on the market that it is difficult to choose a favorite. My children all like to play the picture lotto games, picture dominoes (Kim is starting to play the dot variety), and Chutes and Ladders. The girls are becoming more interested in card games, such as Fish and Old Maid. Concept games help develop number and color concepts and recognition and matching skills as well as giving a child practice in following rules. They are relatively inexpensive. When I first began playing these games with my preschoolers I found that the game was much more successful with parental participation. Once the rules are mastered the older ones enjoy playing these games by themselves.

d. Construction games: There are hundreds of construction games on the market, but if I had to choose only three, I would choose the old standby of Tinker Toys, and then a fairly inexpensive set of Constructo Straws, and to balance it out, a fairly expensive set (that's the only way they come) of Legos.

e. Miscellaneous toys: This category encompasses toys from A to Z. But the essentials are the ABCD toys.

> A is for Airplanes,
> B is for Balls,
> C is for Cars, and
> D is for Dolls.

When I shop for toys I use the following standards to protect both the children and me from unsafe or unnecessary toys.

Avoid toys that:
1. break easily
2. are hard to keep clean
3. may cause injuries (burns, cuts, bruises, or choking)
4. are psychologically harmful (don't agree with my value system)
5. we don't need

Toys are the tools of childhood, but if they aren't selected carefully they can be a waste of money, or worse yet, they can be weapons in unskilled hands.

6. *Books.* Books can be checked out from a library, but it is nice to have a few good books that do belong to the children. For religious instruction, I couldn't do without the ten volume set of *My Bible Friends** by Etta Degering, who wrote the stories for her grandchildren. I have searched the shelves of numerous bookstores, but still can't find any Bible story book or series of books for preschoolers that can compare to the quality of writing and pictures that are available in *My Bible Friends*. *My Good Shepherd Bible Story Book* (by A. C. Mueller) and *Taylor's Bible Story Book* (by Kenneth N. Taylor) are excellent one-volume Bible story books.

The five-volume set of *Uncle Arthur's Bedtime Stories* by Arthur S. Maxwell contains delightful stories about character development. Kevin politely listens to the stories, but I'm sure by three years of age he will be as intently absorbed by the stories as the girls are now.

For concept books, I like Richard Scarry's books. I used to think his drawings were silly, but my children love them. For babies, his *Best Word Book Ever* has everything in it. Then when children begin to be interested in the sounds of letters his *ABC Word Book* is delightful. Every time we read out of these books the children see something new. They especially enjoy finding Lowly, the worm, as he pops up in the most unexpected places.

Good books are expensive. A good children's picture book on high-quality paper with a hard cover will last till the grandchildren come, but the high price per book doesn't allow a very big personal

* Complete references for children's books are in Appendix B.

library. So I have compromised and have gotten a few sets of books from Scholastic Book Services (New York). They have printed well-known children's books on cheaper paper in paperback bindings. By buying the set of books, it is cheaper than buying each book individually, but there are always a few that do not fit my value system and I put them high on the shelf. (For standards on book selection, see Wednesday, September 25.)

7. *Records.* A "childproof" record player is essential so that the children can select and play their own records. I have found very few good records on the bargain table. Most of the time I get what I pay for. Children's records, such as the songs by Hap Palmer or Ella Jenkins, can be purchased from an educational music supply store and are good—and expensive. When I am paying such a high price for a record I make sure I listen to the entire record before I purchase it so that I won't be disappointed later. I like a variety of children's records—music, both religious and secular; stories with an accompanying picture book; and for our older preschoolers I like the Bible stories and character-building stories on record or cassettes. I recommend *The Bible in Living Sound* (Sentinel Records, Box 385, Simi Valley, CA 93065) and *Your Story Hour* (The Character House Library, Box 15, Berrien Springs, MI 49103). These sets are expensive but not for the number of records (or cassettes) per set, nor for the good influence they will have on the children even into their teen-age years.

Many records are now available also in cassette form. I have found cassettes to be very practical since they are less prone to scratches and breaking than are records. It is also possible to make your own cassettes quite easily by either recording your version of the song or story or taping it from a radio program. I have also found the public library to have an excellent selection of both records and cassettes.

8. *Art supplies.* The broom closet next to the family room contains a broom, a few household cleaning supplies, and the art supplies for the children. Watercolor paints, tempera paints, paint brushes of different sizes, crayons, chalk (and chalkboard), scissors, felt pens, white glue, and paste (I make this myself with flour and water) are essential materials for preschool artists. I round out these materials with a good supply of scratch paper, old catalogs

for cutting, and collage materials, like scraps of fabric, macaroni, beans, or buttons.

9. *Friends.* To round out the preschool environment, the children need each other. Having friends over to play is the exception and not the rule at our house. If we lived closer to neighbors, I'm afraid there would be a constant stream of children coming to our gate wanting to participate in the preschool activities I plan. I believe a family needs time by itself and therefore I would make it clearly understood that only a limited time is to be spent with friends. If we lived closer to preschoolers that my children enjoyed playing with, perhaps I would co-operate with another interested teacher-mother. We could share the children and the teaching responsibilities a few hours each week.

Friends are essential, but like toys and books they should be carefully selected. Children learn from their peers the bad as well as the good. Our children are too young to select friends of their own without our guidance. I try to keep the standard simple so that in the future the children can make their own choices wisely and independently. Right now the standard is:

   a. Friends must be kind.

   b. Friends must teach good things.

If friends are unkind or teaching my children bad behavior, then they may not play together. I find this standard not only helps in the selection of friends but it also helps to monitor the children's play. I overheard Kim say one day to a little playmate, "You can't say that because I might learn it and then Mommy won't let me play with you."

These are the essentials for a good home preschool environment. Now I need a curriculum!

Friday, September 6 / The Curriculum

It is the end of my first week as a teacher-mother of our home preschool. At last I have time to organize my thoughts and reflections about the importance of a home education and what I should teach my students this school year.

How did I get myself into this? Certainly it would be much easier to pay the fee and just send the children to a formal preschool. After all, preschool is not new to the children. I have sent the girls two mornings a week to preschool since they were two years old. They loved it. There were a few mornings they were reluctant to go, but on the whole, I felt it had been a good experience for them.

I'm not against a formal preschool, especially when a mother has to work outside her home, which I have done for a few mornings each week since the children were born. A preschool experience can be beneficial if the teacher is perceptive enough to allow the child freedom of choice of a wide variety of indoor and outdoor activities, and if the child likes going. I am, however, against the structured, academically oriented, no-nonsense type of program. I'm still young enough to enjoy school and I think children should, too. No one can convince me little children really enjoy trying to understand abstract things that hold no meaning for them, when the world is so full of exciting, real things just asking curious bodies to hold, hear, smell, taste, and see. But as good as a formal preschool can be, I'm still of the opinion that the best teacher-to-child ratio is one to one, and for young children, there is nothing like a mother and child at home having a good time together.

I guess the biggest reason I got myself into being a teacher-mother is that Kevin isn't toilet-trained yet. It is not because his grandparents don't think he should be, or because he's not smart enough to know where it should go, but because of the combination of his body being not quite ready to accomplish the task easily and his mother not being disciplined enough to sit him on the potty every hour and just after meals, as the books tell you to do.

What does toilet training have to do with how I got to be a teacher-mother? Well, I had it all planned at the beginning of the summer. Kim, even though 5½ and eligible for kindergarten, could continue to go to the same preschool as Kari and Kim had last year. And since Kevin was going to be 2 in August, he could attend, too, thus simplifying my life by having all three children together.

Well, as summer progressed I began to realize Kevin was not going to meet the preschool entrance requirements. He would have his birthday, which was half of it. But in no way was he going to be toilet-trained.

I was also impressed by the following statements, which I read and underlined, by a highly respected author and mother, Ellen G. White.

"It is customary to send very young children to school. They are required to study from books things that tax their young minds. . . . This course is not wise. . . .

"Infancy extends to the age of six or seven years. Up to this period children should be left, like little lambs, to roam around the house and in the yards, in the buoyancy of their spirits, skipping and jumping, free from care and trouble.

"Parents, especially mothers, should be the only teachers of such infant minds. . . ." (*Child Guidance* Nashville, Tenn.: Southern Publishing Association, 1954, p. 300)

These statements were written by a very wise and discerning woman years ago, and I couldn't dismiss them from my mind in light of all the counsel of educational experts today emphasizing the importance of the parents' role in caring for and teaching their own children.

For example, John Bowlby says, ". . . What is believed to be essential for mental health is that the infant and young child should experience a warm, intimate, and continuous relationship with his mother (or permanent mother-substitute) in which both find satisfaction and enjoyment. . . ." (*Maternal Care and Mental Health* Geneva: World Health Organization, 1952, p. 5)

Dr. Earl S. Schaefer strongly supports parents teaching their children during the preschool years, with this statement:

"An awareness of the major role of the parent as educator is emerging from child-development research. . . . The accumulating evidence suggests that parents have great influence upon the behavior of their children, particularly their intellectual and academic achievement, and that programs which teach parents skills in educating their children are effective supplements or alternatives for preschool education." ("Parents as Educators: Evidence from Cross-Sectional, Longitudinal, and Intervention Research," *Young Children*, Vol. XXVII, No. 4 [Apr. 1972], pp. 227–39)

These statements, emphasizing the importance of the mother's role (even in a child's education) during the early years, impressed me. So at a weak moment, I put the question to my girls. "What would you rather do this next year—go to your old preschool [with all of the fancy equipment, toys, and playmates], or have your mother be your teacher at home?" Well, almost before I finished the proposition, they were jumping up and down shouting, "Mommy, Mommy, you teach us; you teach us."

It was not what I expected, so I rephrased the question: "Would you rather have me teach you at home or *get to go to your old preschool?*" Again, the vote for me was unanimous. I was elected even without campaigning!

This decision meant that all three of my children would be together for preschool. But I still needed to be gone two half days a week to work at my office and teach my university students. In the past, on the two mornings the girls were at preschool I had gotten a sitter for Kevin while I worked. But now since I was going to be their teacher, I wanted to devote the morning hours to my children. Then, after lunch when they might sleep an hour or so, I'd find someone to watch them. The search ended at the home of my friend Evelyn Erickson, when she suggested that we exchange baby-sitting services. She needed someone to watch her three preschoolers when she had class. So everything seemed to be working out.

But I had forgotten the first step in planning any educational program. I had memorized it years ago in every education class I took. Then it hit like lightning about 1:00 A.M. driving back home from our vacation: the curriculum! I had everything planned but what I wanted to teach the children.

I had happened to be driving and Jan was sleeping in the back of the VW camper (amid three sleeping children, suitcases, boxes, and a full-grown Doberman).

I heard him attempt to turn over and I asked, "Are you awake?"

"Kind of."

"Then what do you want the children to learn this year in their home preschool?"

I got the answer I deserved: a couple of deep sighs and then . . . silence.

So I started out that first day after Labor Day with only the mental list I had worked out between 1:00 A.M. and 1:40 A.M. of the things I wanted my children to learn about in our home preschool this year:

OUR HOME-PRESCHOOL CURRICULUM

GOD
  His character
  His laws
  His Son

NATURE
  Stars (sun, moon, and planets)
  Plants (emphasis on names of flowers and how they grow)
  Birds
  Animals (emphasis on dogs)

HEALTH HABITS
  Brush teeth
  No snacks
  Drink plenty of water
  Regularity in exercise, eating, and sleeping
  Low-sugar diet
  Good diet
  Eating balanced meals
  Cleanliness

MUSIC
  Hymns, folk songs
  Piano basics

ART
  Self-expression and creativity through a large variety of media
  Concepts such as color, form, shape, texture

LANGUAGES
  Spanish
  German

READING
  Phonics
  Word recognition

ARITHMETIC
  Numbers

Money concepts
Simple addition and subtraction

PHYSICAL SKILLS
  Rope jumping
  Bike riding (tricycle for Kevin)
  Tumbling
  Throwing
  Especially for Kevin:
    Balancing
    Somersault
    Hopping
    Galloping
    Skipping

PRACTICAL THINGS
  Set table
  Load dishwasher
  Clean room
  Make bed

After Jan had recuperated from sleep deprivation, he added the following:

CHARACTER TRAITS
  Integrity
  Honesty
  Industry
  Persistence

When I look at this list, I realize it doesn't resemble a typical pre-school or kindergarten curriculum. I did not write learning objectives, which are usually a part of a curriculum. I left everything open-ended. I spelled out no level of proficiency. In each area I will teach the children as much or as little as their interest and needs demand. These will be my guidelines.

My justifications for my home-preschool curriculum are based on my training and experience in early-childhood education; the background I brought to my training; and certain weak points in my knowledge and experience in which I would like to see my children be stronger.

Circle 10 words in magazine that start with A, L, or T. (love)

Play the "opposite game" with Mommy.

(I say hot, you say cold)

Learn 5 birds.

Make play-dough.

Make bed.

Comb hair.

Cut out pictures in catalog and paste.

Roller skate.

Practice riding bicycle or tricycle.

Look up DOG in encyclopedia.

Monday, September 9 / Activity Cards

Today I had time to start preschool properly. I wrote different activities on three-by-five cards.

I drew little pictures on each card to help the girls read them on their own. They loved the idea. After I read them all through, they took the cards and sorted them into two piles. One pile was of rejected activities and the other of the activities they wanted to do.

It took very little direction from me, and before I knew it they were busily engaged in their preschool projects, leaving Kevin standing by my side.

Now I realize that activities on cards for a two-year-old is too advanced. He can choose what he wants to do, but it is easier for him to make the choice if he sees the activities rather than just hears them read from a card.

Tuesday, September 10 / Television: Is It Educational?

My children love Mr. Rogers. If someone were to ask my girls who they wanted to marry, I think Mr. Rogers would probably come in second, after their daddy.

Some people think TV is all bad or not worth the bother and battles to control what children watch. So they don't have one in the house. But I think there are enough worthwhile programs, such as *The National Geographic* specials and other nature programs, that I like the convenience of having our own TV (and the principal likes to watch the evening news).

I've sampled all of the children's programs, and for preschoolers, Mr. Rogers heads the list. I'm not very wild about some of the most popular children's TV programs. In general, the concepts behind these programs are good, but there are too many things that run counter to my values, like the language ("dumb dumb"), the music (loud and jazzy), and the health habits (eating cookies, sodas, etc.), and all the moppets that are grouches and monsters. On top of all this, I think about the research done on the effectiveness of such programs in helping children learn basic academic skills. In general, the researchers found that a nursery-school program, where a teacher worked with children the whole time, was significantly more effective in teaching children than a nursery school where the children watched TV for one hour of the time. (Herbert A. Sprigle, "Can Poverty Children Live on 'Sesame Street'?," *Young Children* [Mar. 1971], p. 202)

I found a new program this fall that has some possibility. It came on right after Mr. Rogers before we had time to turn the TV off. It's a program to help Spanish-speaking children learn English, but enough of it is in Spanish, so I think it may help children learn Spanish. This just happens to be one of the goals I have for my children this year, so I may add this program to my approved list.

I try to limit the children to a half hour of TV a day (or less). They may choose which of "Mom's approved programs" they would like to watch.

I approve programs on the basis of whether they—

1. *Teach wholesome attitudes, values, and behavior in music, picture, and action.* I have a blanket rule against cartoons based upon this standard. Cartoons characteristically are full of aggressive fantasy, both in words and action. To teach children to use their aggressive feelings in a constructive way is difficult enough without giving them more ideas about inappropriate behavior, which is what they get from watching cartoons. The only exceptions to this rule are the children's specials that have been cartooned and tell a worthwhile story. But these are few and far between!

2. *Are appropriate for preschoolers.* Although some of the family-centered evening programs may teach wholesome values, they were not written for the preschooler. Allowing him to watch some of these episodes often brings many questions into his mind that may worry him, because his own life experiences and level of thinking have not matured to the level of completely understanding or coping with these problems. Also, I believe the evening hours

should be family time. And it is very difficult to have any meaningful family communications with the television blaring away.

3. *Are educational.* Even if one were to find a quiz program or a comedy that was not objectionable by the above standards, I would probably rule these out because they really don't teach the child anything, and therefore, I would consider them a waste of time. If my children would argue that they could watch these while they do something else, I would probably suggest that they could listen to good classical music or the Bible story records and gain from the experience rather than filling their minds with trivia.

I feel idle TV watching is a waste of time. So during the day I help the children save projects that they can work on during their TV time. Sometimes they fold the clothes or clean the family room, but more often they draw or paint or work on the craft ideas presented by Mr. Rogers.

So I believe that with proper planning and standards, the TV can be a part of a home preschool.

Wednesday, September 11 / The Fish Hatchery

Our visit to the fish hatchery was a field-trip experience to remember. The children had never before seen so many fish. There must have been millions of rainbow trout, from spawning-tank size to eighteen-inch adults. What a treat it was to be able to throw the hungry fish a handful of fish food.

The process of growing fish was indeed fascinating. The children were impressed with the aerating system that splashed water high into the air before going into each tank. The owner explained that they could double the holding capacity of each tank with this system, since more oxygen was introduced into the water. The sorting machine was an interesting contraption. There was a large net container, which held the "caught" fish in water until a man could measure them. Then, depending upon their size, he put them into one of five long pipes from which they slid down into the right tank for their size. "I didn't know they made slides for fish!" Kevin exclaimed. "I wish I were a fish!"

Our plans for the year are full of many more field-trip experiences. I'd like to take the children to a stable where they train horses, to a dairy where they can watch cows being milked, to the nearby farm that raises llamas, to the local radio station, to the fire lookout on top of Black Mountain, to the factory that manufactures motor homes, and to the market to watch the baker's wife decorate fancy cakes.

Thursday, September 12 / A Dip Dinner

A dip dinner was the lunch menu for today. It is a unique way to eat and not have any dishes to wash. The children think it is great fun dipping raw vegetables, fruits, and crackers into special dips and popping them in their mouths. They did most of the preparation during preschool time today. They cleaned carrots, celery, broccoli, cucumbers, radishes, and cherry tomatoes. (Other foods we have used are cauliflower, turnips, beets, kohlrabi, zucchini, and apples.) Kevin made the onion dip by mixing a package of dry onion soup in some sour cream. I made the other one by mixing some softened cream cheese with peanut butter. (Cream cheese mixed with drained crushed pineapple and chopped walnuts is also good.) A variety of crackers completed the meal.

Friday, September 13 / Worship

> Lord, in the morning Thou shalt hear
> my voice ascending high;
> To Thee will I direct my prayer,
> to Thee lift up mine eye.
>   Isaac Watts

The children sang lustily as we began our preschool time this morning with a short worship. Then I read to them from *The Living*

Bible the instructions found in Deuteronomy 6:4–9, which I had read earlier this morning for my own personal devotions. "O Israel, listen: Jehovah is our God, Jehovah alone. You must love him with all your heart, soul, and might. And you must think constantly about these commandments I am giving you today. You must teach them to your children and talk about them when you are at home or out for a walk, at bedtime and the first thing in the morning. Tie them on your finger, wear them on your forehead, and write them on the doorposts of your house!"

I then asked each child what he thought this meant. After a few attempts and some "I don't knows," I explained: "God says that we should constantly think about him and teach our children about him whether we are inside or outside and from the moment we get up until bedtime. Do you think God wants us actually to tie his commandments around our finger? Should we make headbands and write "Don't forget God" on them and wear them all day like Indians? Do you think I should write the Ten Commandments on each side of the doorways, so every time you go through the doorway you remember God? It may not be necessary to do those specific things, but the important message that God has for us is that we must do everything possible so we do not forget about God. That is one of the reasons we have worship. Worship is like tying a string around a finger so we won't forget, or wearing headbands, or writing the Commandments on every doorway. Worship helps us to remember God."

True worship is an attitude. No matter what we may have to do during the day, we can do it with God in our thoughts. Therefore, is it necessary to set aside a specific time during the day for worship—especially for preschoolers? Yes, I believe it is. Habits are formed early and if I want my children to establish the habit of beginning and ending the day with God, and thinking about his love all during the day, then I must help them during these formative years to find worship time a delight.

What should be the ingredients of a meaningful worship experience with preschoolers?

First, I would say, make it short. Keep it within the child's ability to pay attention. Maybe five to ten minutes at first. It is better to end the worship time formally when the child is eager and attentive, rather than wait until he is so restless that one must battle for the child's continued interest and co-operation. The ensuing struggle destroys every bit of good the worship experience was intended to produce.

Second, make it fun. Clever, active songs such as "Father Abraham," "I'm in the Lord's Army," "I'm Inright, Outright, Upright, Downright Happy All the Time," and "If You're Happy and You Know It Clap Your Hands," help to add fun and sparkle to worship times.

Today we sang a favorite I found in the Ralph Carmichael songbook, *He's Everything to Me, Plus 153* (Waco, Tex.: Lexicon Music, Inc.). It's called, "I Heard About . . ." To make it easier for the children to remember the different verses, I made flash cards with such things as Noah's ark sitting on a mountaintop, and then for "Zekiel preachin' to the bones," I drew a couple of bones.

Third, get the children involved. Sometimes we imitate the church service and have one child "read" the Scripture (recite a memory verse), another sing for special music, and the third give the sermon (that is, tell a Bible story); or all three might co-operate on any one of the activities.

Sometimes the children pantomime a Bible story for Jan or me to guess. Most of the time they still need help from one of us to get their props organized. For example, one day the children decided to pantomime the story of Noah's ark and insisted that we bring the two-man canoe into the living room to make the production more realistic. That needed Mother's help!

Fourth, read or tell a story. A story is an essential part of the worship time. Everyone loves a good story—especially preschoolers. I suggest that Bible stories should be told rather than read, unless you have found a good book with the stories geared to the child's level of comprehension.

Jan has tried to read some Bible stories from Arthur S. Maxwell's ten-volume series *The Bible Story* (Nashville, Tenn.: Southern Publishing Association), but they are far too wordy with too few pictures to hold the interest of my preschoolers. In a few years these will be more appropriate. The only way that Jan can use these books now is to read the story himself first, and then stand up and act out the story himself in front of the children as he reads the most important sections and tells the rest.

Egermeier's Favorite Bible Stories, by Elsie Egermeier (Anderson, Ind.: Warner Press), is an acceptable book for preschoolers. There are thirty short stories in one volume, but only one picture per story.

For a book that really sounds as though you are reading directly from the Bible, only on a child's level, *The Children's Bible*, published by Golden Press, is the best we have found.

Fifth, don't try to have your worship at the same time as the children's worship. Jan and I have our own Bible study time before the children are awake, so our "family" worship time focuses on the needs and interests of the children. Making children sit through long Bible reading sessions may teach them endurance, but does little to inspire a love for the Scriptures!

Finally, every worship time should include a family ritual. Some families read systematically through a book for worship time. *Little Visits with God* and *More Little Visits with God* by Allan Hart Jahsmann and Martin P. Simon might be good books for this type of ritual. (These books are published by Concordia Publishing House.)

If morning worship is conducted at breakfasttime, why not clasp hands around the table and sing a prayer, such as, "Father, we thank Thee for the night and for the pleasant morning light. For rest and food and loving care, and all that makes the world so fair."

Our ritual is to hold hands and sing, "Jesus Loves Me." Then we kneel as each person prays. "Make it a sentence prayer," the children remind their daddy. Then with heads still bowed we sing, "Alleluja, alleluja . . ." And with a hug and a kiss we are ready to begin our day.

Monday, September 16 / Games

Today was game day at preschool.

Playing the games of childhood, such as "Simon Says," "Ring Around a Rosy," "Hide and Seek," "Musical Chairs," "Follow the Leader," "Red Light—Green Light," and "Tag," can not only be fun, but also something more. They can teach children the importance of following rules.

Rules for games are not so very different from parents' rules, school rules, traffic rules, or societal rules. Rules are there for a purpose. If they cease to serve a purpose then they should be abolished or changed according to the proper methods. When one breaks the rules there are consequences.

The consequences of not following the rules of a childhood game are many. Often the child will be ostrasized from a group, which for a child may be a harsher punishment than we as adults inflict upon children for not following our rules.

Many experiences of following parental rules, as well as following the rules of childhood games, should help children be more willing to understand the need for rules as well as be willing to follow the other rules he will meet in life beyond the preschool years.

Tuesday, September 17 / A Working Mother

Today I was a working woman and a failure as a mother. When I have to leave the house before 8:00 A.M. I'm always rushing and everything seems chaotic. The children, sleepy-eyed with thumbs in their mouths, were hanging onto me as I gently pushed them away to get to my job on time! I guess I should get up earlier so I could spend my usual morning time with them. But that would have meant going to bed earlier, and with everything there was for me to do yesterday preparing to be out of the house today, I just couldn't make it. I really didn't plan on being gone all day. I thought I would go into my office in the morning to catch up and be home by noon. That was wishful thinking. I'd been gone all summer and the news spread quickly that I was back. My phone began to ring and before I knew it, it was 5:30 P.M. and I hadn't even had time to take a proper lunch break.

Then at 5:45 P.M. I was home, ready to assume my No. 1 job—being a mother. The children stood around me screaming for joy and tugging on arms and skirt wanting to be hugged and held. They should come first, right? Yet I knew they were hungry and Jan was expected home in fifteen minutes, so they must wait. What should I get for dinner? In my plans for the day I hadn't gotten this far. I opened the pantry door and scanned down the shelves, selected a couple of cans, tossed a salad together, and we ate. Then the clean-up routine, all the time thinking *preschool*—I should do something with the children or today would be totally lost. So I tried to muster my energy, overlook the disorder that had accumulated during a typical day with preschoolers, and called "preschool time." You should have heard the groans! "Oh Mommy. Now? We're too tired." So I said I'd just read to them. I selected a book and sat down. Kim and Kari stumbled into the living room. (Kevin didn't even bother coming.) After two pages, Kim said, "I don't like that book. I want this one." She forcefully thrust it into my lap.

"I don't like that one," Kari whined. "I want my book."

I suggested a compromise. "OK, first I'll read Kim's, and then yours." There was more squabbling, more whining. Finally I gave up my preschool idea of reading and just held them as I rocked and hummed a lullaby in our oversized rocker. Some things are just more important than learning. And I guess being rocked falls in this category.

Wednesday, September 18 / Rhythm Band

Young children love to play rhythm instruments. I thought I would invest in some for our home preschool until I realized the expense. Instead, the children and I made our own instruments during preschool time today.

First we made paper-plate tambourines. I put a handful of popcorn kernels between two heavy paper plates, and the children stapled around the edges so the popcorn wouldn't fall out. Then they decorated the plates with crayons and ribbons.

While the children were busy with their tambourines, I thumbtacked sandpaper around some of Kevin's blocks. Two sandpaper blocks rubbed together make an interesting sound.

For a jingling sound, the children took jar rings and old jar lids that I punched holes in and strung them on strings, tying the ends together.

I then brought out the lids of my pans for cymbals, wooden spoons for sticks, an empty gallon can for a drum, a spoon for a drumstick, and a small jar filled with dried beans.

And we made music!

Thursday, September 19 / Experiences with Rhythm

"Play rhythm instruments" was the activity card that was the top choice today.

"See if you can play the same rhythm I'm making," I challenged the children. I began by clapping a steady walking rhythm. "Now listen carefully and see if you can follow me when I play the rhythm fast and then slow on the piano. Good. Now you've really got to use your ears and play soft when I play soft, and loud when I play loud. I'm going to try to trick you to see if you can stop playing when I stop. Now let's see if you can march and play as I play the rhythm. Follow me when I go fast or slow."

After the children were following me fairly well, I changed my approach. "Did you know your name has a special rhythm? Kim, say your whole name."

She replied, "Kimberly Kay Kuzma."

"Now say it over and over again. Good. Clap your hands for each syllable of your name."

She clapped three short, fast claps for Kimberly, and then three long but even claps for the Kay Kuzma. Then I had Kari and Kevin join us as we clapped to the rhythm of Kim's name.

"Does my name have a rhythm?" asked Kari.

"It sure does. And it is different from Kim's. Let's try Kari's full name. Karlene Michelle Kuzma." We clapped two short ones on Karlene, paused, two more on Michelle, paused, and then two longer claps for Kuzma. And then we clapped the rhythm of Kevin Clark Kuzma and found it also was unique. Finally we added the rhythm instruments to their name rhythms. I joined in by playing different chords on the piano to the same rhythm.

Playing rhythm instruments is excellent training in listening skills and body control. It takes a lot of co-ordination to put the whole thing together. Children can practice this skill by clapping their hands or stamping their feet, but the instruments do add a unique quality to the activity.

Friday, September 20 / Useful Work

Today was irrigation day. I'm beat, but for the kids it was a high day. It's not every day they can walk through the water with their shoes on (tennis shoes, that is) and build rivers and waterways to their heart's desire. I had to smile as I looked behind me this morning and saw three little ones splashing through the water with rakes in hand following me as I checked to make sure each tree was being watered and, where it wasn't, cleaning the leaves and debris out of the furrows. They are such good little workers, and I appreciate their "help" even when someone slips and ends up waist deep in the water. Though the clean-up operation of removing mud and water from body, hair, and clothes, and the sand tracked in on the kitchen floor sometimes makes me wonder if it is worth the trouble, I always answer yes, yes, yes.

Five years after we were married we finally moved into our dream house and at that time we made a wise investment. I couldn't stand the 4-acre weed patch that was supposed to be a pasture. So we planted 720 grapefruit trees with the plan that some day the profit from the grapefruit trees would help pay for the children's college tuition. But the children also would have the responsibility (as soon as they are old enough) to care for their trees.

I really believe that parents should be responsible for planning activities and projects in which their children can take responsibility, while at the same time learning useful skills, especially since jobs for teen-agers are almost nonexistent. I heard of one family that bought an old car for their sons to work on. After two years of rebuilding, their product was the envy of every boy their age. But even more important is the responsibility these boys had to assume and all the things they learned in the process.

In some cases hobbies grow into jobs. Some families raise show dogs or chinchillas. The list is endless. The secret is helping the children to feel that the project would fold if it weren't for them. It has to be theirs, and at the same time, the family's. As you work together, you learn together and you grow together.

When I was twelve years old, I started to work for my dad in his manufacturing plant each day after school. It was a small company and there were many little jobs I could do as well as anyone else. I was proud at being able to keep up with and most of the time ahead of older, experienced assembly-line workers. My dad manufactured fishing tackle. So I glued floats together, screwed screws in bubbles, attached hooks to lures, painted lures, stapled lures on cards, packaged them in plastic bags, and then boxed them for shipment. As the years went by, Dad even let me run the press that stamped out the lures, and try my hand at office work. As I think back on it, I probably had a chance to do a little of everything.

I was really proud of this job and would often run a good share of the two miles from school to be able to put in a few extra minutes on the job. I have no idea what my hourly wage was. I kept my own record of the number of hours I worked, and Daddy paid me out of his pocket. I'm sure my pay was probably far below the minimum wage. But that really didn't matter. It wasn't the money I was working for, even though it helped pay my private church school tuition; it was the feeling of pride and accomplishment at successfully holding down an adult job that I still remember to this day.

Not every parent has a ready-made job for his underage child as did my dad. Since Jan and I were teachers, we realized our profession doesn't lend itself to children taking an active, responsible role, and so we planted the grapefruit trees. Grapefruit is second best, but it is better than nothing.

Right now irrigating is a special event for our children. I hope to keep it this way for as long as possible. But I know the time will come when weeding and watering will be drudgeries. At that time, I hope they feel responsible enough to keep at it, even through those hot summer months when the rest of the gang is loafing at the beach.

Monday, September 23 / Packing a Project

The university classes began today. I was up early trying to organize myself so I would be able to have preschool with the children and leave the house in some state of order by noon. The children could hardly wait to go visit the Ericksons this afternoon. I hope they are still as eager about this arrangement in a month when the exception becomes the routine.

For the special preschool activity today I decided to plan a project that could be completed at the Ericksons. The anticipation of taking something special to their friends and finishing the project with them should help to bridge the transition from home to babysitter's. The project I selected was to make sugar cookie dough. Kim measured the dry ingredients: ½ cup sugar, ⅛ teaspoon salt, and 2¼ cups flour (I used whole wheat). Kari measured the 6 tablespoons vegetable shortening, 1 teaspoon vanilla flavoring, and 1 tablespoon milk. Kevin broke the egg! When the ingredients were all mixed together, I put the dough into a container with the following instructions for Evelyn: "Dear Evelyn, Here is some cookie dough for the children to bake at your house. Have them roll it out until about ¼ inch thick. Enclosed are cookie cutters of various shapes. Bake on an oiled baking pan at 375 degrees for 10 to 12 minutes. You should get about 3 dozen—if the children don't sample too much raw dough! Have fun. Love, Kay."

Tuesday, September 24 / Collage

Yesterday my children had a wonderful time at the Erickson house. Kevin even took his nap without any problem. In addition they brought home a dozen cookies decorated with different-colored frosting and raisins.

I had wondered if Evelyn was just trying to make me feel good by saying she had an easy time with the children. She had said that in a way having six of them was almost easier than having only three. It really didn't make sense to me, but since I had all the children today, I think I'm inclined to agree. Because each child had someone special to play with, I found that they tended to rely less on me.

The project Randy, Lisa, and Greg brought with them was helpful. Evelyn had packed some styrofoam shapes that are used in packing boxes, a plastic bottle of white glue, and some paper plates for making a collage. I added a few ingredients from the pantry, like dried lentils, split peas, pinto beans, and *garbanzos*. I helped the children color some macaroni with food coloring. After the macaroni dried, the children added these to the collage. The result was really a very interesting project—and one that held their attention long enough for me to accomplish a good deal of my housework.

Wednesday, September 25 / Selecting Library Books

"Surprise!" I called as I greeted the children with my arms overloaded with books from the library.

"Goody, goody. Mommy got us some new books," they yelled as they hugged and kissed me and danced for joy.

They immediately offered to take the heavy load from me. Then, putting the books in a pile in the middle of the sofa, they each started browsing to select what they wanted me to read to them before bed.

The children never seem to tire of a new selection of books from the library. I started getting library books for Kim when she was only two years of age. Every three weeks we get a new batch, and four years later I still don't see any hope of reading all the ones on the shelves. I usually take the children with me when I go to the library, since I believe they should get used to using a library early in their lives so it becomes a way of life for them. A library is a wonderful service—a necessity for a teacher-mother and her preschool children. But tonight I decided it would be fun to surprise the children by getting the books by myself on my way home from class.

From my years of experience in selecting library books for children I have developed some standards to help me in making a quick selection without having to read the book completely through. Since I usually get twenty-five books at a time, I would be at the library all night if I had to read each before deciding whether to check it out or not. Of course, I do make mistakes. But on the whole I have had quite good success with the following guidelines.

1. Books about real animals, things, or people (especially typical situations or emotions preschool children may experience).

2. Books with good illustrations on every page, co-ordinated with the text, with not too much writing per page.

I begin my search for choice library books by browsing through the books that have been previously checked out and returned but not yet reshelved. I figure if other people have checked them out for their children, there may be a better chance of finding a child's favorite than by just starting my search at random. I've come across some great finds this way and I'm saving the librarian the work of reshelving (a small favor for the free library service!).

Once I find a book that I think may have possibilities, I apply my guidelines. Here are some of the reasons behind these standards, and the names of some of the books I selected tonight:

1. *Books about real animals, things, or people.* Books about real things go over better with my family than the make-believe and nonsense books. Before I had children, I used to like Dr. Seuss' *Green Eggs and Ham, The Cat in the Hat,* and all the rest. The rhyme and rhythm, the clever words, the absurd happenings, and the funny drawings sparked a responsive chord in my adult mind (as they do for many older preschoolers and school-age children). So I started getting them for my children. Their response was wrinkled-up, puzzled faces. Not even a laugh. I finally asked Kim why she didn't like them. "They don't make sense," she replied. So I have learned to choose books that my children can realistically relate to and learn from. All the stories with dragons, fairies, and pixies are OUT. I haven't found one I like yet. I'm convinced my children can get along nicely without these make-believe things. There is so much to learn. Why crowd their minds with trivia?

What about fairy tales, like "Snow White," "Cinderella," "Sleeping Beauty," and all the rest? Well, my girls are far from being interested in handsome princes, and marrying and living happily ever after. Leave those plots to the school-age kids, and even then, I question whether they need them. The children do enjoy "Goldilocks and the Three Bears." I think it's the repetition of going from Papa Bear's to Mama Bear's to Baby Bear's things, and being able to project themselves into the role of Goldilocks or the Little Bear. But more important, it's Grandmother's favorite story. And if Grandmother tells it, that makes it special. Almost all of the fairy tales I know are so scary, they frighten even me. Can you think of anything quite so blood-curdling as what the Giant says when he smells Jack of beanstalk fame: "Fee fi fo fum, I smell the blood of an Englishman. Be he alive or be he dead, I'll grind his bones to make my bread."? Children are afraid of enough things in this world. Why do they have to have nightmares about fairy tales and fantasy, too?

The children's favorite books are about things that they do or things that could possibly happen to them, or to animals. It doesn't matter if the characters are people, as in Robert McCloskey's books (*Blue Berries for Sal* or *One Morning in Maine*) or animals, as in Russell Hoben's books about Francis (*Bedtime for Francis, Bread and Jam for Francis,* and others), as long as the story is believable.

Tonight I couldn't resist *Whistle for Willy* by Ezra Jack Keats and *Do You Want to Be My Friend?* by Eric Carle. Both of these books are excellent for the youngest child and are still enjoyed after many readings by my four- and five-year-olds. Since *Do You Want to Be My Friend?* has no words, Kim loves to "read" it to Kevin. Finally, I chose one of Kim's and my favorites: *Small One* by Zhenya Gay. It's a lovely story for four- and five-year-olds, about the adventures of a tiny rabbit who didn't obey his mother. Although Kim loves it, it frightens Kari. She has to leave the room when I start reading about the fox that almost finds the baby. But she returns to enjoy the last two pages when the mother rabbit finally finds her small one.

2. *Good illustrations.* When selecting books, I always check the illustrations and the writing on each page to see if the illustrations are pleasing and there is not too much reading, and whether the two are co-ordinated.

I believe that the younger the child the more important are the illustrations. For example, Kevin won't sit through more than two or three lines per page before he wants to turn the page to see what is next. Good illustrations lengthen the amount of time he will look at one page.

I love beautiful art, so I never can resist Brian Wildsmith's books. Tonight I got his book *Birds* for Kevin and *Puzzles* for the girls. He is such an outstanding artist that his books are worth getting just to look at the illustrations.

Many of the books are read only once, then left on the shelf waiting to be returned to the library. Others are read daily. Tonight as I read through the children's choices, I realized I had found one destined to become a favorite. It is called *Bear Mouse* by Berniece Freschet. The story is about a mother mouse and how she tries to find food in the winter so that she can feed her babies and keep them alive. Mice aren't my favorite creatures, but even I hold a tender spot in my heart for this little mother, "Bear Mouse."

Thursday, September 26 / Bedtime

Getting a good, peaceful, and adequate night's sleep is what I consider one of the prime prerequisites for a successful preschool day. When the children get to bed late, I find they are grumpy wakers, picky breakfast eaters, and cantankerous students. That's why I jealously try to guard the children's bedtime.

Why worry about an occasional late night? Why not just let the child sleep in and start the preschool day a bit later? Fine, in theory. But I haven't met a preschooler yet who followed the theory. With most children, their wake-up alarm clocks go off at about the same time rain or shine—late night or not.

The only thing a parent can do is to realize one may have to live with grouches all morning. Be gentle with their little sleepy souls. Remember, the late bedtime was probably not their fault! Avoid pushing them or persisting in having them perform to your high expectations. Give them an early lunch (since they probably weren't wide awake enough to eat a good breakfast) and tuck them in for a nap. Not too long, or else you are in for another late bedtime—and you want to avoid that cycle.

I'm an advocate of flexible regularity. Double talk? Not really. Every child is different. Some can handle irregularity better than others. Some need more sleep than others. Some recover from late nights easier than others. Flexible regularity means meeting the child's needs within a general plan, rather than rigidly adhering to a routine to which the child must adapt.

Kim is our night owl. I used to fuss with her, threaten her, rock her, rub her back—anything to try to help her get to sleep at what I considered a decent hour for children. And many times, after all of this, I would go into her room an hour later and she would still have her eyes wide open.

Then my mother, who is very conservative with her grand-motherly child-rearing advice, just commented how nicely Kim goes to sleep when she is ready. "Remember," she said, "each child has his own timetable, and his differences should be respected."

This set me to thinking. But there was one technical problem: Kim and Kari share the same room and if Kim got to stay up, then Kari, no matter how tired, would want to stay up. I could have just laid down the law, saying Kim was older and she would get to stay up later. But I really didn't feel like weathering the storm.

So I whispered to Kim, "As soon as Kari is asleep you can get up." It worked like a charm, since Kari was usually asleep in less than five minutes. When Kari wanted me to whisper the same thing to her, I whispered, "As soon as Kim is asleep you can get up." So far, it has never happened. She just cannot manage to stay awake longer than Kim. If Kim really wants to, she can stay awake longer than anyone. I now don't have to fight bedtime. If Kim is tired, she falls asleep waiting for Kari to drop off. If she is not tired, then she knows she can get up in a few minutes and have an extra fifteen minutes with the big people. The arrangement has its added benefits, for now Jan and I have a chance to spend some time with each girl alone; Kim at night and Kari (our early bird) in the morning. Both girls are getting adequate sleep, and bedtime is much more enjoyable.

This is what I do to try to make bedtime a pleasant experience for the whole family:

1. I set a reasonable time and make sure that it is widely publi-

cized. "Eight o'clock is bedtime for children," is the slogan at our house. That means usually fifteen or twenty minutes on either side, depending upon stories, the children's needs, or mother's activities that might crowd in on the children's bedtime schedule.

2. Thirty minutes to an hour before bedtime I start the winding-down process. I try to keep the stimulation at a low level so the children approach bedtime in a relaxed manner rather than being so excited that settling down to sleep is almost impossible. During this time we put the toys away, finish the games, start the baths, and there is absolutely no TV. Evenings are for our family, and TV and family growth are just not compatible.

3. Fifteen minutes before bedtime we go into the final-count-down phase. This routine is followed faithfully each night so the children know just what to expect. When the announcement is made, "It's a quarter to eight," they know that bedtime is inevitable. There is no escaping.

The final countdown goes something like this: Finish baths, put on pajamas, brush teeth (if they somehow escaped the after-supper brushing), storytime, prayers, climb in, lights out, turn on night light, a good-night kiss, a special word for each child with a back rub or love pat thrown in, and finally as I close the door I give my last parental admonition, "Good night, sleep tight, and don't let the bedbugs bite." And the bedtime job has been accomplished—if I'm lucky enough not to hear one last, "Mommy, I'm thirsty."

Friday, September 27 / It Pays to Make the Commitment

I now know why it is important for a mother to decide she is going to be a teacher for her children. During the last week I began wondering: Is this whole thing worthwhile? It seemed as if I had been doing the things with the children that they would have done whether or not I was their teacher.

For example, sorting and matching objects and playing with blocks and dolls. But what happened today convinced me that the commitment I made to be a teacher-mother does make me look at my role as a mother differently. It all started yesterday, when Kim brought out some pieces of material about six inches square that a friend had given her. I was elbow deep in dishwater when she announced that she wanted to make a hat with them. I glanced at the pieces of material and said "fine." (A "no" would surely have created an argument, and I was sure the idea would soon be forgotten.) But bright and early this morning Kim came skipping out of her bedroom clutching those same dear scraps of material, stating that today she was going to make a hat for Kari and mittens for Kevin. I had to admire Kim's enthusiasm and her altruistic motives, but I was less than enthusiastic about the idea. Right after breakfast Kim asked me to thread a needle with a white thread she brought to me. She was obviously going to do this project with or without my help.

A few minutes later when I sat down to write out the cards for preschool, I printed "Make a hat" on one of them and put the card at the bottom of the pile. Preschool time came and the children gathered around me eagerly waiting to hear what the cards said. (See illustration of activity cards.)

Kim didn't hesitate a second in deciding what she wanted to do. "I'm going to make a hat!" she confidently said.

It was obvious to me that sewing those scraps together to make a hat was too difficult for her. How could she best learn?

For her fifth birthday, I had bought her a toy sewing machine. I had purchased the necessary batteries so that everything was ready to teach my daughter to sew. What a disappointment when Kim tried her machine. The stitches raveled out as fast as she could put them in. Sewing itself can be frustrating to both adult and child, but when the stitches ravel out so quickly, it is not worth even trying. So we had put it away in the closet. We had taken it down a few months later to play with it, only to discover that the batteries were dead. And so was my big idea to teach my daughter to sew.

But now Kim was determined to make a hat whether I helped her or not, so impulsively I said, "OK, I'll show you how to use my machine." She got on my lap and quickly learned to control the foot pedal and keep her hands far out of the range of the needle as she guided the scrap of material through the machine. Her interest and motivation were so strong that it took only one time to show her

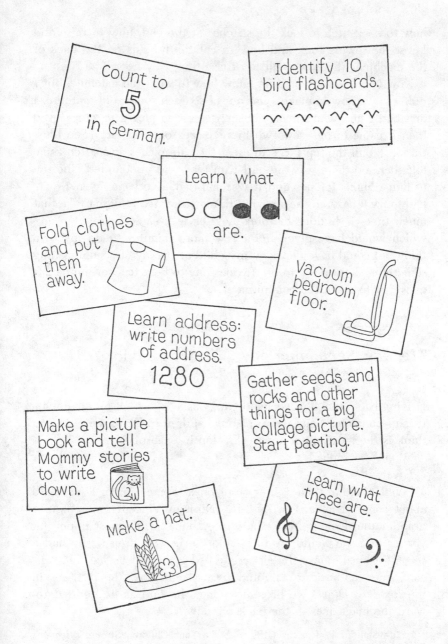

Count to 5 in German.

Identify 10 bird flashcards.

Learn what o d d d are.

Fold clothes and put them away.

Vacuum bedroom floor.

Learn address: write numbers of address. 1280

Gather seeds and rocks and other things for a big collage picture. Start pasting.

Make a picture book and tell Mommy stories to write down.

Make a hat.

Learn what these are.

how to backstitch to lock the stitches at the end, how to raise and lower the sewing foot, and how to cut the threads on the back of the machine. She now could do these things by herself.

Now I had a problem: Kim knew how to work the machine, but I didn't know how to make a hat out of six-inch squares of material. I first had Kim (who sat on my lap) sew two pieces together. And then it came to me—sew two more pieces on the side. (See illustration.) Pull the top piece to meet the side pieces and stitch them together and there was the hat! Kim's joy was unbounded. She ran to find ribbons for ties and it was finished. Everyone, even Kevin, had to try it on. And the amazing thing was, it really didn't take that much time. I shudder to think how close I came to saying "no," which would have given me a few more minutes to do my own thing but could have deprived my child of the joy of accomplishing something she wanted to do. It does pay to be a teacher-mother. It does pay to make the commitment.

Monday, September 30 / Character Traits

Driving back from our weekend trip, I asked Jan, "Of all of the virtues or character traits we want our children to have, what do you think is the most important to develop in each one?"

"Well," he replied.

I waited.

"Well, there are many important ones. For example, I just read about some in an article by Mrs. Norman Vincent Peale.* As a grandmother looking back, she wrote about the six most important virtues that she would try to develop in her children if she had a second chance today. Her list contained . . . ah, let's see . . . self-confidence, enthusiasm . . . and I can't remember the rest. It's in the *Reader's Digest* we brought along," he said as he nodded toward the magazines in the back window.

* Ruth Stafford Peale, "Six Gifts to Make Your Children Strong," *Reader's Digest* (Aug. 1974), p. 157.

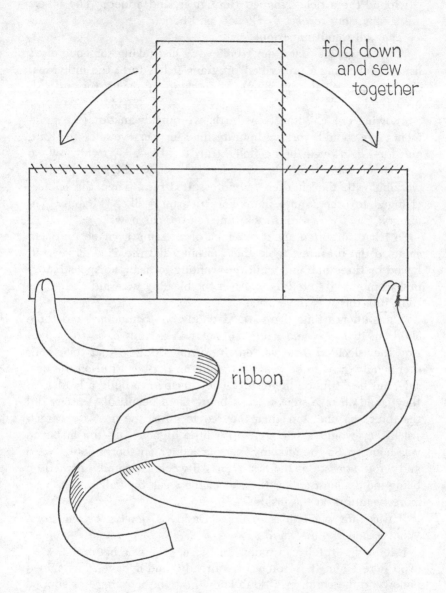

fold down
and sew
together

ribbon

I found the article, scanned through it, and added, "The others are compassion, respect, resilience, and hope."

"They all sound important."

"Yes," I agreed, "but I don't believe in just taking someone else's list and following a prescribed program; it has to fit the individual child's needs. What traits should we include on our list for our children right now?"

Knowing our children from birth, we quickly made some judgments. We should work on honesty for Kim, perseverance for Kari, and for Kevin—well, he's a delightful "terrible two" right now, so just about everything fits. We decided we would start Monday working with the children on different virtues. Then the subject changed to other, more immediate demands, like, "Mommy, I'm hungry. Can't we eat our sack lunch in the car now?"

So I had forgotten about our idea of stressing a virtue until Jan came to the breakfast table this morning like the Pied Piper, followed by three bubbling children wanting to hear the special story he had promised to tell them. After the blessing was said and plates were full, this was the story:

"Once upon a time there was a daddy and a mommy and three children, two girls and a boy. [That was getting close to home.] And they decided they wanted to do something so that their children would grow to be beautiful children; not beautiful on the outside, but beautiful on the inside. They decided to build a ladder, so they could all take steps toward being more beautiful. As they did the things on one step, then they could go to the next step. Each week they would get to step up a little higher. And the first step was honesty. So the mommy made a ladder on the bulletin board and wrote honesty as the first step. All week the family worked on being more honest and at the end of the week they all were a little more beautiful on the inside."

It was Kim who spoke up first. "Daddy, I don't get your story. What is honesty, anyway?"

"Mommy will tell you today for preschool," was his reply.

So here I am. It is 10:00 A.M. already, and I haven't explained honesty to the children. I don't know how the morning has slipped away from me. I just put in my third load of clothes to wash, ordered a winter coat for Kim that was on sale in the new catalog, and I can't procrastinate any longer or the morning will be gone. Here goes!

Later:

I set out paper and scissors and asked the girls (Kevin hasn't mastered the cutting skill yet) to cut strips of paper to make a ladder for the bulletin board. They happily did what I asked, even though the task was far from creative. Then I wrote the word "Honesty" on the bottom rung and explained that honesty was the first step toward having a beautiful character. I then read them the story, "Zacchaeus, the Cheater" from *My Bible Friends* series, as an example of how people disliked a person who was not honest. I explained that we can all be honest if we become Jesus' friend. He will help us not to cheat or tell lies.

"But I still don't understand," said Kim. "What does honesty have to do with being beautiful?"

"Well," I hesitated, "let's go out and see if we can find some roses."

Now the children were really curious.

I pointed to a beautiful-looking bud. "You children are like buds. When buds are very young they still have the green protective sepal surrounding their tender petals. Now, there are lots of bugs and worms that would like to get into the middle of this rosebud and eat the nice, tasty, beautiful petals. As long as the green sepals surround the bud it is pretty safe, but it doesn't want to stay a bud all its life, so as it grows the sepals open up and petal by petal the rose unfolds so you can see its beautiful inside. Worms and bugs are the most dangerous to the young opening buds. If the bud can resist the pests it will usually grow into a beautiful flower."

I then went on to explain, "The green sepals are like Mommy and Daddy, who watch out for you and teach you what is right and wrong and protect you from bad things. But as you grow Mommy and Daddy can't always be with you to teach and protect you. You must make choices yourself about how to stay beautiful on the inside. The worms and bugs are like temptations to be dishonest, and to lie, cheat, and steal. Now is the time when these worms and bugs have the most chance of damaging you on the inside so when you grow up to be full-blooming roses your insides will be all eaten and scarred by dishonesty."

Then I pointed out a rosebud with a wormhole and another open rose with a damaged inside.

"I don't want to grow up having the worms eat out my insides," said Kari, much impressed with the explanation.

"Being honest," I continued, "is the way you keep the worms out so you can grow up to be beautiful roses on the inside. Do you understand?"

"I think so," Kim replied.

I'm really not sure how clearly I explained what honesty is, but I think stories and object lessons are much more effective than a lecture on the definition of honesty. And where can anyone find better character-building stories than in the lives of those persons told about in the Bible and in nature's object lessons?

Teaching about character development is usually done with a hit-or-miss approach. I think most people just assume it all happens naturally. But without a plan there can be serious omissions, and I don't want those to happen in Kim's, Kari's, and Kevin's lives. I like the systematic approach of stressing one particular trait at a time and then going on to another. I guess next week it will be perseverance, and the next week—well, my list is already too long. (See January 1.)

OCTOBER is born
We must move on and beyond
Our mystical dawn

Tuesday, October 1 / When the Teacher-mother Gets Sick

Today I feel terrible. My cold has gone into my head. I can't breathe, my sinuses are full. My body aches. All I feel like doing is lying in bed surrounded by peace and quiet. Lying in bed is not too difficult, but to achieve peace and quiet with three little Indians living in the same house is another story.

So this morning (after they had been playing toboggan over my prone body) when one of them said they wanted to watch TV, I thought, "Why not? Once a year can't hurt them." They turned on the UHF channel at about nine fifty-five just in time to watch the last five minutes of "Sesame Street." A special program for children with Halloween songs and stories followed; they then switched channels and found "The Brady Bunch"; then back again for "The Electric Company" and "Villa Alegre." I couldn't believe it when I came into the family room at noon. For two whole hours my three children had been sitting with their eyes glued to the TV.

It was always hard for me to believe the statistics that on the average children spend as much time watching TV each week as they spend in school—so much time, in fact, that by sixteen years of age, they have averaged the equivalent of fifteen to twenty months of

TV watching, twenty-four hours a day! Now I believe it can happen. If I hadn't established some controls, they could have started watching the children's programs that begin again at about 3:00 P.M., then watched an hour of the news and then the evening comedies. What a waste of time!

As I forced myself to prepare the children a decent lunch, I came to the conclusion that first of all a teacher-mother should never get sick, and second, if sickness does come (even after carefully guarding her health), she should teach her children how to take care of themselves without having to resort to a television baby-sitter.

When I feel good, it takes every bit of energy I can muster to keep up and ahead of my children. But when I feel bad, teaching them is a most difficult task. The quality of life in our whole house goes down when I'm down. Not only are the children somewhat neglected, but also sometimes the interactions that they have with me are not what I would recommend. "Don't do that!" "Be quiet!" "No, I can't help you now!" My patience runs short, and even the children's innocent play with their giggling and occasional squabbling grates on my nerves.

The conclusion that a teacher-mother should never get sick, although idealistic, is not realistic. Therefore, I am wondering how I can make today a learning experience for my children. Perhaps if I would only take time with them, they could learn . . .

1. to understand my impatience with noise and interruptions when I'm trying to sleep.

2. what they can do to help me feel more comfortable.

3. how they can play alone without needing my help.

4. to prepare simple food and use paper plates and pick up their toys so I will not have as much work to do.

I think I will call the children to my bedside and explain to them just how badly I'm feeling and enlist their co-operation. I have a feeling the few extra minutes spent with them in this way may help this day to end with the children having a good learning experience, even though two hours of the morning were wasted watching TV.

Wednesday, October 2 / Charades

"How would you kids like to play charades?"

"What's that?" the children asked with puzzled looks on their faces.

"Here, I'll show you how. I'll act out something and you have to guess what I'm doing." I pretended I was sweeping the floor. After they guessed I encouraged them to try. "Act out somebody working or be an animal." With a little help Kevin pretended to be a horse. Kari chose to pound with a hammer and be a carpenter, and Kim acted as if she were a teacher. Then they pretended to be such things as an airplane pilot, a snake, a bird, a swimmer, an elephant, and a turtle.

After preschool the children thought of many other things they could act out, and came to me throughout the day saying, "Guess what I'm doing now, Mommy."

I continued to play the game by asking them to do things by acting them out. For example, I would say, "Time to ——." Then I'd pretend to eat, brush teeth, or take a nap.

At bedtime we played a variation of the game. The object was to tell how the person was feeling by his facial expressions. It was amazing how easily different emotions such as fear, anger, sadness, jealousy, and happiness were identified by the children.

Thursday, October 3 / Action Songs

As a follow-up on the charades we enjoyed yesterday we sang some action songs I learned as a child. "The Battle Hymn of the Republic" was the only tune we needed for these three action-packed songs: "John Brown's Baby," "Mr. Bunny Rabbit," and "Old Mr. Ford."

"John Brown's Baby" is perhaps the best known of the three. Here are the words and actions:

"John Brown's baby [rock arms] had a cold [cough] upon his chest. [Put hand over chest. Repeat this line three times.] And they rubbed [rub chest] it with camphorated oil. [Hold nose.]"

The way you do this is to leave out singing the first action word and do only the action. Each time you sing the song, leave out the next action word and keep singing until it is all action! "Mr. Bunny Rabbit" goes like this:

"Mr. Bunny Rabbit [put hands up like ears] had a fly [say 'Buzz' and wiggle finger as if flying] upon his ear. [Put hand up as if an ear. Repeat this line three times.] And he flapped it [flap arms held against head as if ears] until it flew away. [Wave both arms as in flying motion.]"

"Old Mr. Ford" is my favorite. It has been sung for the July Fourth celebration in my hometown for as long as I can remember. The words and actions go like this:

"Old Mr. Ford [grunt loudly] had a puncture [say 'sssss'] in his tire. [Hold hands and arms above head like a tire. Repeat this line three times.] And he fixed it with a wad of chewing gum. [Make your voice slide down about four notes on 'gum' and back up like a trombone, while pretending to reach in your mouth and pull out the gum to arm's length and put it back in again.]"

All this sounds rather complicated, but the children caught on in a few seconds when they heard and saw it done. They will have a good time singing these songs as we travel or around a campfire.

Friday, October 4 / My Reward

"Mommy, Mommy, come outside quickly! You won't believe the surprise I have for you," called Kim. She was followed by Kari, saying, "Yeah, Mommy, it's real neat."

Well, at least my curiosity was aroused enough to leave my half-typed letter and follow the girls. Outside Kim raced to her bicycle, from which I had just recently removed the training wheels. I must have run behind her for miles, holding onto the seat, trying to teach her how to balance it. Just this morning, Kim had almost started crying over the frustrating experience, and I was beginning to doubt she would ever master it! I watched in disbelief as she got the pedals in just the proper place, put one foot on, and gave a little push with the other, wobbled unsteadily for a second, and then rode her bike the whole length of the driveway, even maneuvering the ninety-degree turn.

I changed my mind right then. The joy of seeing Kim's exhilarating excitement of achieving the almost impossible was worth every minute and more that I had spent helping her. Yes, I will admit: Being my child's teacher is a satisfying job.

Monday, October 7 / "Mary Had a Little Lamb"

What a beautiful day this has been! Not outside—it's one of those early-fall gray days with such a heavy sky you're sure it's going to rain. No one has felt like going outside, but inside I could sing. Everything has gone so well. Kim is bubbling over with joy because she learned to play "Mary Had a Little Lamb" on the piano. It always amazes me to see how much joy a child gets from such small accomplishments (small in our estimation).

Preschool started out in the usual way, sorting through the cards. I didn't even add anything new, since the cards are slowly piling up. If we don't get some of these items done, before long it will take all of our preschool time just reading through the cards. Kim has sorted through them so often she knows pretty much what every card says; not that she can read—she just has her own coding system. If I ask her how she knows that a card says, "Clean your room," she may answer, "Because it's pink," or "Because it only has three words on the card." So today she sorted out the three cards that had something to do with the piano. (See illustration.)

When I made out the cards I had no idea how to go about teaching these fundamental musical concepts. I wish I had had time to check through some method books for teaching music to young children, but since I am a teacher-mother and expected to teach

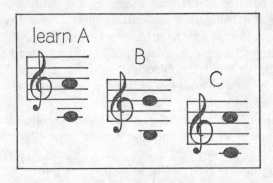

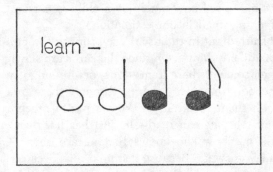

every subject, I sometimes don't have time to read a how-to book for each subject, and I must do what comes naturally. So I used what I call the trial-and-error, common-sense approach. It doesn't always work, but today was like magic. Kim and I started with the card about the ABCs of music.

"Find A on the piano." The moment I said it, I realized what a foolish request I had made. What chance had Kim of being successful in finding an A out of all those unknown keys on the piano? So I tried again. "This key is an A on the piano. It is right between two of these three black keys. See if you can find another A on the piano." In no time eight As, eight Bs, and eight Cs were located. And before I could think about what to do next, she played the A (saying the name of the note), the B, the C, and continued D, E, F, G, and almost said H, hesitated, laughed, and said A, all without my trying to go through each separately. What a lot of words and explanations that saved. So I moved on. Forgetting that you need to know about musical signs and notes before you play anything, I suggested, "I know a song that uses most of these notes. Would you like to learn it?"

"Yes!" The bait had been swallowed.

Three months ago I showed Kim how easy it was to play "Mary Had a Little Lamb." "It only takes five notes and you can pick out the notes yourself. It's easy," I had said. Well, playing "Mary Had a Little Lamb" with one finger, by ear, may have been easy for me, but it was extremely difficult for her. I even pointed above her fingers which note to play next. Still she gave up, frustrated. Three months heals wounds, and when I mentioned "Mary Had a Little Lamb," she seemed eager. I played it once for her, singing along the names of the notes as I went, "E, D, C, D, E, E, E . . ." It finally dawned on me: You don't really need to know notes and all the technical stuff before you can have fun playing music. I found a ragged nursery-rhyme song book I had as a child, and sure enough, there was "Mary Had a Little Lamb" in the key of C.

In just a few minutes, I covered the necessary information Kim needed to know in order to read the music.

"This is a treble clef. You will play every note on the lines where the treble clef is. These notes on the lines tell you which keys to play on the piano. The first note is E. It is on the first line of the staff. The second note is just below the E note. What name do you think that note has?" She hesitated and then the light dawned as she realized the notes' names went up the staff in the same order as the alphabet. I wrote the familiar letter names above the notes on the staff. And then I said, "As I point to the note (with the letter name above it), you play that key on the piano." We did it twice like that before Kevin announced he was "going potty." I ran to the bathroom to catch what I could, leaving Kim alone, and I couldn't believe my ears. From the living room came the most beautiful music I have ever heard—my very first child playing stumblingly through her very first song all by herself! I'm sure "Mary Had a Little Lamb" will always hold a special place in my heart.

But my excitement was small compared to her own. "Mommy, I did it! I did it!" she yelled as she came running to tell me, the ragged song book clutched in her arms.

I shared her moment of triumph before stating reality. "It takes lots of practice to really play 'Mary Had a Little Lamb' well. You'll have to play it over many, many times." Without another word she ran back to begin practicing.

About ten times later she announced, somewhat surprised at herself, "I can even play it without looking at the music." And so she had memorized her first piece.

Today I solved the practice problem. What about tomorrow? So many of the parents I know right now are having to stand over their children or threaten them in order to get them to practice. I would hate to be in that position, but days of not wanting to practice are probably ahead. Wouldn't it be wonderful if every day children could find just the right challenge in music (like Kim did today) to motivate them to practice? But now I'm dreaming.

"Time to go to Evelyn's house. Please get your things ready," I announced. As I carried Kim's bag of things to take to Evelyn's to the car, I noticed that along with Kim's roller skates and dolls was the nursery-rhyme song book. "Kim, what are you taking the song book for? Evelyn doesn't even have a piano."

"I know. I just want to show them that I can play 'Mary Had a Little Lamb' . . . and tomorrow I want to learn 'Three Blind Mice.' "

Tuesday, October 8 / Recipes

Cooking is one of the children's favorite preschool activities. Today they made their own recipe book so they could remember what dishes they liked best that were fairly easy to make. Instead of adding the full recipe, they just wrote the name of the dish and drew a picture of it. Now when they want to cook something special all they have to do is look through their book for ideas.

Here are the recipes the children selected:

Pizza Muffins

1 package English muffins	grated cheese and other
1 can pizza sauce or spaghetti	favorite toppings
sauce	olive oil (or regular) in a
	squeeze bottle

Open muffins on a cookie sheet.
Squeeze a little olive oil on each muffin (a spoon can be used).
Put a spoonful of pizza sauce on each.
Sprinkle with cheese and other favorite toppings.
Broil until cheese melts.

Silly-shaped Cake

Pour cake-mix batter into frozen aluminum dinner containers with various-shaped holes. After baked cake cools, let the children decorate with imitation whipped cream either squirted out from a can, or by knife. With a drop of food coloring the children can add various colors of "frosting."

Fruit Leather

Use any ripe fruit such as pears, peaches, apples (not citrus). Remove seeds (not skin) and cook down to a pulp. Blend in blender. Spread ⅛-inch thick on clear plastic wrap on cookie sheet. Place in warm oven until dry to touch. Leave oven door open slightly.

Bean Salad

Take a can of each of the following:

olives (pitted)	red kidney beans
green string beans	*garbanzos*
yellow wax beans	hominy

Drain off the liquid and mix together. (Older children can cut in tomatoes.) Then pour Italian dressing over it. It's delicious, and there's plenty for company!

Date-nut Candy

With a dull plastic knife cut seeds out of dates. Stuff each date with a walnut piece, almond, or peanut. Eat immediately.

Fruit-juice Popsicles

Use any kind of fruit juice, including the juice from canned fruit. Pour into a small glass and insert a popsicle stick (or spoon). Freeze.

Tower Sandwiches

Spread cracker with softened cream cheese or peanut butter. Put another cracker on top. Keep alternating cracker and filler until the tower reaches the desired height.

Strawberry-banana Milkshake

1 cup cold milk	1 frozen banana
1 cup frozen strawberries	2 teaspoons sugar, optional

Place in blender until smooth.
Serve immediately.

And now for my own favorite recipe. I call it:
The Kuzma Recipe for a Well-preserved Family

Take one happy husband and one happy wife

Add: 3 small children
2 dogs and
1 cat

Mix together with love and care and thanksgiving.
Add a pinch of tears and stir with compassion.
Let settle into a comfortable house.
Fill center with toys, books, food, and laughter.
In summer:

sprinkle with sunshine,
spread with a layer of clear blue sky, and
bake outdoors in a flower-fragranced yard.
Cool in the pool.

In winter:

sprinkle with raindrops,

spread with a layer of heavy gray clouds, and
bake in front of the fireplace until cozy and warm.

Serve immediately.

Wednesday, October 9 / The Middle Child

I remember that Kim knew the alphabet by three years of age, and
surely Kari should know it, too, by now. I really don't believe it is
extremely important that three- and four-year-olds know the alphabet. In fact, kids can do very nicely without it until they are ready
to read and alphabetize things. I do think, however, it is important
for them to learn the sounds of the letters, and parents should play
games with them like, "Guess which letter this word starts with?"
or "What letter makes the m-m-m-m sound?" before first grade. But
just learning the alphabet by rote has very little value.

Now that Kari is four, I just naturally expected that she knew all
the letters. She had listened to the lessons I had given Kim. Kari
sings the alphabet song beautifully (she just mixes up J and K). So
when I sat down with her today with one of Kevin's picture alphabet books I couldn't believe that she didn't know the E or the F,
and many other letters.

I can remember a year ago, when she was just barely three, we
started teaching her some letters. At that time she did well with B
and C, but no matter how many times we told her A, she couldn't
remember it. Finally in frustration I said, "You really have a problem with A, don't you?" After that every time she would see the letter she would say, "Oh that's the letter that gives me problems; it
must be an A."

I now see how important it is for a teacher to plan for each child
individually. I just took it for granted that Kari was catching everything I was throwing to Kim. I really need to sit down and plan
some learning experiences just for Kari.

The thing that really shocks me is how a parent can live so
closely with a child and yet not really know her. If this can happen
in early childhood, when you spend most of your time together,
how much easier it must be to lose contact with a teen-ager.

Thursday, October 10 / Homemade

French fries and doughnuts are not exactly the most nutritious foods that one can give to preschoolers, so I very rarely serve them at our home. A few weeks ago, however, I asked the children if they wanted french fries for lunch. They all, including Lisa and Greg, who were there at the time, shouted, "YES."

So I replied, "OK. I'll need some helpers to peel the potatoes."

Lisa looked at me in amazement and said, "I thought you had to go to McDonald's to get them."

Today I decided to experiment by making homemade doughnuts for our preschool activity. This time it was Kari who looked at me questioningly and said, "Mommy, do you really know how to make doughnuts?"

I'll have to admit, I was surprised how very simple they were to make. We didn't have any of the special equipment like a deep-fry pan or doughnut cutter, so we used a pan on the stove to deep-fry in and a jar to cut out the outside shape and a small tube to cut out the hole. I had forgotten how delicious warm, whole-wheat cake doughnuts sprinkled with date sugar tasted, but I doubt if the children forget.

But of all the homemade products that the children and I enjoy making, there is nothing quite as special as homemade whole-wheat bread. Mmmmmmmm! Just thinking about the aroma and taste of freshly baked whole-wheat bread makes my mouth water. The children enjoy breadmaking at every stage—mixing, tasting, kneading, and eating. The surprising thing is that yeast bread is not very difficult to make. It doesn't take long to mix the ingredients together or to knead. The time-consuming process is waiting for the bread to rise, but that time can be profitably spent on other preschool activities, or tackling my "Things to Do" list.

I think one of the nicest things about being a teacher-mother who stays home a good share of the day is that I have time to treat the family to homemade versions of their favorite foods, and enjoy the children, and the principal exclaiming, "You mean that you don't have to go to McDonald's to get this?" In addition, the children experience a heightened sense of self-worth knowing that they have contributed in the preparation of such delicacies. Here are the recipes we used:

Whole-wheat Cake Doughnuts

4 beaten eggs	3 teaspoons baking powder
½ cup sugar	¾ teaspoon salt
⅓ cup milk	1 teaspoon cinnamon
⅓ cup vegetable shortening	½ teaspoon nutmeg
3½ cups whole-wheat flour	

Beat eggs and sugar till light. Add milk and shortening. Sift dry ingredients together and add to first mixture. Chill. On lightly floured surface, roll dough ⅜ inch thick. Cut out doughnut shapes. Let stand 15 minutes. Fry in vegetable shortening in a deep pan (375 degrees) until brown, turning once. Drain on paper towels. While warm press in bowl of date sugar. Makes approximately two dozen.

Whole-wheat Bread

Set aside to rise: 2 rounded tablespoons yeast sprinkled on ½ cup warm water and 1 teaspoon sugar. (If yeast has been in fridge, use quite warm water.)
Combine the following ingredients and mix:

⅔ cup raw sugar (or brown)	Add yeast mixture, which
⅔ cup oil	should be light and fluffy.
2 tablespoons salt	Add 3 cups flour and mix
5 cups warm water	thoroughly.
Add 7 cups whole-wheat flour and mix thoroughly.	

Sprinkle 3 to 4 cups more flour into mixture as you begin kneading. (Add only enough flour so you can touch dough without sticking to it.) Knead approximately 10 minutes and then let stand for 10 minutes. Mold into 4 pan-size oval balls. Place in greased loaf pans. Let rise for 25 to 30 minutes. Bake at 350 degrees for 35 minutes.

Friday, October 11 / Phonics

Kim is really becoming interested in reading. Today on her own she wrote down some more words she has learned, such as: go, love, Puff, bus, Pat, milk, Kevin, Kari, Kay, Jan, fox, and Mexico. It's probably not what a grown-up would select for a child's spelling list, but these are words that she is interested in and has pretty much learned on her own.

A few years ago I was fascinated by an advertisement in *Parents' Magazine* that shows a 4½-year-old reading third-grade books. Since I didn't know very much about how to teach phonics, I ordered the *Listen and Learn with Phonics*† kit with a 10-day, free-return policy. When it came, my 3-year-old Kim could care less about letters, let alone phonics, so it was not opened until a year later. Now that I have looked at it, I realize I could do by myself what the kit suggests, but it is a little late to send it back!

So now that we have it, I've used it with Kim, listening to the records and looking at the corresponding book. Every time I listen to a record I become more and more convinced that any parent can teach beginning phonics.

Naturally, you start out with the sounds of the consonants, because they don't change. But you have to watch out for the letters with two sounds, like G (as in girl, and as in George).

This kit doesn't mention the names of the letters—only the sounds. I can see the rationale in this. If you want a four- or five-year-old to read, why clutter their minds with two abstract things, the name of the letter and the sound, when in reality it is only the sound that is really needed in reading?

But Kim already had the names of the letters so well in mind that it has not been difficult to associate the sound with the letter name.

I really don't like the "listen and learn" method of learning anything, not even for college students. I think teaching is more effective if it's done incidentally, at that teachable moment, rather than by lecturing. For example, instead of looking at nineteen pages at a

† Career Institute Inc., Mundelein, Ill. 60060.

sitting and hearing a voice say, "This is the *Buh* sound," it seems a lot more meaningful to me to say to children as they are playing ball, "Ball starts with the Buh sound. Can you hear it when I pronounce the word slowly? Now you say it."

I like the idea of illustrating a letter sound to make it less abstract. For example, milk coming out of a bottle sometimes sounds like "buh, buh, buh." Any parent can come up with his or her own list of such illustrations, but here is the list we are using, based on the *Listen and Learn* set of materials.

A‡ (as in apple or "a-a-h" if you saw a worm in an apple)
B   (emptying a bottle of milk, b-b-b-b)
C   (cat coughing as if choking on something, c-c-c-c)
D   (drain sound, d-d-d)
E‡ (eh, as in elephant)
F   (cat hissing, f-f-f-f)
G   (frog croaking, or like the J sound)
H   (panting, h-h-h)
I‡ (I as in Indian)
J   (the beginning sound of jump, as when jumping rope)
K   (same as c)
L   (sound that goes through a wire, l-l-l)
M   (top humming, m-m-m)
N   (as in "No, no")
O‡ (as in octopus)
P   (puffing on a pipe, p-p-p)
Q   (as in quick)
R   (growling dog, r-r-r)
S   (snake hissing, s-s-s)
T   (ticking of a clock, t-t-t)
U‡ (as in umbrella)
V   (as in Valentine)
W   (wind blowing)
X   (as in ax)
Y‡ (*i* sound as in cry, and *e* sound as in yawn)
Z   (buzzy bee, z-z-z)

I think that one of the most clever things that I got from the set of materials is how to remember which letters are vowels. The story

‡ a short sound given

is told of a girl who borrowed some sugar and then went to return it. But she couldn't say the L sound for "lady," so she said, "AE, IOU some sugar." With a few clever ideas such as this, parents can be quite effective in introducing their children to the important world of phonics.

Monday, October 14 / Chain-learning

Sylvia Ashton-Warner, in her book *Teacher* (New York: Bantam, 1971), says that when children have a chance to choose their own words, they learn to spell and read them without difficulty and seldom forget them. I agree.

One day last week Jan said, as he was leaving for work, "Don't let Kevin see the G-U-M" (spelling out the last word for my information only).

That sparked everyone's interest, and immediately Kim said, "What's G-U-M?"

Then I could hear her saying to herself as she headed down the hall to her room, "G-U-M. G-U-M." At midmorning Kim brought me a torn-off corner of paper on which was printed G-U-M. "Look, Mommy," she said, "that's GUM."

Today for preschool, I said to Kim, "I'll give you a prize for every five words you can write on these cards. If you know ten words, I'll take you to the park." Then I made the same proposition to Kari, making it letters instead of words.

There is such a difference in the way children accept challenges and buckle down to work. Kim found a pencil, sat down, and immediately started writing down the words she remembered. Kari just stood looking at me. So I got a pencil for her, arranged the cards, and even got an alphabet book so she could copy the letters she knew. I gave her the directions again and helped her copy the first letter so that she would know exactly what was expected of her. By this time, Kim already had ten words down on her cards—and guess what the first one was? GUM! This was her list:

GUM

FOR

FORD

SEY   (I told her this was backward, so she changed it to YE2.
How many times do you correct a child before frustrating
her? I left it for now. The next time she will probably have
the S right.)

ON   I asked her what this word was, because I knew she didn't
know ON. She said, "NO," so I turned the card upside down
and sure enough it was NO.

SEE

Oꟻ   (which I recognized was OF)

LOOK

LOVE

GO

TO

Finally there was a card that had "∩∩" on it. That really stumped
me. I couldn't even read it. So I asked Kim what it said. "Oh," she
replied, "that's 'McDonald's.'" I had to admit I could see the resemblance once it was pointed out and almost didn't have the heart
to tell her those were just the golden arches that resembled an M,
which was only the first letter of the word McDonald's.

It was Kari's turn next. Troubles, troubles. "I can't do it," she
complained. I sat beside her to support her and *we* got five letters
written down. Ten would have caused a breakdown for Kari. So we
left for the park, with the alphabet book in hand, my hand. Kari
could care less. After playing on the playground equipment for a
while, I pulled out the book. Kari willingly sat down beside me. I
opened it up in the middle and asked her what letter I was pointing at.

"No, no," she said, "that's not the way you do it." She took the
book from me, turned to the first page and said "A," then turned to
the next page and said "B," and continued through the entire book
—not missing a letter. On the surface it looked as if she knew all the
letters. So again I turned at random to a page and said, "What is
this letter?"

Her response was a whispered, "A, b, c, d, e, f, g, h, i . . ." Then
in a loud voice she stated, "I." She was right, but the process by

which she arrived at the answer intrigued me. I turned to another page; again she started through the alphabet and arrived at the right answer. Enough for one day; it was time to play. As she ran off, happy and successful, I began to realize that learning in a "chaining" fashion not only facilitates learning of some things, but also may become a crutch that a child would be better off without. Since Kari likes the way that offers the least resistance, why bother learning the letters as individual entities when you could get to the same place easier (even though more slowly) by starting at the beginning of the alphabet each time? Well, we'd just have to work on it when we have the opportunity. I think I'll do away with the alphabet book for the present. It just reinforces the chaining. I'll start helping Kari to notice letters as they appear in real life—all jumbled up. Hey, I have a good idea: a jumbled-up alphabet book, where all twenty-six letters are presented in a random order only. On second thought, such a book probably wouldn't sell. Grown-ups probably find security in the familiar alphabet just about the same way children do.

Kari is not the only chain-dependent child in our family. The girls get a good laugh from showing Kevin a group of objects and asking him how many things there are. They love to hear him say, "Two, three, four."

But the best example of chain learning I heard was when I was a teen-ager baby-sitting little Barbara. She had just returned from a vacation visiting her uncle Eddie, who lived on a farm. She bowed her head before eating and this was her prayer: "God bless Mommy and Daddy, Trixie and Bingo, and Uncle Eddie has a farm, E, I, E, I, O."

Tuesday, October 15 / Exercising

"One, two, one, two, up, down, up, down . . ." It was my exercise time during the children's preschool activity time. Why not? I find I get plenty of exercise when I include them in my program and they benefit as well. Kevin's my biggest helper. He sits on my feet as I do situps. "One, two, three, four . . . nine, ten," he counts and then starts over again. Sometimes we see if I can do enough situps for the entire alphabet. That's twenty-six of them! When I'm tired and ready to quit, Kevin shouts, "Again, Mommy. Do it again." And I try to comply.

I plan exercises that will be especially helpful for my pre-schoolers as they participate with me. We touch toes as we pretend to parachute out of our planes. We bend from side to side with arms extended over our heads as if we are trees blowing in the wind. When we are hopping on one leg we are monkeys who have hurt a foot; when jumping on two legs we are jumping jackrabbits. With the splits we are bridges over a river that keeps getting wider. Balancing on one foot with the other extended behind is our ice-skating routine. A head stand is an upside-down statue, and a somersault is a tumbling tumbleweed. The most difficult is a boat made by lying on your stomach and grasping your feet and rocking back and forth on your tummy. Groan.

Then comes my leg exercises—which the children think are the most fun. I lie on my back with my feet in the air, and one of the children lies tummy down balancing on the soles of my feet. They extend their arms to the side and become soaring airplanes. Finally, I flip them in the air by lying down and letting them sit on the top of my feet with my legs bent. I have them lean forward and hold their shoulders with my hands and then kick my legs up into the air and flip them over my head.

"Again, again," the children shout. Finally, when I can't hold up my feet and legs any longer, I announce, "The end. This flipping machine is out of order until preschool time tomorrow."

Wednesday, October 16 / Concepts

The children were all trying to blow up their balloons. Kim succeeded, and I made the casual comment, "Kim's balloon is filled with her carbon dioxide."

"Why did you say that?" Kim looked at me quizzically.

Perhaps it was a little academic, I thought, but now that I've gotten myself into it, I attempted this explanation.

"The air around us is made up of gases. There is a lot of nitrogen gas, some oxygen gas, and a tiny bit of carbon-dioxide gas and other gases. You need the oxygen to live, so when you breathe the air into your lungs, the little red-blood cells capture the oxygen. When the oxygen is mixed with food in the blood, energy is released, so that you feel like moving and playing. The gas, carbon dioxide, is also produced. But you don't need it, so it goes back to your lungs and you breathe it out with the other gases you don't need. Since you breathe out more carbon dioxide than you breathe in, the balloon is filled with a lot more carbon dioxide than it would have been if you had blown it up with a bicycle pump."

Kim's expression immediately changed to concern as she asked, "Is the capturing going to hurt me?"

I had to hold back my smile and added, "No, all that capturing that the blood cells are doing in your lungs is what they are supposed to be doing."

I realized then that the explanation was too advanced for her. I would have to repeat this over and over before she really understood the process. In the meantime, I'm going to do some studying on this subject in the encyclopedia to see if my information is correct. As her understanding increases I will be able to explain further how the plants need the carbon dioxide to live and they give off the oxygen that we need to live. Neither of us could live without the other.

Isn't it amazing how many things children must learn about in this world? I could help them get a head start if only I, as a parent, knew more about these things. For example, what specific gases compose the air we breathe? How really does the capturing take place? I think I know so much until one of the children asks a simple question and I have to try to explain.

On the other hand, it is surprising how many things we assume children know about, only to discover they haven't the foggiest notion what we've been talking about. You would think that a four-year-old who has been to church almost every week of her life and who hears religious songs and knows so many herself, would know what a hymn is. I read a story to the children today about hymns and singing praises. One of the questions at the end of the book was, "How many hymns do you know?" Kari didn't hesitate a mo-

ment and said, "I know lots of them—Jesus, Daddy, Opa . . ."
Well, I guess I know lots of those "hims," too!

Thursday, October 17 / A Vacation

Every teacher needs a vacation. This is also true for every mother.
Maybe it is doubly true for every teacher-mother! I can see that
even though teacher-mothers may need a vacation, it is probably
also doubly impossible to take a complete vacation at Thanksgiving, Christmas, or Eastertime, as most teachers do. But an unusual situation has come up, giving me a chance to take a unique vacation. I have been asked to give a paper at the American Public
Health Association in New Orleans, and by coincidence Jan is giving a paper there, too. It all sounds too good to be true. A whole
week alone with my husband in New Orleans!

Some people would shake their heads in disbelief that devoted
parents would leave three preschoolers and go off by themselves.
Isn't this the time that children need their parents the most? This
may be true, but children also need happy parents. And there is
nothing that rejuvenates a marriage more than taking a honeymoon
each year.

Our children are now old enough actually to look forward to having us go away for a few days. They think it is very special to be
able to spend a whole week with their cousins. I gave each of our
children a stamped envelope with our New Orleans address in case
they wanted to draw a picture and send it to us. I specifically
suggested that the girls might draw a picture of themselves doing
something special at the cousins. (Kevin is still at the scribbling
stage!)

The preschool activity today was to pack suitcases. First I asked
the children to tell me what they wanted to take. Next, I modified
and completed their lists by adding what I thought they would
need. Beside each item on the girls' lists I drew a descriptive picture so they would be able to check the lists themselves. As they
put an item in the suitcase, they marked it off the list. I double-

checked their work to make sure nothing was forgotten. I worked with Kevin on the packing project, asking him to bring me various items. He had a good time getting such things as his toothbrush, teddy bear, and blanket.

By eleven o'clock the car was full with everything they thought they might need for a week. As a going-away treat, I packed a surprise picnic lunch for them.

"Where are you going?" Kari asked as I turned off the main road toward the park.

"Are you hungry?" I asked.

"I'm starved," they all replied.

"Then let's have a picnic and feed the ducks before we go to the cousins."

"Oh goody," they shouted. "It's fun going on vacation."

Thursday, October 24 / "Long Distance" Preschool Projects

It was good to have a vacation but it's also good to be home. While we were away we tried to make sure the children had a daily reminder of our love. We called them and sent postcards. But they especially liked the picture letter I wrote them.

So the children could experience as much of our trip as possible, Jan and I kept a scrapbook of the things we did. It contained matchbooks, napkins, placemats, ticket stubs, postcards, and pictures we drew of some of our experiences. We even included the pictures the children had sent to us. Preschool time today was spent "reading" through the scrapbook—and unpacking. They are looking forward to the big homecoming celebration tonight, when Daddy and Mommy take them out to dinner to some "fancy" place where they will be able to collect a matchbook, napkin, and placemat to add to the last page of the vacation scrapbook.

Dear Kim, Kari and Kevin,

👁 love U. 🧍 (Daddy) and 👁

🪚 a big 〰️river 2 day.

We went in a 🚢.

🧍 and 👁 8 breakfast

in a 🪭C place. We

miss U. B.. good.

♡♡ and xxxxx

Mommy and 🧍

Friday, October 25 / Free and Inexpensive Materials

"Oh Mommy, where is that easel you bought for us?" asked Kim right out of the blue.

"What easel?" I replied, trying to act surprised. I had gotten one on sale three weeks ago for the children's Christmas present and was so pleased with myself at having gotten it in and out of the car without the children even noticing. What had gone wrong? I quizzed Kim enough to realize that she knew I had it and wasn't going to accept "no" for an answer. So I decided the children could have an early Christmas present. Perhaps it would be more meaningful at this time than it would be later, when the tree would be surrounded by other presents.

We pulled it out of its hiding place in the garage, and the children helped me with what was going to be the Christmas-morning task of putting it together. By the time it was ready the children all had visions in their little heads of the pictures they wanted to paint on the easel. It was then that I went to the cupboard only to realize, like Old Mother Hubbard, that the cupboard was bare. We needed paint, paper, and brushes.

"Let's go shopping and get everything we need so we can use our easel," they pleaded.

Our first stop was at the local newspaper office, where I used to get free all of the end rolls of newsprint I wanted. Today they charged me for the leftovers. But getting newsprint in this form is still less expensive than buying it already cut, and the children can cut the size pieces they want.

I then started soliciting the wallpaper stores for discarded books of wallpaper samples. These large colorful sheets make excellent easel paper, or can be used for cutting or collage. One store willingly gave us a book, but I ended up paying a dollar each for two more. I think we will use one of the books for the children to have as an art scrapbook, so they can keep their favorite pictures organized. Another book will be used for a scrapbook of dog pictures. The children can start finding dog pictures in magazines, cut them out, find their names, and paste the pictures in a wallpaper book labeled "Dogs." And one of the books will be used for colorful and unique paper for their art projects.

I don't like to purchase paper if I can possibly get it free. I ask Jan to save all the old scratch paper from the office that still has one clean side, and the children do most of their drawing on that paper. Other sources of paper are:

1. printing companies
2. used wrapping paper
3. old newspapers
4. white cards that come in packages of women's hose
5. slightly soiled paper plates
6. cardboard boxes
7. computer printout paper

Our next stop was at the art supply store to buy paint and brushes. I was shocked to find that Kaylor liquid paint, the tempera paint that I like best, had increased in price—so much, in fact, that instead of purchasing a variety of colors, I selected only the primary colors and white. The children will just have to learn to mix the rest of the colors from these. Powdered tempera paint is less expensive, but it takes so much time to mix and I always spill so much trying to prepare it that I like the convenience of the liquid. Since paint was so expensive I was glad I had learned the old nursery-school trick of adding liquid detergent and liquid starch to make the paint go farther. The detergent also helps the paint come out of clothing more easily.

When I priced the brushes at the art store, I decided that the children could use what we have until I find small paint brushes (one-half-inch wide) on sale at a discount store.

On our way home, I spied a big cardboard box behind a supermarket. I couldn't resist this free playhouse, so I stuffed it in the trunk. After I cut a door and some windows, the children should have a good time painting their own house.

With prices as high as they are today, I believe in using the free and inexpensive materials we find around us, rather than paying a high price for everything the children use. In fact, the children really don't need the fancy easel that I had purchased for their Christmas gift. A piece of plywood leaned up against the house with some masking tape or clothes pins to hold up the paper would be just as effective!

Monday, October 28 / Taking a Child to Work

"Mommy, I don't want to go to Randy's today," Kim complained on this rainy Monday morning.

"Why don't you want to go?" I asked.

"Because I just want to stay with you. Please let me go to work with you."

"We'll see," I replied.

I didn't have to leave for work until noon, so we dropped the subject. But when I announced to the tribe, "Get ready to go," she again asked to stay with me. Thinking she would change her mind when we arrived at Evelyn's house, where she would see all of the children playing, I didn't make an issue of it.

I'm convinced that at different times each child has specific needs. From the information I got from Kim, I didn't feel there was any specific reason she didn't want to go (like maltreatment or peer rejection); she just wanted to be with me, which is really a very nice compliment to a mother who is around almost all of the time.

When we arrived at the Ericksons', Kim again said she wanted to go with me, so I said, "OK, you wait in the car while I take Kari and Kevin into the house."

Kim's surprise was obvious. "You mean I can go with you?" When I got back to the car she gave me a big hug.

I enjoy taking my children with me to work. So many children have no idea what their parents do at that mysterious place called "work." I once heard a story about a little boy who was bothering two little girls in the housekeeping corner in nursery school. One girl finally handed the boy a doctor's kit and said, "Here is your lunch. Now you go to work and don't bother us for the rest of the day." The boy left and walked to the other side of the room. He sat down and said, "Work, work, work."

First of all, it is too bad that parents have to work at all when their children are small, but since we have to be realistic, I think parents should give children every opportunity to see and experience what their daddies and, in many cases, their mommies do at work.

When my children were little (before walking), I always took them to work with me. Of course, not every mother is as lucky as I am, having the kind of job where babies are welcome. Since I teach college classes, I don't have to be in class eight hours a day. I have a lovely carpeted office where I have posted office hours; otherwise, I am free to come and go, so much of my preparation for classes I do at home.

Now that the children are older, Jan and I still like to share our work worlds with them. Often when I have to run into my office at odd times to pick up some papers or books, you can see and hear three little ones trailing down the hall after me. When I leave the children in the "principal's office," I'm sure he doesn't get very much done while I'm gone. But fifteen minutes lost during the day can be made up, while if this experience for the children were lost now, it could never be made up.

I was really surprised last year at Kim's observations when I took her with me to one of my classes. After the hour lecture and discussion, she said, "Mommy, I didn't know that's how you teach the students. I thought they would sit on the floor around you!" I agree that the nursery-school method may be more conducive to learning, but slightly unusual for large classes of graduate students. Kim knew I was a teacher, and putting that fact together with her experience in nursery schools, her concept of my job as a teacher was far from reality.

So I took her with me again today. And we had a delightful time. It is so good to spend time alone with just one child. It gives you an extra-special feeling of closeness. And it gave my developmental-psychology students an insight into child behavior as Kim unhesitatingly drew on the chalkboard for an hour, oblivious to the fifty college students who were watching her.

Tuesday, October 29 / Experimenting with Sound

Today we experimented with sound. Kevin sparked the idea as he tapped two quart jars on the breakfast table with his spoon. I was ready to tell him to stop when I noticed the different pitched sounds.

"Kevin, tap the jar with the peaches in it," I said. Startled, he looked at me. Obviously he had expected me to say something else. "Listen," I continued. "Now tap the other jar. Are the sounds just alike? How are they different? Why are they different?" I continued questioning. "Kim, can you match the sounds on the piano?" This was more difficult for the children than I had anticipated. We brought the two jars next to the piano and continued tapping as we tried different pitches on the piano until we found a fairly good match.

"Wow, if we had enough jars we could play the piano on the jars," observed Kari.

"Well, not exactly," I said, "but we could play a tune."

I found a few more jars, and the children filled them with different amounts of water. It was not long before they observed that the more water in a jar the higher the pitch.

My mind is already busy thinking of follow-up activities for future days. I want to take off the cover of the piano and let them see the hammers hit the strings. I hope they will make the observation that the long, big strings have a lower pitch. Then I want them to actually see a large string vibrating as they listen to the sound; then touch the string, stop the vibration and thus the sound. I want them to experiment with my guitar, tightening the different strings and putting their fingers on the different frets and listening to how these change the sound by making the vibrating part of the string shorter.

Then ultimately they will be able to put it all together—the bigger and longer the string, the slower the vibration and the lower the pitch. And the more air space in a jar the more room for the sound waves to vibrate and the lower the pitch.

Wednesday, October 30 / The Teachable Moment

It is interesting how a near family crisis can motivate children to learn about something that otherwise would hold a very low priority. Subject: spiders. Crisis: Kevin rushed to the hospital emergency room.

While playing alone in his room, he had started crying as if badly hurt. I went to investigate and found a limping black-widow spider next to him. His hand looked pink in one area, so I put two and two together. It turned out to be a false alarm. I should have known, since he had stopped crying by the time Jan was ready to leave for the hospital with him and he happily waved to Kim and Kari and said, "Good-bye, girls. I'm going to the hospital." He had a good time with all the doctors and nurses, and even got a free balloon—all for the cost of the expensive emergency-room visit. But we'd rather be safe than sorry when it comes to the health of our children.

Well, all of this caused a sudden amount of interest in spiders, things I've never been fond of. Kim had no difficulty looking up SP and then ID in the Britannica Junior Encyclopaedia until she came to SPIDER. It took Kari a little longer and some motherly encouragement before she found SPIDER in the Audubon Encyclopedia. The children then sat wide-eyed as I read to them. I learned more about spiders in the next half hour than I had learned all my life, and I presume they did, too. We read all about the orb-webbed spiders and their beautiful symmetrical webs, the free runners without webs who have to jump on their prey, and finally about the black widows, who build makeshift, nondescript webs. This all happened last night, after bedtime. But if I had waited until preschool time this morning, their interest would have subsided like the crisis. The teachable moment would have been past.

Thursday, October 31 / Halloween

Spooks, goblins, ghosts, skeletons, and witches. I can do without them, and so could most children. I was amazed a number of years ago when I was studying about children's fears, to learn that school-age children fear most those things that will probably never happen to them, or those things they probably will never see—for example, ghosts, goblins, and corpses. The probability of ever meeting up with one of these is very unlikely except, of course, on Halloween. The most feared animals were tigers and bears, and the likelihood of these creatures prowling around urban neighborhoods is remote. The closest thing to wild animals that a child might see in his backyard would be coyotes, which roam around the Los Angeles area, or our Dobermans on the loose.

Since feared objects are something that seem very real to children whether indeed they are realistic or not, it seems very unnecessary for us as a society to have a special day when we sanction running around the streets at night scaring other people. Therefore, I try to minimize Halloween as much as possible with my preschoolers. But it is unrealistic to try to shut my eyes completely to what is going on around us. The children see the Halloween decorations in the stores when we go shopping, they hear the other children talking about Halloween, they see the costumes that parents are buying and making for their children to wear, the library features books about Halloween, and there are Halloween specials on TV.

I still had misgivings about having my children participate in trick-or-treating when Evelyn and Jim invited us to go begging with them to only a few homes in their neighborhood. I finally said yes. We all started out at four-thirty, when it was still light, and by five-thirty the children had what I considered enough candy and gum to last a year.

Yet, I still have some reservations about the value of Halloween.

1. *What does the day stand for?* Some people call it the birthday celebration of the devil. If this is true, I wouldn't want my children

to participate in this type of celebration, even though it has become a fun-filled American tradition.

2. *Begging.* I am trying to teach my children the importance of giving, not getting. I certainly do not approve of their begging in any other situation. Certainly not for candy and gum. Why should I approve of this behavior one day a year?

3. *Safety.* Halloween has become a very unsafe holiday. Every year tragedies occur when children are poisoned, or hurt with such bizarre things as razor blades hidden in apples. Therefore, people now give individually wrapped candy or gum, and everyone is suspect of homemade goodies, or even good fruit.

4. *Junk the children collect.* I'm trying to cut down on the amount of sweets our family consumes, and Halloween only adds to our storehouse of junk. If it would only become fashionable and safe to hand out good old-fashioned apples, oranges, unshelled nuts, or even carrots, I would have fewer misgivings. Somebody ought to start a campaign for a healthy Halloween.

And yet perhaps the healthiest Halloween my children could celebrate for a healthy value system, mind and body, would be to stay home. Perhaps next year the children can dress up as missionaries and greet other children coming to our door. They could hand out specially wrapped copies of the church paper for children, or some other "healthy" treat.

Why not have a family Halloween party? Carve the pumpkin (as we did a couple of days ago). Let the preschoolers enjoy the ooey, gooey feel of its innards and then roast and salt the seeds. What a tasty treat! Instead of dressing up in scary fantasy costumes, let them dress up in whatever they want to wear that is in the house. Blankets, towels, scarves, parents' or older brothers' or sisters' clothing, or even baby things make great costumes. Invite to your party a close friend or relative, or an elderly person who usually doesn't get invited to such festivities. Preschoolers and the elderly are usually a good combination because it is so easy for the older to give the younger their complete attention. And children do love being the center of attention!

Encourage the children to give a program for the other family members. Perhaps the children could sing a Halloween song they made up themselves. It is really not too hard to do. Choose a familiar tune, such as "The Battle Hymn of the Republic," and help the children to put a few phrases to the melody. For example, "Mr. Jack-o-lantern had a smile upon his face" (repeat three times), "and it lit up on Halloween night."

Pop popcorn. Spread a clean sheet on the floor. Put the popcorn popper in the middle of it. Proceed to pop the corn with the top off of the popper. (CAUTION: Make sure the children sit far enough away so they don't get burned from the popping corn. And remember, popcorn is not appropriate for very young preschoolers, since it can be choked on or inhaled into the lungs. Accidents like this are more liable to happen when the children are overly excited and running around the room.)

Why not serve apple wedges spread with peanut butter? It's a good complement to popcorn—and the children can spread the peanut butter themselves.

If you aren't up to a party, select a few homes of friends or relatives that might be fun to visit. It may mean a drive across town, but it would be more meaningful to all than to allow the children just to run wildly through the streets collecting "junk food" from strangers.

Holidays are for celebration, but I do think it is important for parents to consider carefully what activities they let their children participate in while the children are preschoolers. If standards for selecting activities aren't established early, I foresee it being very difficult to say "no" later on.

NOVEMBER is fall
Leaves and crispness in the air
Warmed by Thanksgiving

Friday, November 1 / Pumpkin Bread

It is time to say good-bye to dear old Jack, our pumpkin. Every year I keep him around for a while, waiting for an extra minute to cut him up and cook him, only to discover when I lift his lid that he has grown a hairy mass of mold, which means I'm too late. Not this year. Not with prices what they are!

The children watched as I began cutting. After the pieces had been cooked and cooled, they helped cut the rind away with plastic knives and mashed the pulp. Then I began hunting through my recipe books to decide what to do with it. Pies were out. Jan comes from Europe and has never developed a taste for good old American pumpkin pie. It's a good thing, or I may never have discovered pumpkin bread. You must try this recipe—you'll like it!

Pumpkin Bread

3½ cups flour	4 eggs, well beaten
2 teaspoons soda	⅔ cup water
1½ teaspoons salt	2 cups (1½-pound can)
1 teaspoon nutmeg	pumpkin
1 teaspoon allspice	1¼ cups chopped pecans,
1 cup oil	walnuts, or other nuts
2 cups sugar	1 cup chopped dates

Combine all ingredients and mix well. Pour into 3 small or 2 large greased loaf pans. Bake in a 350-degree oven for 1 hour.

The children helped make the bread, but in this case the product was so delicious that their greatest help was in eating it. I had to set limits so we could enjoy some for supper. It should make an extra-special dessert when topped with whipped cream.

Monday, November 4 / Preparation for School

How much should you teach your child before he enters school? Some psychologists and even some educators are saying that a child should be taught reading, foreign languages, algebra, and much more. I've just been reading *Give Your Child a Superior Mind** by Siegfried and Therese Englemann and I'm amazed at what they suggest five-year-olds can be learning. Other teachers want to do all the teaching themselves so that the child will not have to relearn things their parents have taught them erroneously. Then there are a few persons saying that a child's brain hasn't developed enough before eight or ten years of age to tackle abstract learning without frustration.

With all of this controversy about early learning, it is sometimes difficult for a parent to decide what he should be teaching his children at home or when he should enroll his child in a kindergarten or first-grade program.

It is true that school systems often begin teaching children abstract concepts such as are found in reading and mathematics before many children are ready to grasp these concepts easily. Therefore, I have chosen not to send my children to these programs until they are ready for this kind of learning. No amount of preparation that parents can give will enable some children to be successful in learning abstractions when their bodies and brains are not physiologically ready. But how much should parents try to teach their children before school?

I'm against pushing children to learn abstract things that have

* New York: Simon and Schuster (1966).

very little meaning to them. But a lot of math and even reading can be made meaningful at a young age if they are taught as the children show an interest in and a need for such information. That's what I think parents ought to teach. If we really watch for the cues, I think we'll find the children are interested in many things that may run a year or more ahead of when these concepts are introduced in school. Why not expose them to this information when it's meaningful, even if they will get it later on in school?

Some people argue that children will be bored in school if they already have learned something outside of school. I think this concept is strange. I'm much more interested in listening to a conversation or lecture on something I know about than on something that is entirely foreign. I like to have hooks on which to hang information. And every time I hear related information I can then react intelligently to it, rather than trying to figure out where to hang the hook.

Children like the familiar even more than adults do. My children love to hear the story "Caps for Sale," by Esphyr Slobodkina. I'm sure I've read it to them hundreds of times. They can tell the story from memory—word for word. Still, when I ask them what they would like me to read, they choose their old favorite.

The idea of preparing a child for the learning experiences he will receive in school or even keeping a child ahead of the schoolwork in a certain subject would be an injustice to the child if the child at the same time were led to have an unnaturally high estimation of his abilities and feel superior to other students. If this happened, the threat of a failure may even be increased when the child found himself in situations where he had not been prepared. This could even lead a child to commit dishonest acts to cover his deficiencies.

The child must have a realistic estimate of his capabilities, but at the same time, he can be taught to excel in a skill he is particularly interested in. He can be helped to develop the attitude of "I can learn." He can be taught that he can be successful in learning difficult subjects. Finally, he can be taught that he is still a worthwhile person even if he does meet with failure and defeat.

I have decided that I'm going to prepare my children for school. I'm going to help them develop the following:

1. a good self-concept
2. self-discipline to tackle tough problems

3. strong characters so they will not resort to cheating in order to be successful
4. skills and information (or at least the readiness for these) before they need them in school
5. how to deal with occasional defeat and failure and still feel that they are worthwhile

To help me in preparing my children for school, I made the following list of skills, information, or characteristics that I want them to master or to have before they start first grade. Once these things are achieved, they should have little difficulty being successful at school.

Knowledge
1. alphabet: be able to write the capital and small letters; be able to write their first and last names; letter sounds; recognition of a few simple words
2. numbers: write 1 to 100; counting; simple addition and subtraction; money values (up to $1.00); shapes
3. practical information: telephone number; address; parents' names; where parents work; birthdays
4. time: how to tell time; months; days of week

Physical Skills
1. ride bicycle
2. roller skate
3. jump rope
4. skip
5. balance on one foot
6. throw and catch a ball

Independence and Responsibility Skills
1. dress and undress oneself
2. tie shoes
3. follow directions
4. take responsibility to do simple household tasks
5. comb hair
6. be eager to go to school
7. make bed and clean room
8. have social skills to make and keep friends

Tuesday, November 5 / Applesauce Day

Today was applesauce day from 8:00 A.M. to 11:00 P.M. No time for preschool? Wrong. Kim worked right beside me helping me cut, cook, and grind a good portion of the four boxes of ripe, Golden Delicious apples, while Kari "baby-sat" Kevin and Greg. When boredom set in, Kim and Kari traded jobs. They both enjoyed their responsibilities. And what is more important than doing a good job of a task that needs to be done? The satisfaction of freezing thirty quarts of applesauce will last a whole year and will be especially strong on pancakes-and-applesauce Sunday mornings. To have a well-rounded education, every child needs an occasional applesauce day.

Wednesday, November 6 / Dick and Jane

I never thought I would find myself singing the praises of "Dick and Jane." I'm sure I must have been brought up on the adventures of "Mother, Father, Dick, Jane, Sally, Spot, Puff, and Tim," but I can't remember any childhood feelings about them one way or the other. But I was taught to be fairly critical during those professional education classes I took, and "Dick and Jane" probably got more than their fair share of criticism. I can just hear myself saying, "Can you imagine any bright five- or six-year-old being interested in dialogues like, 'Oh oh,' and 'Oh see Dick. See Jane. See Dick and Jane. See. See. See.'?" Well, I'm changing my tune. I have a bright five-year-old who loves Dick and Jane.

Last library day I spotted a 1956 edition of *We Work and Play*. I picked it up impulsively and put it in the pile to take home. The book sat on our shelf for a week and a half and no one took note.

One night, Kim came running to me, "Mommy, I think I can read this book."

It was 9:15 P.M. The house was quiet, since my other two had been sleeping for over an hour. So I sat down and Kim began reading. She didn't know half the words, but the story progresses slowly enough and with enough repetition, that when I'd tell her a word once or twice, she was able to remember it. I knew she was only reading by recognition of the words and making no attempt at sounding them out, because she would get words like "father" and "funny" mixed up.

Every five minutes, Jan would call out from the study, "Kim, don't you think it is time to go to bed?" But Kim kept reading, determined to read all sixty-three pages.

Forty-five minutes and a few interruptions later—success! "I did it," she danced and sang. Quite a performance for 10 P.M.

Last night, I tucked a glowing girl and her Dick and Jane book into bed. This morning bright and early she and her book were up, and I heard her tell Kari, "Kari, I can read this whole book. Do you want me to read it to you? Today I will be the preschool teacher."

Kari just looked at her as if she didn't believe a word Kim was saying and questioned, "Really?"

Thursday, November 7 / Roller Skating

Roller skating is a must for preschoolers. And the girls are well on their way toward mastering the skill. They play in the skates, eat in them, and would probably sleep in them if I would let them. It had been a few days since I had prepared any preschool activity cards, so as Kim skated across the kitchen floor on her way outside this morning, I said, "I'll have to make up some cards for you and Kari this morning."

Kim's reply was, "Just be sure to put roller skating on one of them." The cards were never made, since roller skating was the overriding interest. Next week it will be something else. Why should I force diversity now?

I probably wouldn't have thought of roller skating as an appropriate learning activity for four- and five-year-olds unless years ago I had been given two pairs of children's old black shoe skates. I almost gave them away, not thinking that in six years I might have children who could wear them. Instead I let friends use them for a few years and asked that they return them when finished. They have been back a year and the girls have had them off and on a number of times, but they always spent more time falling than skating. This week the tide changed, and it's more time up than down. It is amazing how much fun the girls have had with the skates, even though they are still an inch or so too big at the toe.

Each girl skates differently. Kim has caught on to putting one skate sideways and pushing off to a long glide. Kari shuffles along on short walking steps, getting up enough momentum to roll for a few inches. It is always a temptation to me to give too many instructions. Kim takes this pretty well, and will try what I suggest, but it only frustrates Kari. She must find success her own way. When she feels confident at a certain level of achievement, then she is ready for a "tiny" bit of instruction, but not too much. I try not to ruin her fun with too many and too constant instructions. Sometimes trial and error are more effective than a lecture!

Friday, November 8 / Sickness

Kevin whimpered a few times during the night, so I knew he wasn't feeling well, and Kari woke up groaning. I took them all to the park, since it was a gorgeous day. I thought the change in scenery and bright sunshine might cheer them up. Kim made the most of it, roller skating and riding her bike along the trails, but my sick ones just whimpered and moaned. Even climbing the fascinating play equipment was too much for them. When health is gone, nothing else is right in a child's life. Food doesn't taste good, the park is meaningless, and they could care less about stories. They even complained about going to bed. The only thing that felt good was long, long rocks in our rocking chair. And so the day passed.

Monday, November 11 / "The Three Little Pigs"

I am continually amazed at how much information Kevin catches, even though I think it has been thrown over his head.

About a month ago on "Mr. Rogers' Neighborhood," the story "The Three Little Pigs" was presented with marionettes. I watched the program myself because "The Three Little Pigs" can be a frightening tale. It was done in very good taste, with no one being eaten up. Kari, my sensitive one, walked out of the room a few times, but Kevin just sat there soaking it in. Nothing has been said about it since then, until today, when Kevin poked his head out the door of the playhouse and said to me, "Wolf, don't you come in my house," and slammed the door.

So I played the game with him, saying, "Little pig, little pig, let me come in . . . or I'll huff and I'll puff and I'll blow your house in."

I started blowing and he said, "Don't blow house in. [Pause.] Do again, Mommy."

So we played the game over again and again, each time enjoying it more.

Role playing involves the practice of language skills, social interaction, planning ahead, and the internalization of others' feelings. Role playing is an important activity for preschoolers—even when playing the part of a pig!

Tuesday, November 12 / Writing Books

The girls enjoy doing what I do. Since one of my major tasks has been writing, they announced today that for preschool they were going to write a book. They drew the pictures, stapled them together, and then asked me to write down the story they told for each page.

Writing books helps the children organize their thoughts; it stimulates their interest in words and reading and it is a good means of self-expression.

Sometimes the pictures children draw and the stories they tell reveal real insights into their thoughts and feelings that they might not otherwise share with grown-ups.

In addition, there is a certain sense of pride that the children feel when they see their completed book and when they share it with family and friends. When others read aloud the words that they dictated, reading and writing takes on new significance. What a miracle that their words can be recorded in such a way that other people can say them without ever having heard them before.

Keeping the books the children write is a nice record of the children's drawing skills and interests over time.

In fact, writing books is such a valuable preschool activity, I'm going to write this activity on a card and include it as a regular preschool activity.

Wednesday, November 13 / A Walk Through Town

Today was one of those days for which I thought I was ready. I had everything planned for preschool. I had written activity cards, and even had games and puzzles laid out on the table. That's why, when Jan announced that the car needed the tires balanced and that he had made an appointment for this morning and forgotten to tell me, I thought my day had been ruined. He sensed my disappointment, so hastened to explain that it would take only an hour. The garage was right downtown, so perhaps I could go shopping. But I couldn't think of anything I needed, which, for me, is very unusual.

So I decided to make the best of the situation, and as it turned out, today has been one of the highlights of our preschool year. The beauty of the situation was that for once in my life I had nothing to do for at least an hour. Usually when I take the children to town, it is to dash in one store and out another. Today I told the children that we had to spend preschool time in town and wondered what they wanted to do. They said, "Let's go to the library." So that became our destination.

We left the car in the garage and started out on our walk through town. I was amazed at how many interesting things there are in a small town if one just walks slowly enough to notice them. The children looked in each store window, and we began to talk about all of the different types of stores there are. I explained how each person who owns a store has to earn his living by selling the things in his store to other people who need them. When we came to a pet store, the children begged to go in to see the animals. Usually I would have said I was too busy, too hurried. But today we had time and the variety of fish and animals would have kept us busy for the entire hour. Walking past the service station, we had time to stop to watch a man working under a car that was up on a hoist. We watched a man polish shoes in his open-air shoe-polishing shop.

The most interesting sight was a blind man walking down the sidewalk. The children noticed him about a block away as he hit his red-tipped cane against the wall of the building. We saw him stop at the street until the cars stopped, and then he crossed. Finally he stepped up on the curb and walked on past us. The children were fascinated as they watched, but it was not until he was past us that they began asking questions about blindness. I then wished that I had stopped the man and had the children ask him the questions. I'm sure he would have been happy to talk to us. But when the idea finally came to me he was out of sight. We'll just have to walk through town again someday and hope that we'll see him.

As we walked past the city hall, the children noticed a stepping-stone path through a little garden. Of course, they had to try it. It was a delightful minigarden that I had driven past numerous times but had never noticed before.

We had a chance to talk about safety concepts: such things as crossing the street at a crosswalk, looking both ways, and waiting for the green light or the walk sign to come on. The children have had plenty of experience with green lights, but a walk sign was new. We talked about not starting across the street when the walk sign was blinking, because there wouldn't be enough time to get all of the way across the street before the cars started across.

When we got to the library we leisurely selected our books and then retraced our steps, which included the stepping-stone garden and another stop at the pet shop. The car was ready long before we got back.

When Jan got home tonight, my first question was, "When do you think the tires will need balancing again?" His answer made us decide we'd better not wait for that excuse before going on a walking trip through town again.

Thursday, November 14 / Typing

Typing is a skill that every child should acquire.

In typing, as with other skills, perfection and speed come with practice. Are the preschool years too soon to begin learning how to use the typewriter? Today one of the preschool activity cards said, "Type as many letters, numbers, and words as you know." Kim has used the typewriter before and has learned where to place her fingers on the keys. I am quite insistent that she use the correct fingers from the beginning. Kari is at the stage of experimentation, and for her, any finger will do. Kevin is at the stage of "Don't touch unless you are sitting on Mommy's lap and she says it is OK to type."

A typewriter isn't a toy—at least not ones that work well enough for preschoolers really to be able to use. I prefer an electric typewriter, which allows ·tiny fingers to type without much effort.

Some people color-code the child's fingernails with the corresponding keys. Kim has been able to catch onto the system without that crutch.

Spelling and reading often come more easily to a child than physically printing out words. If a child is allowed to type, he can compose words and stories faster than he could if he had to print them. As the skill is developed, homework can be typed, thus saving the child much time, while at the same time saving the teacher time trying to decipher poorly printed or written words. As far as I'm concerned, teaching a child to type benefits everyone.

This is an example of Kim's work at the typewriter:

```
fr.;for;fimi;ford;karlene;kevin;milks'abcdefghijkl

opqrstuvwxyz2220 ono'on;off;noyes;brokbrck    ;245
```

Kari has her own style:

```
11111111111111111111111111111111111111111111111111
22222222222222222222222222222222222222222222222222
33333333333333333333333333333333333333333333333333
44444444444444444444444444444444444444444444444444
b3b3vb4jmnsnfvkajkjkjiuyhghggbxhhhbvb3bm,wkkdfxs.
gdhfjhmnsnfvkaj jkjkjiuyhghghgbgbg dmkcmc, mskjfo
dfhie ruiieurjdhgjxmzcndkas  dcjy  7ekzxj 85093mx
huiuiuiuiuiuiumznxmnc mxz1dpolz ,,m mx,mx,zmmz,mx
```

Friday, November 15 / Puppets

Paper-bag puppetry is a good activity for preschoolers. Even the youngest can paste on construction-paper eyes, ears, and noses. But easy to make, easy to break. I have found that they last about one day when the children really use them in their play.

Sock puppets are a little more difficult to make, but they do last longer. I always keep a sackful of old socks that have lost their mates. (I think my washing machine eats them.) The simplest way

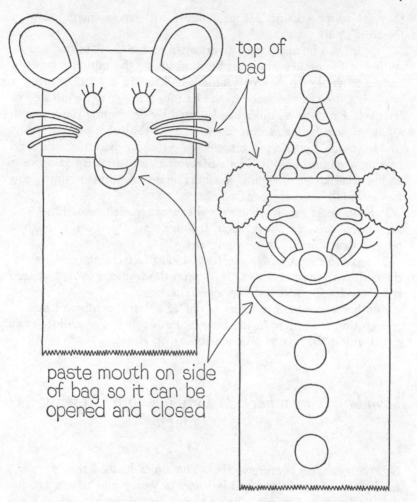

top of
bag

paste mouth on side
of bag so it can be
opened and closed

to decorate a sock is to put a glass (or darning egg) down into the toe and then paste or sew on eyes and ears, or whatever else a child may want. To make a mouth is a little more difficult. I make a slit in the appropriate place and sew an extra piece of material into the hole. Our puppets always look homemade. But I think it is more important for the children to co-operate in the creative activity than to end up with a perfect puppet. Puppets are for imaginative play anyway, and if they don't look exactly like the animal or thing they are supposed to be, it just takes a little more imagination on the child's part.

Puppets can be made with a variety of materials. A mitten can be stuffed or the child's hand can be used inside the mitten puppet to have a movable mouth. A styrofoam ball makes a good head for a puppet. A hole can be made in the ball for a finger to be inserted as the neck. Paper-towel tubes can be used by decorating the top with a hat or yarn hair and drawing a face on the tube. Stick puppets can be made by using a tongue depressor or popsicle stick and pasting a picture onto it. The variety of decorations for puppets is endless: yarn, twigs, sequins, washers, material, ribbons, straw, cotton, rickrack, feathers, paperclips, etc.

Puppets seem to stimulate verbal expression. It is sometimes easier for children to speak their feelings and thoughts through a puppet than directly to someone else.

I keep a large picture frame (on which I have hung curtains) for the children's puppet shows. They prop the frame up on a box, and the show begins without even one rehearsal.

Another easy stage to make is out of a large cardboard box by just cutting a window in the box, like a TV set. The children can crawl inside the box to produce their own show.

Monday, November 18 / Patience and Growing Things

Our patience has been rewarded. The avocado seed that we stuck toothpicks in and submerged halfway in water four weeks ago has sprouted a root. I guess it helps to put the avocado seed in water with the pointed end up. What a beautiful object lesson to help teach patience to me and my children.

Today the children asked, "Mommy, what else can we grow?" So we submerged in water half of a sweet potato and cut off one inch of the top of a carrot and placed it in a shallow pan of water. If all goes well we should soon have a sweet-potato jungle, and the carrot should send up new green leaves. Our job now is just to be patient. That is the character trait we will be stressing this week.

Tuesday, November 19 / Preparation and Active Observation

Today, I handled my home preschool just as a nursery school, and I'm pleased with the results. *Preparation* is one key. Yesterday I cleaned house, so this morning when I woke there was very little housework needing my immediate attention. That meant I had time to read to both girls in bed before I even got up. Then I stirred paints while stirring the oatmeal, so preschool was ready to begin immediately after breakfast. It is amazing how quickly the kitchen can be put in order after breakfast if there aren't a lot of things left out from the day or week before to work around or put up. By eight-thirty all four children were painting at the easel. (Greg is here early today, since Evelyn is trying to get a paper written and preparing to take an exam.) I anticipated that this activity wouldn't last long, so I wrote activity cards, put a game on the table for the girls, and got the blocks out for the boys. It worked like clockwork, just the way the books say it does. As a child finished one activity, he moved on to another interest center or started on another card activity.

This was how I discovered the second key to teaching a successful home preschool. It is *active observation*. I don't mean washing dishes and overhearing the squabble and chitchat going on in the playroom. I mean being in the playroom—watching, listening, and participating. I mean being interested in what the children are doing, not just interested in getting them to do something so that I can hurry off to make beds, or get another room vacuumed. I mean being close enough to step in when I'm needed to help someone across the frustration hurdle or to referee a boxing match from the beginning so that I know the cause of the boxing. I mean watching for the moment I might be able to facilitate learning, rather than pushing for it. By planning and actively observing, the preschool day was so successful that I even had time to work individually with Kim on the *ook* words. Kari played teacher, putting a letter like *b* or *c* or *t* in front of the *ook* and letting Kim do the pronouncing. Before I knew it, I had read four stories to the children and it was outside time.

Good things happened there, too. Kevin for the first time steered the tricycle and pedaled at the same time. What an achievement! His feelings of success shone all over his face. When "Mother" Kari organized the playhouse and her three children (Kim, Kevin, and Greg), I decided I could slip into the house for a few minutes. I actually read one whole page before the children called me to rescue a stray cat that Sarnoff, our Doberman, had cornered in a tree.

Another stray cat is exactly what we do not need. Three wild cats living out in the wood pile and Tiger, our yellow tomcat, are enough. The stray was such a lovely, gentle cat. He came right inside the fence to be with the children, even though Sarnoff was about to eat him alive.

The children had such an enjoyable time in the playhouse that I served them lunch out there. Then more stories and naps . . . and now my reward: four happy, sleeping children and time of my own. It was well worth it.

Wednesday, November 20 / Stories About My Children

Last summer, when we were vacationing in Laguna, Kari was fascinated with all of the flowers growing in the neighbors' gardens. In Redlands, where we live in the midst of citrus groves, we just don't have neighbors with flowers. As Kari admired all of the flowers, the temptation to pick them was overwhelming. Daily she would come back to the house with a handful of posies.

"Kari, don't pick the flowers," was my plea, but it didn't seem to help.

These past weeks, as I have thought about each child's characteristics, I have decided it would be fun to capture some of the incidents in their lives by writing a story about them.

For me, creativity comes in spurts. It was during supper that the inspiration for Kari's story came. "Kari, don't pick the flowers," I muttered to myself.

"I'm not picking flowers," she said. "I'm eating supper."

I excused myself and in a while came back with this little story in rhyme:

I Love the Pretty Flowers

"I love the pretty flowers.
    I love them, yes, I do.
I love the pretty flowers.
    So I'll pick one or two."

Kari was singing and picking.
    Singing and picking was fun.
She picked some yellow flowers
    Then picked a purple one.

Mommy was busy talking
    To neighbor friend named Fred.
She noticed Kari picking,
    So turned around and said . . .

"Kari, don't pick the flowers.
    They don't belong to you.
Picking others' flowers
    Isn't nice to do."

Kari said, "I'm sorry.
    I'm sorry I made you sad.
I love the pretty flowers
    And picking makes me glad."

Mommy went in to iron,
    And Kari soon forgot
She shouldn't pick the flowers;
    She gathered quite a lot.

She hurried home to Mommy
    To show the bright bouquet
Of pretty flowers she had picked
    While singing all the way.

But Mommy said, "Oh Kari,
   You disobeyed me, dear,
You should not pick those flowers!
   How can I make that clear?"

Kari said, "I'm sorry.
   I'm sorry I made you sad.
I love the pretty flowers
   And picking makes me glad."

To help Kari remember,
   Her mommy kept her home.
There were no flowers to tempt her.
   But Kari longed to roam.

She sang, "I love the flowers.
   I love them, yes, I do.
I love the pretty flowers.
   I'll only touch a few."

Once more Kari was singing
   Her special flower song.
She smelled and picked the flowers
   As she wandered along.

Her mommy wasn't watching
   For she was cooking stew.
When she saw Kari's flowers,
   She said, "What shall I do?"

Kari said, "I'm sorry.
   I'm sorry I made you sad.
I love the pretty flowers
   And picking makes me glad."

Then Mommy said, "Remember.
   Remember what I say.
If flowers belong to no one
   Then picking is OK."

So Kari started wandering
   And singing on her way.
"I love my mommy so much,
   I'll find a gift today."

"I love the pretty flowers.
    I love them, yes, I do.
I love the pretty flowers.
    I'll only pick a few."

"I'll make my mommy happy
    If I can only find
Some pretty flowers growing wild,
    Where nobody will mind."

Soon Kari found some dandelions
    Growing free and wild.
She stopped and thought most carefully,
    "These must be for a child."

She gently picked one dandelion,
    Then two and three and four.
"I'm picking them for Mommy,"
    Kari said, and picked some more.

Then running just as fast
    As her little legs could go,
She gave them to her mommy
    And said, "I love you so."

Then Mommy picked up Kari
    And hugged her very tight.
"Oh Kari, Mommy loves you,
    Dandelions are just right!"

After I read the story to her, she smiled and exclaimed, "That's me!" She then carried it around for the rest of the evening and slept with it under her pillow.

Naturally, Kim wanted a story written about her. And then Kevin said, "Me too." So for their bedtime stories I told them each a true story about themselves, promising I would write the stories down later.

It would be fun to have these stories published in a book* or children's magazine, but the biggest joy for me is just seeing how

* Some of these stories have now been published. See Kay Kuzma, *The Kim, Kari, and Kevin Storybook* (Mountain View, Calif.: Pacific Press Publishing Association, 1979).

the children have reacted to having a true story actually written about them. I recommend this as a project for any parent who is interested in raising his child's self-esteem.

Thursday, November 21 / Death

Liza (our beautiful "mother" Doberman) died last night. Jan felt the loss even more than the children. This was his first dog; the dog of his dreams, his Mona Liza. Because I am somewhat uncomfortable with death, it is difficult for me to be comfortable introducing the children to the finality of it.

At the breakfast table we broke the news to the children. "Liza's dead."

"How did it happen?"

"Why did she die?"

"Poor Liza!"

And then almost immediately they asked, "Where is she? Can we see her?"

I hadn't expected this. But when they insisted on seeing her, I led them to the laundry room where she lay "deathly" still (the term now has meaning), legs stiffly out to the side and stomach bloated. They stood looking in silence.

"What is death?" Kari asked.

"Death is like a sleep. You don't know anything that is going on around you."

"Will Liza ever wake up?"

"I don't know. The Bible doesn't tell us what will happen to animals."

"When I die will I wake up?" asked Kim.

"Yes, the Bible tells us that when we die Jesus will wake us up again."

To help the children fully understand the finality of death, we allowed them to watch as Jan dug a hole in the grapefruit grove and buried Liza. The children were full of questions.

"Daddy, why do animals and people have to die?"

"Because," he answered, "there is sin in this world and where there is sin there is death. In heaven there is no sin so there will be no death. Won't that be wonderful?"

"Why do we have to bury Liza?"

"Dead flesh soon begins to decay and smell."

"What happens to Liza now that she is covered with dirt?"

"Her skin and bones will rot or decompose. That means they will break down into smaller pieces and finally become part of the dirt."

"Does that happen to people, too?"

"Yes, it does. But because Jesus never sinned and He died for us, He has the power to make all His people alive and whole and take us to heaven."

Even when it comes to the explanation of death, children deserve truthful answers, although sometimes we have to say, "I don't know." Death is hard to understand, especially when it breaks up families and friends, children and pets. But what a promise of hope we have for the future! It is our responsibility to instill this hope in our children rather than leave them frustrated, worried, and frightened when they encounter death.

Friday, November 22 / More Phonics

Phonics was on the agenda today. I took five envelopes and wrote the following letter combinations on them: "at," "ook," "et," "an," and "oor."

Inside each envelope I placed letters that, when combined with the letters on the envelope, would make a word. For example, in the "at" envelope I placed B, C, E (which makes a different-sounding word), F, H, M, P, R, S, and V. As Kim would place each letter in front of the envelope letters she would sound out the letter and try to figure out the word by putting the "at" sound with the other letter sound.

I was surprised how easily she was able to make the new words after she caught onto the first few words. Later we verbally continued this game in the car, when I asked Kim such questions as, "When I put M in front of the 'at' sound, it spells ——?" By the end of the day, Kari was catching on and sometimes beat Kim to the answer.

Monday, November 25 / Cutting

Kevin has just discovered that scissors cut. Until I watched him concentrate on the task today, I didn't realize that it takes so much thought and co-ordination to hold the scissors, get the paper between the blades just right, and squeeze down. Kevin noticed nothing else and worked for almost ten minutes making three little cuts in a piece of paper. I tried to show him how to hold the scissors pointing away from him, but he insisted on holding them toward himself, with his fingers stuck in the wrong way. When he tried it my way, he couldn't get the scissors open in order to cut. Turned the opposite way, he had success; so as far as he was concerned, that was the only way to do it! I'm just glad I had a pair of children's blunt-tipped scissors so Kevin could practice cutting without danger of hurting himself.

Tuesday, November 26 / Big Red

I don't know why, but stray animals seem to flock to this shelter. We keep the humane officer of the police force busy just picking up dogs that have decided to make our home their home.

Yesterday, a beautiful but thin and matted Irish setter came by and wouldn't move from our front gate. He nearly drove Sarnoff (who was inside the fence) wild. Big Red (we give every stray at least a name) followed Jan everywhere. When we left the house by car he followed the car for half a mile. We thought for sure he would just keep going, but when we got home hours later, there he was. Jan then figured he must belong to someone in the closest housing project, a mile away. Jan took him there and left him, thinking such a loyal dog would surely go home. Well, he did. Within an hour he was back at our front gate.

It's always hard to do, but I decided we would have to call the humane officer. When he came, I walked out holding this loyal, gentle dog by the collar. It was a good thing I did, or he would have torn the officer apart. I've never had a dog "protect" me before. I was so impressed I almost didn't want to give him up. The dog struggled to keep out of the dog cage, but superior strength won out.

This situation impressed the children too, and they asked questions that they hadn't asked before, such as:

"Why do the police have to pick up Big Red?"

"Where are they going to take him?"

"Will his owner find him?"

"What happens if no one wants him?"

"Do they keep him in a cage at the dog pound?"

I told them as much as I knew, but I painted the picture as bright as possible. And then thinking about preschool, I asked, "How would you children like to go on a field trip today—to the animal shelter?" And so we did.

Teacher-mothers must be flexible in their planning in order to take advantage of educational opportunities as they arise. I could have scheduled this field trip for next week—that's what I would have done if I were a "real" nursery-school teacher. But now that I'm a teacher-mother, I have the advantage of being able to take off with my three preschoolers at a moment's notice. And the educational opportunities that I can offer my children, therefore, can have much more value, because they come at the time when the children's interest is at a peak.

Wednesday, November 27 / Mathematics

The best kind of principal is one who gets involved in the teaching aspects of the children's education. Our principal is no exception. He doubles as the mathematics teacher. Every evening (there are exceptions) the girls have a private math class. Jan likes to work with them individually so he can be sure they understand the concepts he is trying to teach them.

His reference books are:

Give Your Child a Superior Mind by Siegfried and Therese Engelmann (New York: Simon and Schuster, 1966).

How to Raise a Brighter Child by Joan Beck (New York: Trident Press, 1967).

Let's Play Math by Michael Holt and Zoltan Dienes (New York: Walker & Company, 1973).

Games for Individualizing Mathematics Learning by Leonard M. Kennedy and Ruth L. Michon (Columbus, O.: Charles E. Merrill Publishing Company, 1973) (good for schoolchildren, too).

His workbooks are the following:

Creative Math Experiences for the Young Child by Imogene Forte and Joy MacKenzie (Nashville, Tenn.: Incentive Publications, 1973).

Discovering Mathematics: A Readiness Book by Anita Cieslinski (Charles E. Merrill Publishing Company, 1967).

Modern School Mathematics by Ernest R. Duncan, et al. (Houghton Mifflin Company, Boston, 1972).

Mathematics—Grade 1 (*Learning About Numbers*) by Irving Adler (Golden Press, Western Publishing Company, Inc., Racine, Wisc., 1973).

Mathematics—Grade 2 (*Mastering Addition and Subtraction*) by Irving Adler (Golden Press, Western Publishing Company, Inc., Racine, Wisc., 1965).

Jan uses the reference books to get ideas for mathematical games and activities that he can play with the children. He picks and chooses those things that sound most interesting and match the children's learning capabilities.

The workbooks are to give the children practice in the basic fundamentals of mathematics. The children go through them systematically, and some evenings they do ten to fifteen pages, depending on the difficulty of the work. Jan keeps busy just reading the instructions to the children. I don't know how he would handle more than two children! With individualized instruction each child can progress through these workbooks at his own pace. The workbooks are quite similar, so there is a lot of repetition, but the children don't mind as long as they get over the material quickly.

If I had to choose only one workbook, I think I would start with *Discovering Mathematics* and then continue with *Modern School*

Mathematics. There are probably many other workbooks that are just as good as these. I do think it is worth shopping around until a parent finds exactly what he thinks his child would be interested in.

Above all, mathematics should be fun and should be practical. During the preschool years I don't believe that children necessarily need a time each day to do mathematics, if parents will teach them the concepts as they do other things around the house. But Jan enjoys this special time with the children and they think mathematics with Daddy is just about the nicest thing they can do together.

Thursday, November 28 / Thanksgiving

"Make a joyful noise unto the Lord, all ye lands. Serve the Lord with gladness: Come before His presence with singing. Know ye that the Lord He is God: It is He that hath made us, and not we ourselves; we are His people, and the sheep of His pasture. Enter into His gates with thanksgiving, and into His courts with praise: Be thankful unto Him, and bless His name. For the Lord is good; His mercy is everlasting; and His truth endureth to all generations." (Ps. 100)

Jan was reading as we sat at our places at our bountifully laden Thanksgiving table. It was hard to imagine times and people with less, when we have so much. Each person then told what he was most thankful for this year. The children's responses were numerous and varied. "For each other, for my mommy and daddy, for Jesus, for my kitty, for our dogs that they can have puppies, that I will have a birthday, for Christmas, for rainy days, for Mommy getting us candy, that I can write, for our house, for preschool . . ."

Then we sang, "We Gather Together to Ask the Lord's Blessing . . ." Jan loves this majestic hymn of thanksgiving. The children listened, for they had no understanding about "chastening" and "hastening to make His will known," or "wicked oppression" and being finally able to "cease from distressing." Why is it that we are always most thankful when we have passed through terrible times? Why is it that we so often forget to thank God during the fruitful days and years of our lives? This hymn reminds me once again how thankful we should be for our country and for freedom to worship as we please. It seems such a small thing now, since we have grown accustomed to this luxury. But Jan is not too old to remember Europe during World War II and the oppression of people and religion. To help the children understand the words of this song, he told them the story about how his family would gather to worship with two other families in a small house in Nazi-occupied Poland, when laws forbade such religious meetings. His family of six would come one by one, sometimes carrying a birthday present or a bouquet of flowers so as not to arouse suspicion.

He told the children how he would walk past the meeting place if someone were watching him, then circle the block and return. He told how they would open their hymn books and read the words of

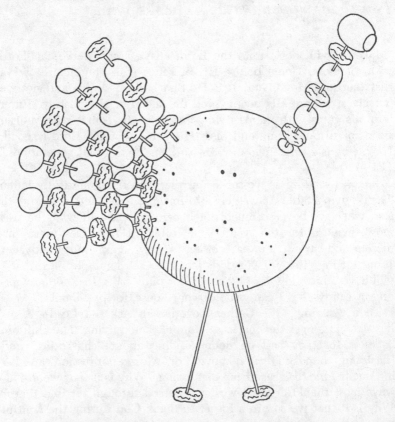

the hymns. They took no chance that someone would hear the singing and report their meeting. They read from the Bible, but someone was stationed at the window to watch for unexpected visitors, so the Bible could be hidden at a moment's notice. No wonder this hymn holds so much meaning to him. Let us not take this wonderful country and the freedom that it allows for granted.

I was glad I hadn't forgotten preschool on this special day, because the fruit turkeys that the children had made for the table centerpiece received ample compliments from our guests. While I peeled potatoes and made cranberry sauce the children were kept busy making turkey feathers by pushing raisins and cranberries on toothpicks. They then stuck the toothpicks on one side of a piece of fruit (apple, orange, lemon, or pomegranate) to make the tail feathers. On the opposite side a decorated toothpick became the neck, and a pimiento-filled olive became the head. Toothpick legs with raisin feet finished the creations. (See illustration.)

The children enjoyed sharing their thank-you books with our guests. It took a good week of cutting pictures out of magazines and pasting them on pages and writing the thing that they were thankful for under each picture. The first page said, "Thank you, God, for . . ." Then the following pages had such pictures and words as "flowers," "dogs," "food," etc.

Later in the afternoon, when the dishes were once again gleaming and the refrigerator was bulging with leftovers, I leisurely sat at the piano and thumbed through the hymnal. There are so many beautiful songs of praise and thanksgiving. Where should I begin to find just the right special one to teach our children? Finally I decided on the canon, "All Praise to Thee." The verses are not only short and meaningful to a child, but also, after they are learned, the children can sing them as a round.

> All praise to Thee, my God, this night,
>   For all the blessings of the light!
> Keep me, O keep me, King of kings,
>   Beneath Thine own almighty wings!
> Praise God, from whom all blessings flow;
>   Praise Him all creatures here below;
> Praise Him above, ye heavenly host;
>   Praise Father, Son, and Holy Ghost.
>   Thomas Ken

As a fitting close to a day of thanksgiving, Jan read Psalm 150. "Praise ye the Lord, Praise God in His sanctuary: Praise Him in the firmament of His power. Praise Him for His mighty acts: Praise Him according to His excellent greatness. Praise Him with the sound of the trumpet: Praise Him with the psaltery and harp. Praise Him with the timbrel and dance: Praise Him with stringed instruments and organs. Praise Him upon the loud cymbals: Praise Him upon the high-sounding cymbals. Let every thing that hath breath praise the Lord. Praise ye the Lord."

Friday, November 29 / Letters

In an early childhood-education class I learned that young children should first be taught to recognize and write the small-case letters. The rationale for this was that basic reading books use small letters first. I have tried very hard to follow this counsel with my children and I have failed. Capital letters seem to dominate our environment. Capital letters glare down from signs: "STOP," "SHELL," "TEXACO." And capital letters even rule the typewriter keyboard. My experience with children leads me to believe that during the early preschool years there is nothing wrong with teaching children the capital letters as the first step of letter recognition. My rationale for this is:

1. Probably the first word most children learn to write is their name, which, of course, begins with a capital.

2. Individuals other than teachers usually write words for young children using capitals, such as DOG or CAT.

3. The capital letters are more easily identified. For example, D P B Q look quite different to a child, while the small letters d p b q look confusingly similar.

4. Because capitals are larger, they may be easier to write.

5. Knowing small letters is primarily important for a child to learn to read.

Children should be taught that each capital letter has a small partner. Sometimes the partner looks alike but is just smaller (Ss, Xx, Cc, or Oo). Sometimes the partner looks very much alike (Tt,

Kk, or Uu), and at other times it looks so different it doesn't even seem related (Aa, Rr, or Dd).

By the time children are ready to begin school they should be able to recognize not only the capital letters but also their smaller partners. In addition, the child should know how to write his name using the *small* letters.

Because children usually copy letters before someone actually teaches them how to make the letters correctly, the letters are often formed incorrectly, at least as far as first-grade teachers are concerned! For example, Kim and Kari both instinctively started to form letters and numbers needing a straight vertical line by starting at the bottom and drawing up. Kari has started to make an O by drawing clockwise rather than counterclockwise. Once these habits become ingrained into a child's motor behavior, they are very difficult to change. When I call this to Kim's or Kari's attention, they resist my instruction. I've warned them that in real school the teacher will make them write the correct way.

"OK," they reply, "we'll do it right then."

But what my children don't understand is that the more they practice a motor skill the wrong way, the faster they get at it, and to start over is just like starting at the beginning. I can just hear the teachers who get my children after me, lamenting, "If only that mother would have left the teaching to us . . . ! She taught them all the wrong way. And now we have to start over again!"

What they will never know is that it was my lack of teaching that caused this problem!

The following instructions are from *Palmer Method Manuscript Writing*, Easy to Teach Series (grade 2) by Fred M. King, and used by permission of A. N. Palmer Co.

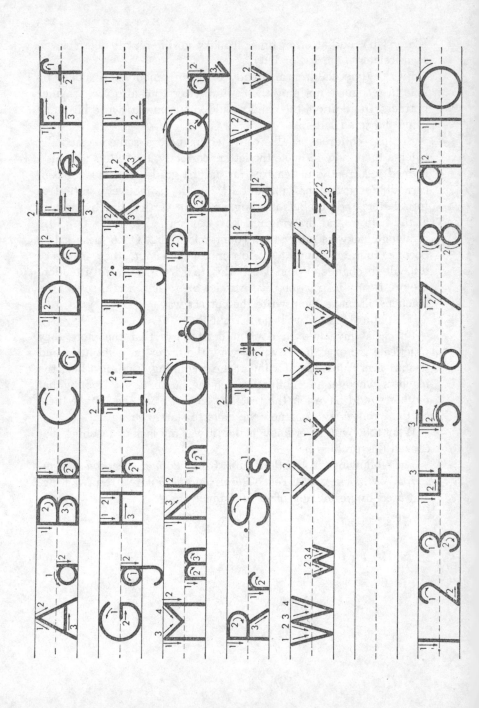

Winter days come short
But DECEMBER lingers long
Its spirit is love

———————❖———————

Monday, December 2 / Preparing for Christmas

"Silver bells, silver bells, it's Christmastime in the city . . ." I sang
as I prepared waffles and applesauce. I could tell it was going to be
a hot day. The sun was shining and the oranges were almost ripe
on the trees outside my kitchen window. But it *is* December, and
December means festivities, holidays, and Christmas. I love the season so much that I didn't want to waste a moment. After our special
breakfast, the first activity was to carry in from the garage all the
boxes of Christmas ornaments and decorations that help in a small
way to make our Southern California home reflect the season.

When Jan and I were first married, we invested in an artificial
Christmas tree, thinking that we could save money by using this
tree for a few years. Now it has become so customary to decorate
the Christmas tree the first week in December that our artificial
tree may become part of our family tradition. A real tree just will
not last the entire month that we enjoy ours. So twig by twig the
children literally put it up. This is their tree. They are free to make
decorations for it and to touch it as much as they wish. After I have
the lights strung on the branches, the children decorate it with balls
and tinsel and their own creations. Sometimes I can't help but give
some guidelines, such as, "The ball will look prettier hanging so that

it doesn't sit on another branch," or "See how long you can make the tinsel fall." Once in a while their creations are such that I am tempted to add my finishing touches or hang the decoration on the back of the tree. But then I remember that Christmas and our tree belong to the children.

Today is also the day to begin preparing our traditional season's greetings. I always include a special message from the children. I try to make it a *family* letter and not just *my* letter. In the past I have asked the children what they wanted for Christmas and have included their lists or asked them what they thought Christmas was for and given their answers. Today I asked each of the children to draw a pencil drawing of the Kuzma family at Christmas. The girls are especially proud that their artwork is to be duplicated for all to see. And I'll have to admit that the Kuzma Christmas letter will be unique!

Tuesday, December 3 / Impatience

Today I lost my temper.

I can try to make excuses for myself. I was tired. The house was a mess and I was trying my best to change that situation. Someone had just telephoned with disturbing news. I expected Jan home very soon and supper wasn't ready. The children had been acting like giggling bunny rabbits hopping from one thing to another all afternoon, and forgetting to put anything back. So when they all three bounced in the back door and without the slightest notice tracked and slipped and slid across the freshly waxed, still wet kitchen floor, I blew up.

I felt badly the minute I yelled, "Get out of here! Can't you see there is wet wax on the floor?" Their hopping and giggling instantly stopped and they looked innocently down at the floor. When they finally realized what they had done, they were unhesitatingly apologetic and offered to fix it up. But my anger had not yet cooled and I retorted, "Just get out of here. All you kids have done today is make messes for me to clean up," I exaggerated. "Daddy is going to be home in a few minutes and now [again I exaggerated] I have to start waxing the kitchen floor all over again. I've had it!"

They sadly retreated out the door that they had so joyfully entered just minutes before. As I repaired the damage (which was minor), I remembered a statement made by Ellen White that I have tried to practice: "Mothers, however provoking your children may be in their ignorance, do not give way to impatience." (*Child Guidance,* Nashville, Tenn.: Southern Publishing Association, 1954, p. 245)

Where had I failed? What circumstances led me to vent my anger on these little ones who learn so easily by my example?

Frustration leads to anger, and anger leads to impatience. I first erred by letting myself become frustrated. Perhaps I had attempted to do too much in one day. Perhaps I was feeling a little guilty that I hadn't worked as closely with the children as I should have done today. Perhaps I was frustrated by their earlier behavior, yet so absorbed in my own job that I didn't feel I had time to do more than just verbally instruct them to pick up their toys rather than making sure the task actually was accomplished. I should have handled my frustration earlier, but I didn't.

My frustrations led to anger. I was obviously angry with the children before they slid through the kitchen. I was angry that they were not helping me; that they were making noise; that they weren't obeying my orders. I should have acted at that point by saying to them calmly, yet with meaning, "I'm angry. I need your help. Kim, you pick up the dolls. Kari, you take your clothes to the bedroom. Kevin, you put the blocks in this box. You have five minutes. If your job isn't done by that time, I will not have time to read you a story tonight."

But I did not act early enough, and I let my emotional temperature continue to rise to its breaking point—impatience. If it hadn't been the waxed floor, it might have been the spilled dog food, or the broken cup, or . . .

My impatience led me to say things to the children that I really didn't mean. I exaggerated and made the situation look worse than it was, and I didn't stick to the topic at hand—slipping on the wax. I brought out the dirty laundry (other things that they had done that day that had made me angry) and I threw it all at them at once. It was really not fair of me, and they knew it.

I'm glad I can learn by my mistakes, and I'm doubly happy a child does not hold grudges. I resolve today to be a better teacher-mother tomorrow.

Wednesday, December 4 / Play Dough and Persistence

Last night as I was cleaning out the refrigerator, I found some old play dough (also known as baker's clay). I got it out, and all three children played happily with it for over an hour. They probably wouldn't have gone to bed then if I hadn't promised, "Tomorrow we'll make new play dough for preschool." So that has been the big activity for the day. It's like a miracle potion, guaranteed to keep children of all ages happy and creatively occupied for hours!! At least it works that way for my children.

Before the breakfast dishes were washed this morning, I was helping the children measure out the ingredients: two parts flour to one part salt, and enough water to make a good, nonsticky consistency. We added a tablespoon of oil and blue food coloring. Then each began making "his own things." Kevin is at the squishy-feeling stage and is very happy to make different shapes like balls, pancakes, and weiners with his lumps of dough. But the girls prefer using rollers (round cylinder blocks) and cookie cutters and cutting out "delicious" cookies. They even think the salty dough tastes good! Ugh! The children put their products in the warm oven to bake, and they come out rock-hard in three or four hours.

Last year we made play-dough Christmas tree ornaments. We cut out the shapes we wanted with cookie cutters, put a small hole with a pencil point in the top for the string to go through later, and baked them in a warm oven (150 degrees) until they were hard. Then we spray-painted them. On some we added glue, glitter, and sequins. We tied pretty ribbons through the holes and gave the ornaments to relatives for Christmas. For Grandma and Grandpa we made hand-print plaques by taking a large lump of play dough and rolling it into a thick oval pancake. After the hand prints were made, we baked the plaques hard and sprayed them bronze. I think the play-dough plaques look nicer than the hand-print plaques made with plaster of Paris.

Play dough can also be used much like clay, making snowmen and birds' nests with eggs. I like play dough because when it dries, it's not crumbly and doesn't need to be fired in a kiln.

Later: The house is quiet for the moment so I am back at my desk. The morning went well, but I still haven't solved the problem of keeping three children busy at different things at the same time.

Kari left the dough first. I suggested that she practice writing her name, since library day was coming and the only way to get a card of her own is to write her own name. I put the model on top of the page, but she still has difficulty with the K. She makes it like a straight line with a capital C attached. I remembered some old practice cards someone had given me. The cards have only one letter to a card, but give both capital and small letter, and then space for the child to write in crayon, which can be wiped off of the plasticized surface. After I found the cards, Kari sorted through them, trying to pick out the letters in her name. Then Kim came in, wondering what we were doing, and said, "I want to do that, too."

"No, this is for me," Kari replied.

"Mommy, she won't let me play," whined Kim.

Then Kevin joined the scene, "Mine."

"No," grabbed Kari.

"Dumb dumb," replied Kevin. (He has just learned that this gets the biggest reaction of all!)

"I've had it," I said, as I walked out of the study. "I'm going to get the mail."

They all immediately forgot what they had wanted so badly just a moment before and tagged along with me.

The two-hundred-yard walk to the mailbox did us all good. After the girls cleaned up the play-dough mess, I read them stories and then suggested we practice singing some of the Christmas songs. Then outside time. Lunch. And now I realize, as I am back at my desk, that I was unable to help Kari follow through on another task. The letter cards are still sitting here half sorted. Tomorrow I must try harder!

Thursday, December 5 / Jan's Night In

It was my night out, and Jan's night in. I returned from my meeting at about nine-thirty and Jan mentioned, "The kids just went to bed." This could mean one of two things: Either the children were so obnoxious that they wouldn't go to bed when they were supposed to and it took till nine-thirty to win the battle, or they were having such a good time that their daddy decided to be extralenient about bedtime. I didn't ask.

At ten-fifteen the phone rang. It was my mother in Colorado. Even though it sounds as though she is next door, I practically yell, just because it is long distance. My wide-awake Kim, whom I believe could recognize the sound of a long-distance phone call in her sleep, jumped out of bed to talk to Grandma. "I like all kinds of gum. . . . Don't forget to bring us some sugarless gum."

After the call, Kim said, "We played lots of games tonight."

"What kind of games?"

"The first one was 'Hide the Treasure.' We hid a ruler and said 'hot' or 'cold' to guide each other to the hiding place."

Kim continued, "Then Daddy drew pictures and we had to put them on our backs and we had to guess what animals we were by asking each other questions."

"What animals were you?" I asked.

"I was a cat and a fish. Kari was a horse and a cow."

I said, "You mean that your daddy can draw a cow that you can recognize?"

"Well, they thought it was a zebra at first," Jan explained. "But since they couldn't read words on their backs, I was limited to the animals I thought I could draw."

Kim added, "The game we liked best was 'Guess the Animal That Carries You to Bed!'" I had never heard of that game, so I asked Jan where he got it.

"I had to think of something fun to get them to bed," he explained.

"Daddy acted really funny, just like he was the animal."

"What animal did everybody ride?" I asked.

Kim explained, "Kevin got to ride a dog and a cat, Kari got a donkey and a bee, and I got a camel and a horse."

After Kim had gone to bed for the second time, I asked Jan where he got the idea of game night. "I had to do something to keep everybody happy and busy, so I thumbed through the book we got a couple of years ago, *1,000 Family Games,** and found the first two. I thought up the rest. You know, we really ought to look through some of our books once in a while; there are probably some other suggestions of games and activities the children would enjoy."

Friday, December 6 / Paper Folding

Today I did just as Jan suggested. I thumbed through my collection of books about things to do if you have run out of ideas yourself. In one book I found a few paper-folding ideas, which immediately sparked the children's interest and reminded me of some paper-folding ideas I enjoyed as a child.

The dog puppet was simple enough for even Kevin to make, and before I knew it we had three paper dogs barking at each other. Just follow these instructions for your own paper puppet.

1. Start with a square of paper:

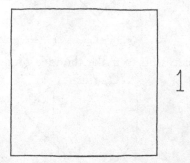

* Pleasantville, N.Y.: Reader's Digest Association, 1971.

2. Fold it in half diagonally:

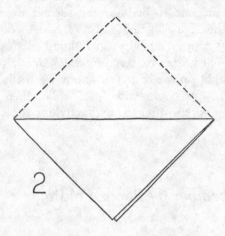

3. Fold the corners down for ears:

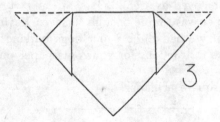

4. Fold the end pieces up to make the face rounder:

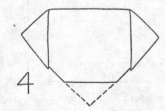

5. Draw in the face:

I stapled the edges right under the ears so the puppet wouldn't come apart. I made sure I left plenty of room for the children's hands.

The love knot was easy too. After writing a special love note on a sheet of paper, fold it over a number of times so that it is very narrow and long.

1. Then fold one side over like this:

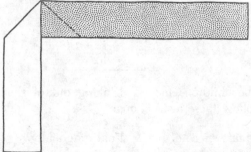

2. Fold the other side over backward, like this:

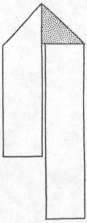

3. Then fold again backward:

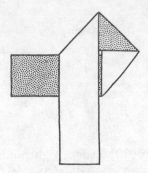

4. Then lift the flap over the other end and you have tied a love knot:

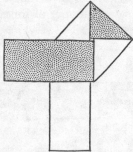

Finally, the children enjoyed drinking out of their own paper cups. Just follow these instructions:

1. Take a square piece of paper. Fold diagonally.

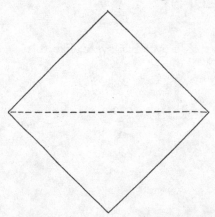

2. Then fold one side like this (make point A touch point C):

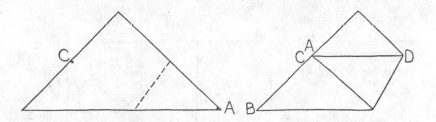

3. Then do the same thing to the other side, making B touch D on the opposite side. Then fold down the top edges.

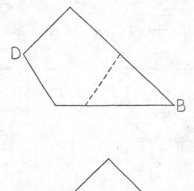

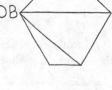

If it resembles a cup, treat yourself to a drink—of water, of course.

But of all the paper-folding activities, the twirly birds make the best toy.

1. Take a rectangular piece of construction paper and crease along the dotted line:

2. Follow the cutting lines:

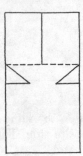

3. Then fold on the dotted lines and paste the folded base together:

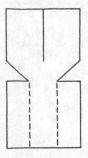
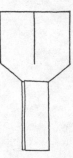

4. Bend one side of the top in one direction and the other opposite. The side view of the finished product should look like this:

Then stand on a chair and watch it twirl to the ground. The girls' bunkbed became our launching site.

Monday, December 9 / Carols vs. "Nuttin'"

There is never enough time in the year for me to sing, play, and enjoy listening to Christmas music. One of my favorites is the old German carol, "Still, Still, Still." I decided that I would like to learn it by memory so that I could sing it as I went about my housework. At the same time, the words seemed so simple and repetitive that I felt this would be an ideal song to teach the children. So I began to sing.

Still, Still, Still

I sang this lilting lullaby over and over again, but the children just couldn't seem to get enthusiastic about it.

Then, digging deeper into a stack of old music, I came across "Nuttin' for Christmas,"† which I remember singing as a child. I opened the music and sang the song through. Immediately the children urged me to sing it again. After singing the song three times, Kim said she knew the song by memory and didn't want me to help her with the words. There are three verses, so I couldn't believe it as she sang almost perfectly about such terrible things as breaking a bat on Johnny's head, hiding a frog in sister's bed, spilling ink on Mommy's rug, making Tommy eat a bug, and buying gum with a penny slug.

Why is it that children are so eager to fill their minds with songs about nonsense and trivia, when they could just as well be learning a carol of beauty and value?

Should we as parents guard our children from such make-believe songs as "Santa Claus Is Coming to Town," "Rudolf the Red-nosed Reindeer," and "Frosty the Snowman"? Is this really what we want them to fill their minds with? What do I really value? What is the true meaning of Christmas, and how best can I use this beautiful season of the year to help my children to become more like that babe in the manger?

Tuesday, December 10 / Guessing

I just read a newsnote about a speech made by an educator named Frank Smith, who suggests that we ought to allow children to have fun with reading by encouraging them to "guess" the next word.

At first I said, "Guess? Never. Children should sound out the word." But these two arguments convinced me that guessing isn't so bad.

1. *Words have too many meanings.* When you see a word in isolation, it is very difficult to know the meaning, since so many words have multiple meanings. I never really thought about it before, but

† Words and music by Sid Tepper and Ray C. Bennett.

words like "table," "house," and "shoe" can be either nouns or verbs. That can be confusing to even grown-ups if they don't put the word in context and guess at the meaning. To make matters worse, many of the most common words have the most meanings.

2. *Phonics doesn't work in isolation.* Phonics is a tremendous aid to pronouncing most words—but it's not the only answer. For example, there is not a single letter that doesn't represent more than one sound, and not a single sound that doesn't represent more than one letter. Mr. Smith said that one researcher, using only the 6,000 most commonly used words, came up with 211 rules for pronunciation. Can you imagine adults, let alone children, ever learning 211 rules for pronunciation? So what phonics specialists do is call it 10 rules and then have 201 exceptions.

With all of the exceptions to the rules of phonics, it is a wonder anyone ever learns to read. It seems to me that the best readers use a combination of word recognition and phonics and guessing. Word recognition is important for those simple everyday words that occur constantly.

But when it is an uncommon word that one is deciphering, then one needs to use both phonics and guessing to discover the unknown. Phonics gives clues to word pronunciation; then a child must use his own experience and rationale according to the context of the word, to "guess" the correct word.

Children should know that a parent or a teacher will accept intelligent guesses and will not be constantly reprimanding or correcting them.

I can remember how I used to hate to read aloud because the teacher corrected every word. When I finished I had no idea what I had read because I was too busy reading words to worry about what they meant. When Kim read her "Dick and Jane" book, I remember the impulse I had to correct her when she made a slight error in words such as saying "funny" for "father." But I kept still, and sure enough after a few more words, she corrected herself. By allowing Kim to correct herself I did not make her feel that she had made a mistake. Constantly correcting children can make them feel like failures. Also, by wise guessing Kim was able to figure out the word herself, and I have a feeling that she will probably remember it longer than if I told her what the word was.

And so as I search for clues on how I can better teach my children to read, I must be open enough to add to word recognition, phonics, and to phonics, that very unscientific-sounding term—guessing!

Wednesday, December 11 / Spelling Lists

Backward or forward, there is something special about the spelling lists of a five-year-old. Why is it that children seem to write backward just as easily as forward—and sometimes more easily?

It all has to do with a child's brain development and the establishing of a dominant hemisphere. Children who have a difficult time learning left from right (read words like WAS as SAW) and tend to be somewhat ambidextrous are still in the process of establishing a dominant hemisphere of their brains. Writing backward for these children is just as natural as writing forward because their brains do not easily distinguish the difference. This is a natural developmental process, and usually by eight years of age, children no longer have difficulty with directionality. If the problem continues past this age (as it does for many children), it makes it almost impossible for them to do well in reading. If forced to read in a school program, they begin to feel like reading failures, and this can affect their feelings about their abilities for years. But if a child is allowed to begin reading on his own time schedule, when his brain dominance has been established, he will feel successful and can usually catch up with his peers without difficulty.

What should I do now? Kim is only five. Writing backward is to be expected. Therefore, I'll not make a big point of correcting her. I'll first show I appreciate her efforts, then gently point out that the beginning of the word needs to start on the left side of the paper. When individual letters are written backward I'll put my hand over hers and move it in the correct way, forming large letters. Tracing letters may also help. Making letters is a learned motor skill. It is perfected only after much practice. Encouraging children to practice the correct direction is important, but should not be forced to such an extent that children hate writing altogether.

Thursday, December 12 / Role-playing

Role-playing is an important part of childhood play. It helps children clarify different roles that they may (or may not) have to assume in real life. By pretending they are someone else, they gain a better understanding of the feelings and attitudes that another person may have.

I like to keep a box of dress-up clothes available for children to use when acting out Bible stories. Blouses, shirts, pants, scarves, hats, long pieces of colorful material, belts, old negligees, and even a crown and scepter help to make the play seem more realistic.

As Christmas approaches, the children have become more interested in the birth of Christ. Today the girls played out the Christmas story themselves without any help. They had gotten the book *My Bible Friends,* which has the story of Christ's birth, and had dressed themselves as much as possible like the pictures in the book. They brought the rocking horse into the house, and Kari sat sidesaddle on it and had a baby doll under her robe. When I walked in on their play, Kimberly-Joseph was just saying to Karlene-Mary, "Darling, it won't be long now and we will be to Bethlehem so you can have your baby." They were embarrassed and started giggling when I stopped to watch, but I encouraged them to continue and told them that this would be an ideal skit to do for family worship.

After the doll was born, they let Kevin be baby Jesus. By playing through this story, I am sure they had a better understanding of the feelings and responsibilities that Mary and Joseph had, and the story of Jesus' birth became more meaningful.

Friday, December 13 / Christmas Decorations

When it comes to art, I enjoy a good-looking product, but I strongly resist telling a child every move to make. Originality and

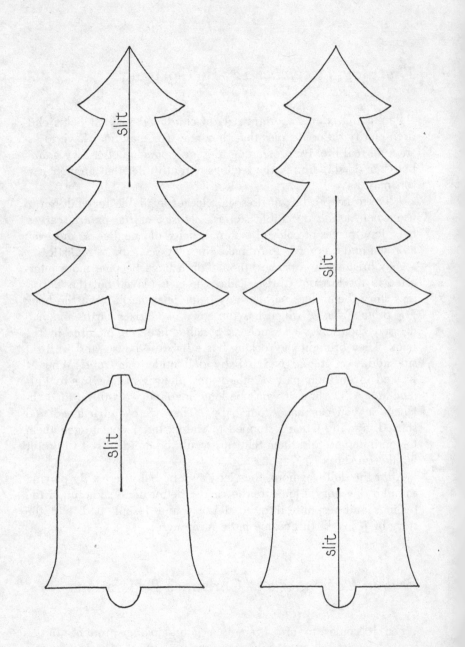

the process involved in the creation are far more important than a perfect product. A delightful Christmas-tree ornament can be made by any preschooler by sticking round toothpicks into styrofoam balls. We made them today, and after these were sprayed with paint or artificial snow, they looked like ornaments I would buy for the tree. Even Kevin enjoyed this activity and depleted my toothpick supply by his perseverence.

The children also made old-fashioned construction-paper chains and hanging decorations in the shape of Christmas trees and bells such as I used to make as a child before we had styrofoam balls. I drew the pattern for them, then they copied it, cut it out, and put the two pieces together by slitting the top of one piece and the bottom of the other.

To feel free enough to be creative, children must have a variety of materials on hand and know they won't be made fun of for creating their own things, even though no one else has ever seen anything like them before.

To me, Kim's and Kari's Santa Claus is priceless. The raw materials were just red construction paper and white scrap paper, an orange crayon, and some watercolor paints. They used a paper punch to make the eyes, scissors to cut out the figure, and glue to paste everything together. There is no pattern for this Santa—it is one of a kind, and I appreciate its uniqueness.

Monday, December 16 / Vacation in Baja

Christmas vacationtime. Time for teachers to get a vacation, right? Wrong. One thing I've learned: Teacher-mothers seldom get vacations. Since each day is filled with new wonders for my preschool children to discover, I want to be there to enjoy these precious, once-in-a-lifetime moments. So I want to be "on the job" every day with them.

Just for a change, we are heading down to Baja California for eight days of sunshine (I hope). The nineteen-foot-wide road is

not very wide, but adequate to take us across the deserts to the
Sea of Cortez, our destination.

Vacations in our household are usually family affairs. We enjoy
going somewhere that has something for everyone. As much as Jan
and I enjoy snow skiing, the children are too small to enjoy the
slopes with us. Vacations are not to be wasted in motels and restau-
rants. Those are conveniences for business and convention trips. As
far as children are concerned, if you've seen one motel or restaurant,
you've seen them all. So when Jan and I consider our vacations, we
try to choose some place we will really enjoy; a place where we can
be truly relaxed and come back more rested than when we left
home; a place where our preschoolers can find plenty of enjoyable
things to do that take very little adult guidance.

When it's winter vacationtime, we often head south to Mexico,
where we can sit in the sand and soak up the sun and splash in the
surf. For Jan, the most adventurous member of the family, there is
snorkeling and canoeing. This year Grandma and Grandpa from
Colorado are coming along; also my sister Joanie, her husband,
Dick, and one-year-old Timothy, too. It's really destined to be a
family affair.

I once asked a group of college students to list the things that
tended to pull family members away from each other, and then to
list the things that pulled their families together. It was interesting
that the things listed as pulling families apart (work and school)
were the things to which, out of necessity, we must devote the largest amount of time.

In contrast, vacations and family celebrations were high on the
list for pulling families together. And yet only a few weeks or days
a year are devoted to these activities, which tend to strengthen
family ties.

I have always loved vacations. Of all the memories I have from
childhood, the clearest are of our family vacations. Now, as a parent, I realize that vacations involve so much planning and preparation that it would be easier just to stay home.

But if we stayed home, our children would be deprived of that
closeness that being away together can bring. So when I add up the
pros and cons, it seems worth all of the extra bother. If I ever get

packed, we'll be on our way. It's vacationtime, not for me as a teacher, but for our family. The fact is:

> I like it when I'm there,
> smelling fresh clean air;
> sitting on the beach
> leisure within reach.

> But oh the job before!
> The getting-ready chore!
> Packing this and this,
> I wonder what I'll miss.

> And when I've got it in,
> I know I cannot win,
> for soon we'll turn about
> and have to take it out!

Tuesday, December 17 / Getting Acquainted

What a beautiful day! Now that I really am relaxing on this remote Mexican beach, I can truly say that the packing and the long trip were worth it. I am amazed how children seem to have a good time wherever they are. I'm not particularly fond of driving for long distances, but the children could have traveled for another few days before they grew tired of playing in their grandparents' camper. Now on the beach the children have invented their own games in the water and on the sand. Watching the children play together makes me very happy that we decided to have more than one child, fairly close together. Jan and I have had our times of trouble with our three, but now that they are older and can truly interact and enjoy each other, I can't imagine life without them.

Joey, an eight-year-old boy and the only child of a young couple camped down the beach from us, wandered up our way a few hours ago. We had seen him last night and again early this morning, sitting by himself on the beach. He did look lonely, so I suggested to the girls that they invite him to come over to our camp to play.

As he walked slowly up the beach, he kept watching the girls playing on the air mattresses in the water. Then he stopped, and without a word started interacting with them in a hesitant sort of way. Without a word of introduction, the girls accepted him into their play. A few minutes ago, I asked Kim and Kari their new friend's name. Neither of them knew—it had never occurred to them to ask. A child's getting-acquianted game is so different from an adult's getting-acquainted game. Adults care first about facts— names, occupations, hometowns—while a child asks:

Do you like boats?
Do you know how to swim?
Do you have a brother or a sister?

They want to know about a person's interests, skills, or possessions.

It is fun for the children to make new friends, but when there are no friends to play with, I'm glad they have each other. And as long as our children remain close to each other, they will probably not experience that miserable feeling of loneliness.

Wednesday, December 18 / An Adventure with Nature

Yesterday we heard the snorting from shore and saw their black bodies leaping rhythmically in and out of the water. They appeared close to us, yet still too far away to identify. Some said porpoise, but some said they looked so large that they must be whales, perhaps a herd of killer whales. The children were excited that we had seen them, whatever they were.

Today, we departed in our inflatable canoe to explore a tiny island offshore, completely forgetting the animals we had seen in those waters such a short time before.

Kari stayed behind with the grandparents to go shelling in the shallow water. I left her with this admonition, "Try to find five different kinds of shells while we are away." Kim and Kevin got on their life jackets and climbed in the canoe with Jan and me. We didn't realize our bay was so sheltered until our light-green shallow water changed to a foreboding black, and the whitecaps lapped at the tiny canoe, which had minutes before been in peaceful waters. I was apprehensive as the thought flashed into my mind that we were in the very same waters in which we had seen those black sea creatures the day before. What if?

The rocking of the boat lulled Kevin to sleep. Then we saw them coming toward us. We were directly in their path. I looked back at Jan, and his look acknowledged that he had seen them, too. I didn't say anything to Kim, but it was only seconds until she saw them bearing down on us. She was hysterical with fear. Jan stopped paddling. There was nothing to do now but to let them pass. As they drew closer and circled our canoe, we recognized them as porpoises. But that didn't reassure me of our safety, since natives had told us about the curiosity of the porpoises. Sometimes they even nuzzle a boat. "But don't worry," they had said, "they are very smart animals, and if they turn a boat over they will often hold persons up to the surface with their noses."

I spoke reassuringly to Kim, who was holding onto me frantically. "Don't worry. They are only curious porpoises. We are lucky to get to see them so closely. Notice how they spout each time they dive out of the water. That's how they breathe."

In minutes they had moved on to their feeding ground, where we could see them circling about and hear them snorting in the distance. When our canoe once again glided into our green, glassy bay it was with our prayer of thanksgiving for our safety.

Kari met us and proudly exhibited her shells: ". . . and here's a scallop shell and I also found six sand dollars." But it was Kim who had a whopper of a "fish" story to relate. She learned more about porpoises in that five-minute experience than I had learned in thirty some years! I only wish I had thought to wake Kevin. It was probably a once-in-a-lifetime adventure with nature.

Thursday, December 19 / Campfire Stories

We were sitting around the campfire, the stars overhead brighter than ever in the moonless black sky. Earlier, as we walked along the beach, we had been fascinated with the phosphorescent waves, and now we could hear them lapping at the shore. Faces of loved ones shone yellow in the firelight. It was good to be all together. Somehow a fire brings people closer.

"Tell us a story, Grandpa," the children begged.

Grandpa told stories of his boyhood and his experiences with his three brothers. He told about the pranks he pulled as a boy. My sister and I kept reminding him of other stories until finally we reminded him of the skunk story. Grandma left at that one, insisting that children shouldn't hear such stories, because they might get ideas. But with this introduction, the children yelled insistently, "Oh please tell us, please tell us."

After the story about Grandpa's experiences trying to catch a family of skunks, the children were still not satisfied. "Grandpa, tell us one more." When Grandpa said that he was all out of stories, the children groaned.

Finally someone suggested, "I know what we can do. Why doesn't one person start a story and then the next person will continue the story and we'll keep going around until everyone has as many turns as they want?"

Kim began the story, "Once upon a time there were three bears and they lived in the forest in a nice little house. But one day their house burned down. They were so sad they didn't know what to do, so they went down the road and . . ."

Uncle Dick (a social worker) continued: ". . . and they waited and waited and finally a car came by and the people in the car said, 'What can we do to help you?'

"The poor bears told them that their house burned down and they didn't have anything to eat. So the people took the bears into town to a social worker who helps people like that. The social worker was surprised to see the bear family. He said he helped people, not bears. But when the bears began to cry, the social worker felt sorry for them and asked them what they needed. They said they needed a house to live in, so . . ."

Grandpa (a real-estate broker): ". . . so, the social worker said, 'I don't think I can help you. You need to go to a real-estate agent. They are the ones who find houses for people to live in.' So the bears went to a real-estate agent, and he said, 'What can I do for you?' The bears said that they needed a house to live in. The real-estate agent asked, 'How much money do you want to spend on a house? It costs money to live in a house.' The bears started to cry. 'We don't have any money. What can we do?' "

Uncle Dick contributed: "Go see your social worker. And the social worker told them that they would have to get jobs so they could earn money. But . . ."

Aunt Joanie (a "retired" nursery-school teacher since having a baby of her own) continued: ". . . but the bears said, 'How can we go to work? We have a baby bear to take care of.'

" 'Well, you could find a good nursery school for your baby and then you could work while the baby is at nursery school.'

" 'What a good idea,' said the bears. 'These people have thought of everything.' So they went out to find a job . . ."

Kari's turn: ". . . they went looking and looking and they were so sad. They didn't know what to do. 'I know,' said Mommy bear, 'let's ask over there.' But they didn't know what to do either. Finally they went out on the road and a car stopped, and the people inside said . . ."

Daddy (who is a statistician) said: " '. . . The probability of your finding a job at this time is very poor, since so many people are out of work. But if you want, I can give you a ride back to the forest.'

"So the bears got into the car and drove back to the forest. They then decided that the forest was not such a bad place to live after all, and they lived happily ever after."

THE END

Friday, December 20 / Child's Play

This morning on the beach Kim and Kari were both pulling on different ends of an air mattress, yelling, "It's mine; give it to me!"

Finally, Kim said, "Kari, you're not supposed to fight with your husband. Say 'please.' "

So Kari obliged, "Please, husband," and the air mattress was happily handed over! It makes me think of that Bible verse, "And a little child shall lead them."

Later Kim and Kari were playing "dying." "Oh!" sighed Kari. "I'm having a heart attack! Quick! I'm dying. I'm dead."

"Oh my," said Kim, with a smile on her face, "I'll have to breathe in your mouth." She held Kari's nose and breathed in and out about five inches away from Kari's open mouth. Guess what? It worked!

"Come," shouted Kari as she jumped up. "Let's play 'Adam and Eve.'" The girls ran a short distance down the beach to begin their new drama. I was curious, but too lazy to follow.

"Besides," I thought, "playing Adam and Eve would probably be more fun without a snoopy mother watching and writing down each word." I'll just have to imagine the rest!

Many times parents who want to be effective teachers of their children think they must be constantly teaching. This is not good. Children need time to play without adult interruption and supervision. Play is the best way for children to learn to relate to each other. Play is an excellent vehicle for vocabulary and concept development. Play encourages children to test out reality. So as a teacher-mother I'm very content just to sit here on the beach and allow my children to continue to develop their minds, bodies, and relationships through their uninterrupted play.

Monday, December 23 / Memories of the Beach

The children dug clams today. The small sandbar in our bay is filled with the little creatures, and when the tide goes out, they are there for the children to find. Digging for clams is like digging for hidden treasure. You know it is there someplace, but when it is discovered, it is always a surprise. The children had a delightful time filling their buckets, and then, at the day's end, we scattered them back over the surface of the sandbar for the tide to cover, so someone could rediscover them again tomorrow after they burrowed back down under the sand.

There is so much to learn from the ocean. The children all knew what a clamshell was before digging for them, but they usually see only one of the two shells. Actually to see where these creatures grow, and to feel them while they are alive, to try to pull their shells apart only to give up because their muscles are stronger than ours—these are things that no book can portray to a child with the same meaning as the real experience. Preschool can be effective at one's own home, but there is a time to leave home and start discovering some of the wonderful world of God's creation beyond our own backyards.

Today we must leave this paradise. We will try to wipe the sand from our shoes, but we will never be able to wipe away the memories of the octopus hidden in shallow water under a tree branch, the underwater trail of the conch who thought he was hidden in the pile of sand at the end of the trail, and the colorful tropical fish we could view by looking over the side of our canoe down into the shallow water in the coral bed. We will always remember the clams and the porpoises and all the other sights, sounds, feelings, tastes, and smells that a new environment brings to us. This vacation was not a vacation from preschool. Perhaps it was the richest preschool experience the children will have all year.

Tuesday, December 24 / Watercolors and Christmas Eve

I took a watercolor painting class in college and I learned one thing: It's a lot harder than it looks. With oils and other media you can cover up your mistakes. It's not so easily done with watercolors. The teen-age girls who were camping next to us on the beach in Baja made watercolor paintings as they sunbathed. Kim was fascinated as she watched them. Today is our first day back home, and Kim has been sitting at her table a good share of the day making watercolor paintings. Some of them show a striking resemblance to the ocean scenes that the girls were painting at the beach. I think it is really important to expose children to different art techniques and to watch artists at work. The inspiration this kind of experience can bring is far superior to an artificial attempt to create the motivation to learn and experiment with something new.

Later:

Tonight was Christmas Eve. Since I am older and don't believe in Santa Claus and mistletoe, one would think that some of the excitement of Christmas would wear off. But it hasn't. I love to celebrate this night in our traditional family way. After a simple supper of hot soup, Jan gathers the family around the Christmas tree. He either reads from the Bible or tells the Christmas story. Then each person says what he would take to Christ if He were born in our town tonight. After prayer we talk about what our gifts to Christ would be this Christmas season, and then we open our gifts.

Tonight, Kim selected the first gift and took it to the person whose name was on the package. After that gift was opened and everyone exclaimed over it, the next gift was distributed. In this way each person has a chance to see what everyone else has received. After the gifts, we took pictures to record the event for posterity, sang some carols, and Jan and I tucked three sleepy children into bed. After everyone was safely in bed, I filled their stockings with fruit and nuts and little wrapped packages. This year I got them each a package of decorative seals, a religious-card game, and a package of sugarless gum. I always put an orange in the toe of each sock. I think this is from my childhood days when oranges in Colorado were a real Christmas treat. While I filled stockings, Jan cleaned wrappings off the floor and then we collapsed into bed.

I try not to say anything about Santa Claus during our Christmas celebration. He just doesn't seem to fit into our home! The children know he is a fairy tale and they enjoy singing songs about him, but they know that they get their presents from real people, not because they are good, but because they are loved. When my children were babies, I used to delight in taking them to see the department-store Santas and having a picture taken with them. Before they were two years of age, however, I found out that, instead of immediately falling in love with these fat, roly-poly, jolly old fellows, they were scared to death of them! Now I realize I can leave Santa Claus out of Christmas completely, and my children enjoy it just as much. Certainly the beauty and intrigue of the true Christmas story are far more meaningful to children. They love babies and identify with the Christ child more than with a silly old red-faced adult whom grown-ups have manufactured.

Wednesday, December 25 / The Real Mary

The Christmas carols are playing and it is a time of reflection. What is the meaning of Christmas? How can we become like that Christ child who was born in Bethlehem so many years ago? I think about Jesus' mother. This was her first child. I wonder if she was frightened, being away from friends and relatives who customarily helped when a child was born. I wonder how Joseph felt, not being able to find a room for his new bride. Certainly he wanted to provide the best for her. I wonder how they felt as labor started and they had no place to stay. I wonder how long she was in labor. This was her first, and the first is always the hardest. I wonder if an angel instructed Joseph on what to do to help her. After the baby came, I'm sure Mary was exhausted, since she had traveled so far, and labor is hard work. I wonder how they felt when their privacy (if you can call having a baby in a barn private) was suddenly interrupted by the curious shepherds. I wonder how long they had to stay in the barn before Joseph was able to find some other place for them to live.

So often we think of this Christmas story in relation to the pictures that have been painted about the stable scenes. Mary looks radiant, her gown is spotless. As I contemplate on how it probably was in reality, I marvel all the more that Christ, the Son of God, would choose to come down to this world for us. This world is such a wicked place. The amazing thing is that Nazareth, the place where Jesus grew up, even had a reputation for its wickedness. "Can any good thing come out of Nazareth?" How did Mary and Joseph raise the boy Jesus under what I would consider less than perfect conditions? I'm sure he must have spilled his milk and torn his clothes like all children do because of their immaturity. I wonder how his parents handled these incidents so that Jesus learned appropriate behavior? What a challenge and responsibility to care for and teach God's special son, Jesus!

But then, Jan and I too have been blessed with the responsibility of caring for and teaching three little ones, whom God calls his daughters and son. "Lord grant us the wisdom you gave to Joseph and Mary so long ago when you sent your very own Son to this earth to be our Savior. And thank you, Lord, for Christmas each year to remind us in a special way of your great love."

Thursday, December 26 / Signing Off

The next few days will be filled with the fun and pleasures of the holiday season and preparations for the new year. So I'm signing off for now so I can plan for a more effective preschool experience during the new year.

Sunday, December 29 / Birthday Stories and Potato Pancakes

"Happy Birthday to me, Happy Birthday to me . . ." sang Kim as she jumped out of bed this morning. "Mommy, tell me the story again about how I was born and had a bump on my head and had the brightest eyes of all the babies in the hospital."

So with Kim, Kari, and Kevin snuggled up next to me in my warm, electric-blanket-heated bed, I told her again her favorite story. When I was finished, Kari wanted her story, and of course Kevin didn't want to be left out. I am surprised how much the children enjoy hearing about how they were born. Each child is so unique, and so is their birth experience.

When I finished the story of each of their birthdays, they eagerly climbed out of bed to begin their day. I lay there a few more minutes reflecting on my experiences giving birth and the subsequent joy of mothering each baby. But my babies were growing up and it was time to start Kim's sixth birthday celebration with her favorite breakfast of potato pancakes.

This is how I make potato pancakes: I finely grate three or four raw potatoes and add an egg and seasonings (salt and onion powder), then fry on a skillet like regular pancakes. (If your blender has a grating speed, you can put all the ingredients in the blender until all the potato pieces are grated.) I serve them heaped with applesauce and apricot syrup (the syrup that is left over when I can apricots via the hot-pack method).

This is a breakfast truly fit for a birthday girl.

Awake! A New Year
Unbroken resolutions
JANUARY's here

――――――――――――――――――――――――――――――

Wednesday, January 1 / Character-development Curriculum

How refreshing it is that once a year there is a time to start again. Another day, and yet a new year. A time to resolve that the days ahead will be more meaningful than those in the past. Jan and I look forward to New Year's Eve each year, not so much as a time for celebration, but as a time of fellowship and reflection. A quiet, unhurried evening with our closest friends and our children is a balm to our year-older, ragged souls.

Last night, after an early farewell, we enjoyed a quiet ride home with our three sleeping children bundled in blankets in the back seat. It was so good to be able really to communicate. When I can sit next to Jan without competing with three preschoolers and we can talk to each other without interruptions, it is almost as if we were still single.

As we drove, we talked about New Year's Eves in the past and how it used to be, but we both knew we wouldn't want to retreat to the past, not after we have experienced the joys (and tribulations) of being parents of preschoolers.

After the children were all snug and warm in their own beds, it was our turn to think seriously about New Year's resolutions. We both agreed that our greatest desire is to have children with beautiful characters. As we heard the bells and horns in the distance welcome the new year, we made our first resolution—"to work out a system of teaching character development to our children, first thing in the morning." Then we snuggled close to each other, happy that we had each other; happy that we can work together teaching our children; happy for the new year, with its boundless possibilities.

This morning we began the task of developing a program of character development for the children. Jan suggested that we would be wise to follow Benjamin Franklin's method of stressing one virtue each week for thirteen weeks and then start over again the next quarter with the same thirteen virtues. We thumbed through Ben Franklin's autobiography* until we found his list of virtues.

The following are the thirteen virtues stressed by Benjamin Franklin:

1. *Temperance:* Eat not to dullness; drink not to elevation.
2. *Silence:* Speak not but what may benefit others or yourself; avoid trifling conversation.
3. *Order:* Let all your things have their places; let each part of your business have its time.
4. *Resolution:* Resolve to perform what you ought; perform without fail what you resolve.
5. *Frugality:* Make no expense but to do good to others or yourself; that is, waste nothing.
6. *Industry:* Lose no time; be always employed in something useful; cut off all unnecessary actions.
7. *Sincerity:* Use no hurtful deceit; think innocently and justly, and, if you speak, speak accordingly.
8. *Justice:* Wrong none by doing injuries, or omitting the benefits that are your duty.
9. *Moderation:* Avoid extremes; forbear resenting injuries so much as you think they deserve.
10. *Cleanliness:* Tolerate no uncleanliness in body, clothes, or habitation.

* *The Autobiography of Benjamin Franklin* (New York: Pocket Books, 1954), pp. 103, 105.

11. Tranquillity: Be not disturbed at trifles, or at accidents common or unavoidable.

12. Chastity: Rarely use venery but for health or offspring, never to dullness, weakness, or the injury of your own or another's peace or reputation.

13. Humility: Imitate Jesus and Socrates.

We both liked the system, but we felt we should choose the thirteen virtues that we felt were most important for our children to develop, rather than just copy those Franklin thought were good for him. This led to a search of the virtues mentioned in the Bible.

I read again 2 Peter 1:5–7, where Peter mentions the character traits that are important for spiritual maturity: faith, virtue, knowledge, temperance, patience, godliness, brotherly kindness, and charity. Then I looked over Paul's list in Philippians 4:7, where he mentions the importance of being true, honest, just, pure, lovely, and of good report. In Matthew 5:3–12 Christ mentions the importance of being poor in spirit, meek, merciful, pure in heart, peacemakers—and then He says to "rejoice and be exceeding glad."

Finally, after much deliberation, we arrived at our own list of thirteen character traits we wanted most for our children. Our list includes the following with our own "homemade" definitions.

1. Faithfulness: Complete trust (confidence or reliance), loyalty, allegiance to some person or thing, hope, unquestioning belief in God.

2. Orderliness: Regularity, neatness, tidiness, good behavior, lawfulness.

3. Self-discipline: Temperance; self-control; moderation; patience; submission to authority and control; self-discipline is the result of orderly conduct.

4. Happiness: Joy, contentment, merriment, cheerfulness.

5. Perseverance: Continuing to do something in spite of difficulties or obstacles, steadfastness in purpose, endurance, diligence.

6. Honesty: Truthfulness; integrity, fairness, and sincerity; genuineness; purity.

7. Thoughtfulness: Consideration of others, kindness, gentleness, carefulness, attentiveness, heedfulness, thankfulness, love, reverence, courtesy, helpfulness.

8. *Efficiency:* Ability to produce the desired effect with a minimum of effort, expense, or waste; working well; competence, ability, capability.

9. *Responsibility:* Obedience, trustworthiness, dependability, reliability, answerability, ability to distinguish between right and wrong and to think and act rationally, and hence be accountable for one's behavior.

10. *Respect:* Feeling good about self and others; self-esteem; self-confidence; treating self with consideration and courtesy; courage.

11. *Enthusiasm:* Intense or eager interest; inspiration, zeal; fervency; ardor; optimism.

12. *Humility:* Absence of pride or self-assertion; modesty, meekness.

13. *Peacefulness:* Freedom from disagreement or quarrels; harmony; serenity; calmness; contentment; quietness; tranquillity; silence; absence of mental conflict.

Our next task was to search the Scriptures to find the Bible texts that the children could memorize each week to help them remember the importance of the character trait we were trying to emphasize. We used the King James Version, since that is still the most widely used version of the Bible, but we did make some of our own adaptations, such as changing "thou" to "you." On the longer verses we underlined the portion of the text we would use for Kevin, but we would try to help the girls memorize the entire text, since they were older.

Even though we listed a variety of texts that could be used for a given character trait, we will select out of this list only one per week actually to be memorized.

Since one of our earlier goals was to help the children learn hymns, we felt that this could be incorporated into our character-development program. So from the hymnal we selected songs that would correspond to the weekly trait.

To round out our character-development curriculum we wrote down the topics for stories that would help the children remember the traits. We divided these into three areas: Bible characters, great people (both historical and current), and other miscellaneous topics. We plan to scan through some religious storybooks for children and select stories that illustrate the character traits we are stressing and tell these to the children during the appropriate week.

We also listed the activities we could do during the week that would help the children remember the character trait, or practice the trait.

Finally we designed a weekly chart to keep track of the specific character-building plans for each week. At the top of the chart we listed the Bible text and song we would try to learn. Then for each day of the week there is space to record stories and activities we plan to use to emphasize the character trait.

We will make copies of the chart and fill it in with our weekly plans either on Saturday night or Sunday morning. If we think of things during the week and do them with the children, we will try to write these down, too, so that we will have an accurate record each week of what we have done with the children in the area of character development.

We are still somewhat uncertain about how to evaluate the children in this area. But we are hoping to observe a change in their behavior as well as noticing them talking about these character traits in their work or play. Therefore, we have left a space at the bottom of the page for our comments and evaluation of the children.†

It's a new year and a new plan, but Jan and I are the same "old" parents teaching the same "old" children. Perhaps after following this plan for a year, Jan and I will have learned how to be better models for our children in this important area, and we will all be better individuals.

Monday, January 6 / Faith

To help us in our study of faith this week, I placed two questions on the bulletin board for the children.

† This character-development plan is available in the book *Building Character* by Kay and Jan Kuzma. A companion volume of children's stories emphasizing these character traits is Kay Kuzma's book *The Kim, Kari, and Kevin Storybook*. Both are available from Pacific Press Publishing Association, Mountain View, Calif.

"In what should we have faith?" was the first, and the responses of the girls were particularly interesting:

That Jesus will come
That I will grow up and be a big girl
That Kevin can learn how to go to the bathroom by himself
That I won't use cigarettes when I grow up
That we will have Christmas every year

"How should we be faithful this week?" was the second question. These are some of the answers given by the children:

Praying   Reading stories
Keeping New Year's resolutions Obeying Jesus
Brushing our teeth   Having preschool every day
Eating food

These questions give the two different aspects of faith that I think are important to stress to young children: (1) We must have faith, especially in God and in the Bible. (2) We must be faithful so others can have faith in us.

Tuesday, January 7 / Thank-you Notes

It is so easy for my children at Christmastime just to receive and forget to say "thank you." Since many of the gifts they received came from relatives living miles away, it is difficult if not impossible to say "thank you" in person.

Today for our preschool project I suggested that the girls make their own thank-you cards by folding a piece of paper and making a watercolor picture on the front. I wrote a short note that they could copy in each card. It sounded easy to me, but it took them most of the morning to finish two cards, the motivation wearing very thin as time progressed. So I suggested that if they just made the paintings on the front, I could write the inside notes. But the cards that were the most fun to make were those on which I wrote the names of the items and asked the girls to draw the pictures of the items.

I don't feel that it is good to give children tasks that are so difficult or require so much time that they become frustrated. Writing thank-you notes should be a pleasant, joyful task. "Oh be joyful and give thanks. . . ."

Wednesday, January 8 / Ideas for Art

The children get so many of their ideas for artwork by seeing something someone else has created or by actually watching the person make the product.

Today after Mr. Rogers' program, Kari went to the art-supply cupboard, selected a piece of red construction paper, took the white glue, and dribbled the glue all over the page. I was tempted to tell her she was using too much glue (it is very expensive), but sometimes we adults are too cost conscious when it comes to children's creativity. Kari then took her paper with the wet dribbles of glue outside, went to the sandbox, and sprinkled sand all over it. I figured she must not be very interested in the picture to cover it with sand. But after a few minutes she picked up the paper, shook off all the loose sand, and presented to me a most unique piece of artwork. I'm sure she must have observed Mr. Rogers making a similar sand drawing on his program.

When I took Lisa and Greg home today, Randy had just gotten home from school with a snowman picture made from applying tempera paints with a sponge. Kim immediately asked him how he made it. After learning the secret, she was eager to return home so she could make a similar picture for herself.

Thursday, January 9 / Kevin's Colors

Any 2½-year-old who can distinguish a motor boat from a canoe, and a steamship, and a tugboat, and a sailboat, and a cargo ship, and a speedboat ought to be able to distinguish red from blue. Unless, of course, the child is color-blind. I am beginning to think that may be Kevin's problem.

I have been taking advantage of every opportunity to teach Kevin the names of colors. All the books about child development say that "normal" children should be able to learn the names of the colors by two years of age.

When Jan realized how color-retarded Kevin was, Jan took over Kevin's color instruction. Finally, two days ago, Jan decided that Kim might be a more effective teacher. "Kim," he said, "I'll give you a stick of gum for every color you can teach Kevin." Kim would do anything for gum. For two days now she has been working on teaching Kevin the color white. She takes him by the hand and leads him through the house pointing out everything that is white.

"Kevin, touch the wall. See, the wall is white. Say white." And she goes on to the next white object. Finally, she points to an object of another color, when she is sure he has learned white, and asks, "Kevin, what color is this?"

"White!" he shouts.

"No, Kevin," pointing to a white object, "this is white, not this."

Tonight I decided it was my turn to see if I could teach him a few colors. I got out a large pegboard game with large, beautifully colored pegs.

"Kevin," I instructed, "put a red peg in the hole." He picked up a peg. "That one is a blue one. Say 'blue.'"

"Blue."

"What color is it?"

After a long pause, "Green."

"No, it is blue. This one is a green one. Find another green one."

He shuffled through the colored pegs in the box and finally, after much thought, he selected one. "This is a green one," he said.

"Kevin, that is a yellow one. It is the same color as your pajamas. Put the yellow one in the hole."

He picked up a red peg. "Kevin, what color is that one?"

"Blue."

"Kevin, this is a blue one (holding up another peg), and the one you have is a yellow one. Remember, the yellow one is the same color as your pajamas. Your pajamas are yellow and this one is yellow."

At about this time, Kim came in with a little red VW car. Kevin immediately picked up the car and started crawling around the floor with it. "Vrummmmm, vrummmmm."

"That's a red car you have. Do you like your red car?"

"I'm going 'vrummmmm' with it. Mommy, you put up colors now."

"OK, Kevin," I said, realizing I'd lost. "You can play with your red car."

I left and went to the study. A little later he came in, vrumming his red car. "Kevin, what color is your car?" I questioned.

He stopped and thought. "Blue? . . . Yellow?"

"Kevin, it's red."

"Mommy, you play with red car," he offered, as he placed it next to my typewriter and left the study.

"I can't believe it," I spoke aloud to myself. "How can such a bright boy be so dumb?" I really don't think he knows one color from another. If he knew them and were teasing us, he would forget the game occasionally and say the right answer, wouldn't he?

But then I consoled myself. Why really does a 2½-year-old have to know his colors? They will still be there when he is 5. Perhaps it is more important at this age to know the difference between a motorboat and a sailboat and all of the other different kinds of boats than to be able to name the colors.

Friday, January 10 / Building

At 7:00 A.M., when I had heard the cement trucks drive up across the street, I remembered that the neighbors were pouring the cement foundation for their new house. That sounded like a good field trip for my preschoolers. As soon as breakfast was over, teeth brushed, dishes done, and beds made, the children climbed into the big red wagon and I pulled them over to where the cement trucks were pouring. After they watched for a while and placed their handprints and names in the wet foundation, we headed home, pulling a wagonload of scrap wood to be glued and nailed together for wood sculptures.

A building site can be a dangerous place for unsupervised preschoolers, but with the proper preparation and limitations and parental care, it can also be a fascinating place filled with priceless learning opportunities. In addition, it can be a very profitable place for teacher-mothers who have learned to identify junk that can be valuable assets to the preschool program.

One day when we visited another home that was being built, the children picked up bent nails, screws, "play coins" from the electrical boxes, bits of wire, and pop-bottle caps. They glued them to heavy paper plates, then sprayed the plates with bronze paint. What delightful wall hangings! In fact, the children gave one to their grandmother for her plate collection!

Today the children built boats with the wood scraps. Kim's boat had a railing all around it made with a row of nails and some colored telephone wire that the telephone repairman threw away. Kari's boat was made of graduated pieces of wood nailed on top of each other. Kevin glued a small piece of wood on a larger piece and then painted his creation with tempera paint. When it was dry I sprayed it with quick-drying clear lacquer. With our boat productions completed and a small picnic lunch packed (for the children— and the ducks), we headed to the park to launch the boats in the fish pond.

Monday, January 13 / Memory List

To help bring some practical order into our lives, I made a memory list of all those things the children needed to remember to do during the day. There are so many things that I forget unless I consult the list. By writing these things down and daily placing stars beside the items that the children remember to do, perhaps a routine can be established so that the children will need fewer reminders in the future and we can live a more orderly existence.

Memory List

7:00   Make beds; get dressed and put away pajamas; set table for breakfast
7:15   Breakfast story about character traits
7:30   Clear table; brush teeth
8:00   Play
9:00   Preschool
11:00 Practice piano
12:00 Lunch; brush teeth
1:00   Rest; practice piano
4:00   Park
5:00   "Mr. Rogers' Neighborhood"
5:30   Set table; clean family room
5:45   Supper
6:00   Brush teeth; clean up play things; practice piano
6:30   Worship; Bible story; church school lesson study
7:00   Play
7:30   Bath; get ready for bed; put dirty clothes away
8:00   Bedtime

Tuesday, January 14 / Chicken Pox

Yesterday I thought I had discovered another advantage in keeping young children home and becoming a teacher-mother, rather than sending them out into the world to be educated in groups. They aren't as likely to catch contagious diseases. Chares, a six-year-old cousin, caught the chicken pox from the other children in her kindergarten class and had to spend Christmas in bed. "Poor Chares," everyone was saying. As soon as the isolation period was lifted, my girls were the first ones to throw their arms around her and welcome her back into society. *Today* I discovered that just because I have decided to be the children's teacher and have preschool at home doesn't mean that they won't catch contagious diseases. Kari just broke out with chicken pox. I can see the handwriting on the wall: Kari this week; three weeks later, Kim (and Kevin, if they both decide to get it at the same time), or three weeks later still, Kevin. I could be homebound for nine weeks!!!

Because Kari didn't feel well, I was challenged to find some preschool tasks that would take her mind off of her illness and yet not require a lot of exertion.

So today we turned our house into Redlands General Hospital. Kari pretended she had a very serious disease. (Just look at the spots!) Kim was the doctor with her emergency-doctor-kit equipment ready for action. Her main responsibility was to make Kari comfortable by rubbing calamine lotion on the itchy pox.

Kevin was the accident victim and had so many injuries that he kept both Dr. Kim and Patient Kari busy wrapping him up with splints and bandages. I was the hospital administrator, cook, and housekeeper all in one.

We made up the sofa bed in the family room. (Who wants to be stuck off in a bedroom to commiserate one's physical ailments all alone?) Seeing the hustle and bustle of normal life mixed with the novelty of a new bed in a new room took some of the unpleasantness away from Kari's poxed condition.

We equipped the "hospital room" with a pitcher of ice water, glasses and straws, books and magazines, a bouquet of "flowers" (weeds were the only thing growing in the yard at this time of the year), and a bell to call the hospital staff when in need. With the long extension cord we even put the telephone at the patients' bedside so they could call their friends and tell them about the chicken pox. Kim did the dialing and then handed the phone to the patients to tell their stories.

When both patients were either saturated with lotion or wrapped in bandages they listened to records and kept their hands busy stringing necklaces of buttons, beads, and macaroni.

Then as a special feature for Kari I planned a treasure hunt through the children's picture dictionary. I read the instructions, Kari followed them and came up with the answers, and Kim wrote them on the appropriate blank. These were the instructions:

1. Look up HOUSE
2. Count the windows in the house and turn to the page with the same number. _____
3. Find something red on this page. What is it? _____

4. How many letters are in the word for the red thing? _____

5. Add the number of windows with the number of letters for the red thing. _____

6. Turn to that page and you will find what we are going to have for dessert. Write your answer here: _____

I introduced the girls to cutting snowflakes by folding paper three times. (Fold in half once. Fold that in half once more, and then once again.) Then they cut notches in the folded edges. It helps to use thin paper. Kevin enjoyed tearing shapes out of paper and pasting these onto construction paper.

By the time Jan called, "Hi, everyone, I'm home," all three children were lying in the "hospital" bed sipping frosty blended fruit drinks‡ while Mr. Rogers serenaded them. It was a good day, even though it was a chicken-pox day.

Wednesday, January 15 / String Play

Today as the children were playing with some ribbons and string, I suddenly remembered the fun I used to have with my friends doing what we called the "cat's cradle." It is impossible to explain how to do it to a four- or five-year-old, so I showed them. I did the first step, then transferred it to one of their hands and showed them how to do the second step, which would make the "cat's cradle" into the "barn door." Then I did the same thing to show them how to make the barn door into the "fence." Then I transferred it again to them to show them how to make it back into the cat's cradle. Kari tried a few times, but in frustration she gave up and wouldn't even try again, even when I coaxed her. Not Kim. She wouldn't give up even if the odds were a thousand to one against her. She stuck with it, and when we finally got through a whole cycle, her joy was unbounded. Over and over again we did it. Then she had to share her

‡ Blend together approximately 1 cup fruit juice, banana, peaches, apricots, or other fruit, and a tray of ice cubes.

success. She was so proud, it was the first thing she showed Jan when he got home. Kari just watched, saying nothing.

Later in the evening, Kari picked up the string, worked for a while, and finally got it around her hands in such a way that it made the first cat's cradle. She hesitantly showed it to me. I was thrilled with her attempt to try something that had been so difficult and frustrating, and I could tell that she was pleased, too. But she still wasn't ready to go on.

It is so important to respect the differences in each child and not to push one ahead of his level of competence, but rather just to encourage, encourage, encourage and be willing to praise the smallest advances.

Thursday, January 16 / Jumping Jingles

This morning I took Kim to visit a first-grade classroom, where I thought she might possibly like to attend next September. During recess time the children jumped rope, actually running into the turning rope and back out again. Kim was fascinated. Even though she knew how to jump by starting when the rope was still, she would not even attempt to do it when invited by the other children to jump with them.

When we arrived home, the first thing Kim asked was for me to teach her how to run into the rope. We purchased a fifteen-foot piece of half-inch nylon rope and burned the ends to prevent raveling. We tied one end to the jungle gym, and I began turning the other. It took only a few tries before the girls got the feel of running into the turning rope. As I turned I began to recall all the fun I used to have in my rope-jumping days. A part of the fun was the silly jingles we used to say while jumping. I must have known fifteen or twenty of them, but the only ones I could really recall were *Teddy Bear* and *Blue Bells*.

I know that *Teddy Bear* had dozens of verses, but I could remember only "Teddy Bear, Teddy Bear, turn around; Teddy Bear,

Teddy Bear, touch the ground." So I started making up my own
Teddy Bear rhymes. For example:

> Teddy Bear, Teddy Bear, tie your shoes;
> Teddy Bear, Teddy Bear, read the news.
> Teddy Bear, Teddy Bear, wave hello;
> Teddy Bear, Teddy Bear, learn to sew.
> Teddy Bear, Teddy Bear, wash your clothes;
> Teddy Bear, Teddy Bear, touch your nose.

Blue Bells starts with the rope just swinging back and forth:
"Blue Bells, cockle shells, ezie, izie over . . ." until the word
"over," when the rope starts going over the child's head.

Once I started chanting jumping rhymes, Kim and Kari wanted
more. I asked a ten-year-old friend, and she told me three more
rhymes that I'm sure I used to know as a child.

Down by the Ocean
Down by the ocean, down by the sea,
Johnny broke a bottle and blamed it on me.
How many lickin's did he get? One, two . . .

Little Dutch Girl
I'm a little Dutch girl, dressed in blue.
Here are the things I used to do.
Salute to the captain;
Curtsy to the Queen;
And turn my back on the mean old King.

Down in the Valley
Down in the valley where the green grass grows,
There sat Kim as sweet as a rose.
Along came Kevin and kissed her on the cheek.
How many kisses did she get that week? One, two . . .

I remember that this was one of my favorites. There was always
a great amount of motivation to jump just as long as possible!

As the girls began to ask for more, I decided that I would just
make up some of my own jingles. Using the basic form of *Down in
the Valley,* the children and I came up with such things as,

Down in Redlands where we go to school,
There sat Kari by the pool.
Along came Kim and pushed her in.
How many times did she get a lickin'? . . .

or

Down in Redlands where I have a house,
There sat Kim as quiet as a mouse.
Along came Kevin and he said "Boo!"
Kim started crying, "Boo hoo, boo hoo."

One thing about making up verses as you go: You never manage to say the same thing twice. It is always a surprise to the children. And to my amazement, I found that they were quite good at making up their own jingles. They didn't always rhyme, but neither does some poetry.

Friday, January 17 / Give Me an F

Today is the end of the first semester of preschool. It is evaluation time. Evaluation for most teachers means assigning grades to their pupils. But I'm wondering, as a teacher-mother or as teacher-parents: Is it more important to assign grades to our children, or to assign grades to ourselves?

Everyone likes to get good grades. A good grade for some children may be an *A* (as in achievement), while others would be happy with a *C* (as in co-operation). *A*'s and *C*'s may be fine for children, but for mothers and fathers, the *F*'s are the most important for success.

The first *F* is for *Fast:*

A parent must be fast to get everything else done so that he can take time for activities with his children. When small children aren't around, when they are napping, or listening to records, or playing their own games and don't need close adult supervision to dampen their fantasy, that is the time to work with utmost speed to accomplish the things that parents need to do. If a mother is not very fast, and has a long "Things to Do" list, then the time she spends with her children is given only halfheartedly. Half of her attention is focused on the things she should be doing and how she will be able to find time to do them.

I'm not immune to this dilemma. The other day I was sitting at my desk while the children were gathering around "writing letters and books." Kevin was standing beside me, saying, "Mommy, I need you. I need you. Mommy, I need you." I was vaguely aware of a voice in distress, but I was thinking of how to begin a long-overdue letter.

Kim stopped her work, came over to me, looked me in the eyes, and said, "Mother, Kevin is speaking to you." Well, he did need me. He wanted his already sharp pencil to be sharpened again!

The second *F* is for *Fun:*

If a parent is not fun to be with, then his children will begin to spend their time with other people who are fun to be with. Parents are the key to the atmosphere and mood of the home. If parents are fun to be with, happy and cheerful, the chances of having fun-to-be-with, happy, cheerful children are greater.

Last week I was trying desperately to get my daughters' bedroom in order. This meant going over everything completely with a fine-tooth comb to find all of the missing puzzle pieces, belts of dresses, and misplaced socks and shoes. The more I cleaned, the more upset I became at how much junk the girls had stored in their closets and drawers since the last "spring cleaning" time. They were working with me in this joyless situation, since I had decided that this would be our preschool activity for the day. I complained loudly, and none of us were having any fun.

Finally Kari said, "Mommy, why don't you go clean your own closet and let us clean ours?"

I don't blame her for wanting me out of the way. I was certainly no fun to be with.

I do want my children to enjoy my company. Right now, because they are still under my jurisdiction, they really don't have much choice. But before long the peer pull will be strong. And if the children don't think Mom (and Dad) are fun to be with, then it will be very difficult keeping them home.

The third *F* is for *Fair:*

No one likes a person who isn't fair. But it's sometimes very difficult for an adult to decide what is fair. For example: Is it fair that both girls should go to bed at the same time? How does one explain to the younger child that the fair thing to do is to let the older child stay up later because she doesn't need as much sleep?

Is it fair to expect all of the children to do the same amount of cleaning? How do I handle the complaint, "Why do I have to clean up all this mess by myself?" How can I explain that it wouldn't be fair to interrupt Kim's paper folding right now, because she is trying to finish her project as a surprise for Daddy before he comes home?

I personally think that the fair thing to do is to respect each person's individuality. Not all of us need or want to be treated the same. I'd really like my children to learn that at times each one of them will receive special consideration, because each is different. It's really the only fair thing to do, but how do the eyes of a two-, a four-, or a six-year-old look at such obvious differentiation?

I ask myself, "Is it fair to take my frustrations out on the children?" This week has found me terribly rushed. I don't know how so many deadlines can come due at once. It is so easy for me to say "yes" to requests two, three, and four months in advance. In the far future, anything seems possible. But as time flies, I approach the deadline and wonder, "How did I ever get myself into this?" And because I'm rushed, frustrated, angry, and tired, it is very hard not to take it out on the children.

Little things can be explosive. Kim and Kari, trying to be helpful, emptied the dirty dishes out of the dishwasher (thinking they were clean) and put them all away. I had just spent fifteen precious minutes loading the dishes into the washer and then had to play hide-and-seek trying to find them on the shelves. But it was really not their fault. It is not fair for me to take it out on them.

The fourth *F* is for *Firm:*

The important thing is to say what you mean and mean what you say. I agree with this principle, but when the children sometimes plead and cry, I often end up giving in. I know theoretically that a parent should always say "yes" to a child's request unless the parent has a very good reason for saying "no." This allows a parent to stick to his "no" and explain it to the children. But this is very difficult to put into practice. It is easy for me to say "no" to a request to go outside when I'm too tired to get up for the tenth time that day to get out three sets of coats, boots, scarves, and mittens.

Right now it is very hard to be firm about eating between meals. The oranges in our yard are ripe and hanging there temptingly on the trees. I sometimes give the children a drink of orange juice between meals. However, we do have a firm rule at our house: No eating between meals. Last week when I found the children sitting in their playhouse peeling and eating oranges, I reminded them that they should not be eating between meals. "But Mommy," Kim replied, "it is too hard for us to squeeze the oranges by ourselves and we didn't want to bother you, so we are eating them." That sounds very logical and considerate. Was this a time to be firm or not?

Jan and I know that many things we do as a family, or don't allow our children to do, are contrary to the standards and values of other families. It is difficult sometimes to explain to our children why we have certain standards and other parents don't. We are vegetarians and some of our friends are not. We have told our children that we do not eat meat because meat is not the best kind of food for our bodies, and that we want our children to grow up to be healthy and strong. The children then asked, "Don't Jane and Jim's mommy and daddy want them to grow up to be healthy and strong?"

We have found that it is very difficult to answer some of their questions. Perhaps the easiest and simplest explanation is, "This is the Kuzma way of doing it."

I'm convinced that our being firm helps the children feel secure because they know just what is expected of them. When they decide to go against these expectations, then they should not be surprised if there are certain consequences.

The fifth *F* is for *Flexible:*

At first it may seem somewhat contradictory to talk about being both firm and flexible at the same time. I believe that a parent has to be firm when it comes to moral issues (what is right and wrong) and family values (what is healthful, good, and kind), while at the same time a parent must be flexible in his expectations for his children and the plans he makes for them. Once a parent has spent a lot of time planning a certain activity for the children, preparing all of the necessary materials and setting things up, it is difficult to be flexible enough to change all these "excellent plans" to follow what the children really want to learn and do. One day last week, I had decided which activities I thought each of the children should do. I mixed the paints, set up the easel, put out the paper, and fully expected the children to do what I had planned for them. As it turned out, all they wanted to do was play house. And when I say play house, I mean they start from scratch (a clean family room) and move in all the things they need for their play. By the time they are ready to "play house" their closets are empty. I know no matter how much I fuss and fume and remind them that they will have to put everything back, I will end up having to help them with the clean-up. Should I be flexible enough to allow them to play house even though I have planned other activities? Yes, I believe I should. Children grow from making choices, and the only way this can happen is when grown-ups are flexible enough to let children make their own decisions when it is appropriate.

The sixth F is for *Forbearance:*

Almost every day the children do something that could raise my blood pressure. Yet it doesn't help to rant and rave. It is the calm, quiet talk that seems to work the miracles. But it takes a lot of patience and forbearance to handle the situation in this way. A few days ago, Jan asked Kari to be sure to put away the paper dolls in the family room before going out to play. Kari forgot. He could have made a big issue over it, but instead he just called her to come to him in the family room. She took one look around and immediately began picking up the dolls. No additional comments had to be made about the incident.

The final F is for *Forgiveness:*

When childish mistakes are made, a parent must be full of forgiveness. Young children don't hold grudges, and it does parents no good to hold them either. This only causes children to harbor feelings of resentment and guilt.

Some parents feel that children should say "I'm sorry" for every unacceptable action. This is good if the words are a true expression of their feelings. But too many times a child is forced to say the words even though he does not feel sorry. A child should not have to ask his parents for forgiveness in order to be forgiven. If the child knows the parents are willing to forgive even before he says "I'm sorry," then the "I'm sorry" often comes more easily, because he knows it will not be rejected.

Children who live in an atmosphere of forgiveness will be more willing to attempt difficult tasks, knowing that if they happen to fail or make a mistake they will be met with understanding and not criticism.

Certainly, not all the *F* qualities are good. With diligence I have tried to avoid failure, fighting, fatigue, fault-finding, faltering, fear, feebleness, forgetfulness, frustration, and fussing.

By avoiding the negative *F*'s and striving for the positive ones, perhaps, by the end of the year, I can grade myself higher than an *A* for *Average* and give myself an *F* for being a *Fabulous* parent.

Monday, January 20 / Self-discipline

"Once upon a time there was a chipmunk who loved nuts and seeds." This was the beginning of one of Jan's breakfasttime character-building parables, which he created to interest the children in the importance of self-discipline, the third trait we planned to emphasize in our character curriculum. He continued, "Every nut or seed this chipmunk saw he had to have for himself. He had a nice cozy home that he had burrowed out under a rock and on one side he kept his storehouse of nuts and seeds. When he would go outside his house, he would spend all his time gobbling up all the food he could find. He never had time for anything else, like being kind to others and reading his Bible. When he got so full he could hardly budge he would carry home the rest of the nuts and seeds and place them in his storehouse. He loved nuts and seeds so much that he even fought with other chipmunks if they happened to find a nut or a seed that he wanted. He just couldn't control himself. If he saw a nut or a seed, he had to have it no matter what.

"As time went on, the chipmunk got fatter and fatter until he could hardly waddle along. He ended up fighting with more and more of his friends over their nuts and seeds because it was easier than looking for his own. Soon nobody wanted to play with him any longer and he lost all his friends.

"His mommy and daddy told him to eat just what he should and save only what he could use before it spoiled, but he wouldn't listen. All this time his storehouse of nuts and seeds kept growing.

Nuts and seeds soon filled his living room and his kitchen and his bathroom and his bedroom so he didn't even have any place to sleep. Soon the food began to rot and his whole house smelled. So he burrowed some more rooms under the rock. When they were full he burrowed some more until at last he burrowed out all the dirt under the rock, and the rock fell down, smashing his nuts and seeds and destroying his house."

"Poor chipmunk!" The children were shaking their heads by this time. "Too bad," they lamented.

"Do you think he deserved what happened to him?" Jan questioned.

"Yes, he was selfish."

"Did he need all the food he found?"

"No, he just thought he did."

"Why didn't he do what his mommy and daddy said?"

"Because he didn't want to obey."

"So it's not enough for a mommy and daddy to tell children what to do. Children must be willing to listen and control themselves. Is that right?"

"Right," the children chorused.

"That's what self-discipline is all about," said Jan. "And that's what we are going to be studying all week."

Telling stories is an excellent way to emphasize certain points without pointing fingers. A Bible story can be effectively used when it fits a certain situation, but when I can't think of one, I find that a pretend story, like the chipmunk story, works well. Christ was the master storyteller, and his parables were far more effective than merely exhorting his "children" with lists of "thou shalt nots." Perhaps we as parents would find our teaching more effective if we followed more closely the master teacher's instructional techniques.

Tuesday, January 21 / Personalized Songs

Children not only like to hear stories about themselves, but they also enjoy personalized songs.

The song "A Mouse in His House," which I learned as a nursery-school teacher, is Kevin's favorite. This song has as many verses as Kevin can think of animals that could be in his house—lion's roar, cat's meow, monkey's shriek, snake's hiss, and on and on. When Kevin thinks of an animal whose sounds I'm unfamiliar with, I substitute action, such as, ". . . and this is what he does, hop, hop . . . ," and we continue singing.

Mouse in His House

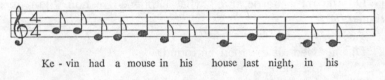

Ke - vin had a mouse in his   house last night, in his

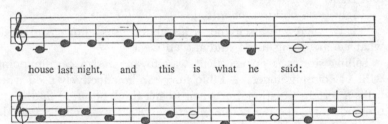

house last night, in his   house last night, Ke - vin had a mouse in his

house last night,   and   this   is   what he   said:

Sweak   Sweak
Sweak Sweak   Sweak Sweak Sweak Sweak Sweak Sweak Sweak Sweak· Sweak

Sweak   Sweak
Sweak Sweak Sweak Sweak   Sweak and   that   is   what he   said.

SOURCE UNKNOWN

Wednesday, January 22 / Preparation for Play

I am sitting at my desk enjoying overhearing the children playing church school in the next room. They have all ten dolls lined up on the floor. "OK," said teacher Kim just a few minutes ago, "it is time for you children to say your memory verse. Repeat after me, 'Thou shalt not help us steal.'"

The girls have worked hard in preparing their church school program. Each "teacher" made a set of cards, which they have observed their own teachers using, to remind them of what came next in the program. Kim laboriously typed each of her cards (letters and numbers in no particular order), while Kari drew a couple of animals and scribbled on the rest. They punched holes through the corner of each card and then put them together with a safety pin so they could flip them easily.

They have their felts and flannelboard set up on one side of the room. Their church papers are neatly folded by the doorway, to give out to the "little children" at the end of the program. They even have stickers to paste on each paper if the dolly says her memory verse correctly.

When it comes to elaborate role-playing, as this church school program has become, it appears that the most fun may be in the preparation for the play. Their motivation is high and they very rarely need my help. Of course, they also enjoy the play, but it often does not last half as long as the preparation. Then comes the clean-up, and that's where they include me, whether I like it or not! But the privilege of listening unnoticed (as I'm doing now) to hear their ideas and expressions is reward enough for a teacher-mother.

Thursday, January 23 / Original Paper Products

I enjoy teaching the children and then standing back and letting them do their own experimentation based upon the fundamental information I have given them.

Since Kim has gotten the idea that you can make many things by folding paper, she has come up with her own ideas. They are simple, but they are hers.

First she made a basket by just folding the paper in half, stapling up the edges, then stapling on a paper handle.

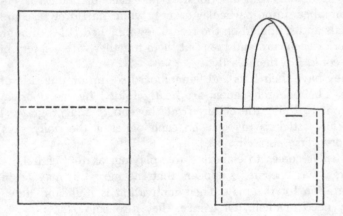

Next she made a more elaborate basket by folding the paper diagonally, then folding over the edges, stapling them together, and adding a paper handle. (See illustration on next page.)

But the thing that surprised me most was the envelope she came up with. She wanted an envelope, so I mentioned that she could make her own. She said, "But I don't know how." So I told her to take an envelope apart and see how it was folded. Now we have an abundance of homemade envelopes. And Kim has had the satisfaction of figuring out how to do it by herself.

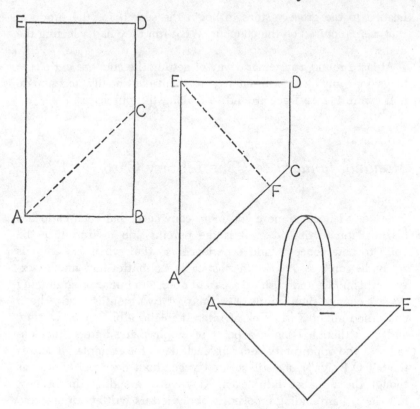

Friday, January 24 / Coupons

"Clip and use coupons" was the preschool activity for the day. First, the children went through all of the magazines that had accumulated during the past few months and cut out the coupons. What fun they had—and it took most of the morning. They then organized these into categories, such as soap, food, etc.

I asked each of the children to choose those items they wanted to purchase, and after I gave my approval to their selections we headed to the grocery store to begin the search for the products that were pictured on the coupons. What fun they had selecting the items.

At last I found a systematic way of getting the coupons out of the magazines and used without having them continually accumulate and expire before I get around to making the purchases.

Monday, January 27 / The Library Card

Every day I become more and more convinced that each child has his own innate timetable. It is the parents' job to introduce the child to new concepts and experiences so that when the child is ready, he can blossom. But in most cases, no matter how much worrying, planning, and pushing a parent does, the initial programming doesn't change significantly. For the past two months I have been concerned about Kari's lack of interest in the alphabet or writing, and even though I made a point of emphasizing letters "incidentally" as the opportunity came up each day (for example, "There is the S T O P sign"), she still seemed to go about her carefree way as though the alphabet didn't exist. Now, all of a sudden, in the past few days, I am finding crooked, wobbly letters written all over everything. Sometimes she copies words in books, and sometimes she writes line after line of miscellaneous letters and proudly brings them to me to have me read them. "Mommy, what did I write?" After I try to pronounce all of these sounds, worthy of some language from outer space, she breaks into giggles and goes back to her writing.

Today for preschool I threw out the challenge, "Kari, if you can learn to write your name today without any help, I'll take you to the library and you can get your very own library card." A few months ago, when Kim got her library card, the challenge of writing her name was too difficult for Kari even to attempt. But now she felt ready to tackle the challenge, feeling that she might have a chance for success. While Kim and Kevin were busy putting together puzzles, and I was making beds, Kari sat in the study writing her name over and over again, copying from capital letters that I had printed on the top of a page. It seemed only yesterday that I had to stand over her to keep encouraging her to finish a task. And now, with a feeling of confidence, she was motivated enough to persist on her own. It takes a lot of little successes to feel good enough about yourself to tackle the big things. After a while she came to me with a whole page full of wiggly KARI KUZMAs. "Kari, do you think that you can write your name without looking at the model? You can't look at anything when the librarian asks you to write your name." She eagerly said "yes." I drew a line on the paper and put an X in front of the line, as the librarian would do, and asked her to write her name. She had no trouble with the KARI, but no matter how many times she tried KUZMA, it was always mixed up. She couldn't remember whether the U or the M came before the Z. To help her, I made up this song to the tune of BINGO, "There was a girl who wrote her name, and Kuzma was her name—O, K U Z M A, K U Z M A, K U Z M A, and Kuzma was her name—O." After singing the song a few times, she went back and tried again. Success. So we were off to the library.

Just before we went in she asked me to sing that song again. We stopped and sang it a few times, and she went in for her first exam. She was brave to try, having just learned her name. Kim had been writing her name for a year before she attempted to get her card, so it had come quite naturally for her. The librarian handed Kari the card with the line on it for her signature. Putting an X at the beginning of the line, she said, "Write your name here." Kari took the card and sat at the table. I took Kim and Kevin to the opposite side of the room to look at books. I waited and waited. I'm sure I felt more agony than Kari did. What was taking so long? Finally she brought me her card, and as I feared, the M was before the Z. Should I help her? Finally I said, "Kari, the letters in your last name are mixed up. Think about the song and try again." She went back, erased the whole thing, and started over. Again we waited. Again she brought the card back, and again the letters were mixed up. Only this time the Z was in front of the U. Again I sent her back, and again we waited. I was beginning to wish we hadn't been so hasty. She erased the whole thing and started once more. Finally she came back. I sighed a sigh of relief. All the letters were there, all in their right order. She hesitated to take the card to the librarian, so I went up with her. The librarian smiled as she looked at the smudged card and said, "Good for you. You really worked hard, but you did it." (May the Lord bless that librarian.) Then she said, "Just to make sure everyone can read it, I'll type your name right below where you wrote it." Then looking up at me she said questioningly, "K-A-R-I K-U-?" She hesitated, and I added "Z-M-A." Kari beamed the whole time. Then the librarian explained how important it is not to lose your card, because you would have to pay ten cents for a new one—unless your mother washes it. "If that happens, just bring back the metal tag and you will get a new one free."

"I don't think my mother will need to wash it," said Kari, shaking her head "no."

She then scurried around trying to decide which four books she would check out while Kim carried her twenty-five up to the desk to be checked out. Kari's selection was interesting: a book about porpoises and another about killer whales. I wonder why? She chose a book titled *North American Birds* by Vera Dugdale, and finally one for Kevin, Lois Lenski's *The Little Family*.

Tuesday, January 28 / "Twenty Questions"

"I'm thinking of something that is mineral."
  "Is it in the Old Testament?"
  "Yes."
  "Is it before Noah?"
  "No."
  "Was it after Moses?"
  "No."
  "Was it during Moses' life?"
  "Yes."
  "Can you pick it up in your hand?"
  "No. . . ."
And so the questions continue until one of the children shouts out the answer.
What better way to learn about the Bible than through stories

and games? We started playing "Twenty Questions" with familiar objects, for which the children knew the answers without seeking help. Then we graduated to Bible topics. Sometimes Kari and Jan team up against Kim and myself. When we choose Bible topics it is often easier for the children to answer the questions if they can check their answers with an adult.

Jan and I sometimes have to go back to the Bible to make sure about a certain answer.

"Twenty Questions" is a family favorite. Often as we are traveling in the car, someone shouts, "Let's play 'Twenty Questions'! I'm thinking of something that is animal!"

Wednesday, January 29 / A Spanish Song

Since foreign words can sometimes be learned in the context of a song more easily than by drill, the idea struck me that we could translate some of the children's favorite songs into Spanish. They already knew how to count to ten in Spanish, so we started out

The Seventh Is for Jesus

JESSE F. MOSER   GRACE BURKE ANDERSON

One, two, three, four, five, six for us, One, two, three, four, five,

six   for   us,   One,   two, three, four, five,

six   for   us,   The   sev - enth   is   for   Je - sus.

Used by permission.

with their old favorite, "The Seventh Is for Jesus," and substituted the Spanish words for the numbers. That turned out to be so easy that I asked my Spanish friend to translate the rest of the song for us, and these are the words:

Uno, dos, tres, cuatro, cinco, seis para nosotros [repeat three times]
El septimo esta por Jesus.

Thursday, January 30 / Teasing

I took the girls to the library story hour this morning. When I returned a half hour later, I found both of them in tears.

"What's wrong?" I asked as I took them into my arms.

"Those big kids are calling us babies. And they said that they were going to get us and . . ." their words were lost in a flood of tears.

This was obviously my girls' first experience with the cruelty of teasing.

"They are just teasing you," I said.

"We know that, and we don't like it."

I then realized that since they had not had experience with teasing before, they had no idea how to handle name-calling and threats.

I took them to the side and explained, "There are two ways you can handle teasing. The first is to go away and ignore it and don't show that you are hurt in the least bit. The second is to stand up and show them who is boss. Since I am here to support you, we should really help those children learn that they should never tease anyone again. Perhaps you should go back over to them and say something like this, 'No one likes to be teased, and it was a very unkind thing for you to do. I forgive you for being unkind, but *never do it to me again.*' Speak in a firm, strong voice, as if you really mean what you are saying, but don't show any anger. Then immediately turn around and walk away. If you need me, I'll be here."

The girls mustered their courage and went back over to the scene of the crime. I followed closely. And couldn't resist adding my maternal emphasis after the girls' speech by saying, "I mean it, kids. I *never* want this to happen again."

On the way home we had a good talk about how cruel and unkind teasing can be. I reminded them that teasing, even if it is done in fun, always hurts someone's feelings.

"I'll never ever ever ever tease anyone," said Kari, shaking her head.

"Me neither," agreed Kim.

It was a good lesson for all of us.

Friday, January 31 / String Art

The children and I love mailtime. I'm glad our mailman is a regular ten forty-five man. The anticipation is so high it would probably be unbearable if it were much later. The children have begun to read the names on the letters. They sort out Jan's mail from mine, which I'm just as happy about, since Jan's large stack is really quite boring to me—financial letters, salary checks, bank statements, and advertisements. I have gotten so I don't even look through his pile. My pile of two or three letters is a little more interesting.

But it is indeed a high day when we receive a letter from my mother. The children can recognize her letters instantly, since they always contain enough sugarless gum for at least two days—which is quite a goodly amount for our family.

I sit down in the midst of whatever I happen to be doing and don't even feel guilty about the time I spend reading the news from home. It is a rare occasion when a package comes in the mail. We always know when a package is arriving because the mailman, who delivers the mail via car to our mailbox out by the road, always drives up to our back door and honks the horn twice.

"Mailman Jim is here with a package," the children shout. Today was one of those rare occasions. A box of about fifteen books Jan had ordered a few months ago finally arrived. We sorted through all the books that had been purchased for birthdays, anniversaries, and Christmas gifts for friends and relatives for the coming year and concentrated on the few we got for ourselves. Among them was a book *String Art,** by Lois Kreischer. I immediately began thumbing through it and couldn't believe all of the fancy designs one could make. I always have admired string pictures and have looked with awe when the owner said, "I did it myself." When I saw the advertisement for the book, I decided that if they can do it, I could, too.

An added justification for purchasing the book was that I could teach Kim and Kari how to do string art during preschool time.

The children showed an immediate interest in the book, so forgetting everything else we had planned to do today, I went out into the garage to find a suitable piece of wood to put the string design on. I found one that didn't look too bad. Since the children wanted to do the string picture right now, I couldn't take time to varnish it. I just gave it a quick coat of silver spray paint, which dried as fast as it went on. We made the size circles we wanted on a piece of paper with a compass (the girls had never seen one used before, even though it had been in the desk for years), and then marked on the paper pattern where the nails should be put. We placed the pattern on the board, and everyone started pounding.

Of course, Kevin had to do it, too. I got an acoustical tile board, which is softer than wood, for him to use.

After we had nailed in all the nails we selected a color of yarn and started stringing. I was surprised at how simple the basic pattern is. Neither Kim nor Kari had trouble doing it. But Kim was much more interested and stayed with the project until we had three circles completed, two of them with two different colors of yarn. After it was finished (less than twenty minutes), I hung it on the wall. The girls were overjoyed. I suggested that it looked good enough to give to Oma (Jan's mother), who was going to have a birthday tomorrow. We took it down, and Kim wrapped the gift all by herself. I couldn't have done a better job. I'm now sold on string art for Christmas gifts. This is one gift a child can make "almost" all by himself, and it looks professionally done! Here's how:

* New York: Crown Publishers, 1971.

1. Draw a circle the desired size on a piece of paper.

2. Divide the circle into halves, quarters, and eighths or more, until the lines crossing the circle are about a half inch apart.

3. Put the paper on a piece of selected wood, painted, varnished, or finished as you like.

4. Pound in a nail at each place where a line crosses the circle line.

5. Remove the paper.

6. Tie a piece of yarn to one of the nails (A).

7. Basic design: Cross with the yarn to the opposite nail (B), and then back to the nail beside the original (A) nail, or (C). Then cross to the nail beside (B), which is (D), and keep working around the circle. When the circle is completely filled in, tie off the string on a nail close to (A), but do not use (A), since you don't want the tie to show.

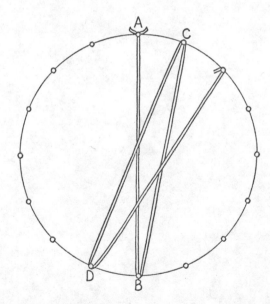

8. Variation: See figure on next page. Tie another color yarn to a different nail. Go a third of the way around to a nail (E), and back to a nail beside the starting nail (F), and continue working around the circle. This makes a smaller border around the first circle.

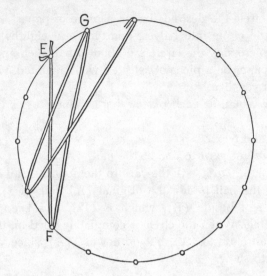

Good luck.

FEBRUARY hearts
Are shaped by loving parents, Tenderness, and Prayers

Monday, February 3 / Perseverance

In planning how best to emphasize the character trait perseverance, I decided to list all the Bible stories I could think of where perseverance paid off. I'm impressed with what I found. What beautiful illustrations to share with the children this week. I hope they will be as convinced as I that perseverance does pay off. Here is my list:

Noah continued to build the ark for 120 years, and he was one of eight who outlived the Flood. (Gn. 6)

Ten times Moses went to Pharaoh to ask him to let the Israelites leave, and with God's help they were freed. (Ex. 7–11)

Ruth gleaned in the fields when I'm sure she didn't feel like it and won the love of a godly and respected man. (Rt. 2)

The Israelites continued to march around Jericho seven times. If they would have stopped short the walls would never have come tumbling down. (Jos. 6)

Jehoash persisted in gathering money and working until the Temple was repaired after years of disrepair. (2 K. 12)

The Wise Men did not give up following the star, even though their journey took many days and nights. (Mt. 2)

The parables of the one lost sheep (out of a hundred) and the one lost coin (out of ten) teach persistence until the lost is found. (Lk. 15)

But Bible stories alone will not be enough to encourage persistence. In addition, here are a few ideas that might help:

1. Plan enough time for the children to finish an activity comfortably.

2. Plan projects that can be finished in a short time, so ·the children will experience the good feeling of having accomplished something.

3. Give more encouragement, including helping them if necessary before they become frustrated, reminding them of the interesting activity that will follow, or even making a game of finishing.

4. Reward them when they finish, by noticing their work, putting it on the bulletin board, or just giving them a hug.

Tuesday, February 4 / Chicken Pox (the Second One)

It happened right on schedule: Kevin has the chicken pox!

Wednesday, February 5 / A Test

It's 11:00 A.M. and all through the house,
Each child is playing like a busy mouse.
I take a deep breath and sit down to write,
After a glance at the kitchen's terrible sight.
Breakfast dishes are piled on the table so high
All I can do is sit here and sigh. . . .
I'm convinced if I don't get things done before eight
The rest of the housework just has to wait.
But at least we have had a good preschool day.
And that is the most important thing, anyway.

The rhythm may not be perfect, but the sentiment is clear. Today really was a delight. But to keep it fun and productive, I had to be there. Every time I thought things were going well and that the children could carry on by themselves, I would silently take a step toward the door. And things seemed to fall apart. Kevin couldn't get the puzzle piece in the right place, and instead of persistently turning it around until it fit, he would start banging with his fist on the puzzle. Or Kari, just as I thought she had caught on how to do the dot-to-dot alphabet book, would say, "I can't find what comes after L." After a number of earnest requests from Kevin, "Mommy, *please* play with me," and from Kari, "Mommy, I need your help," I decided it was best just to forget the dishes and enjoy the children.

I started out today by giving the girls a test. Last night as I was trying to get caught up on some of my reading, I found in the August 1974 *Parents' Magazine* a screening test to determine whether children are ready for school. Of course, I had to try it with my preschoolers.

Kim enthusiastically tackled every task, but if the task was unfamiliar or looked a little difficult, Kari wouldn't even attempt it. This kind of behavior really concerns me. Psychologists say that this is typical behavior of children with a low self-concept. It is safer not to try anything new than to take the chance of possibly failing. In this way the child protects his self-esteem. He can always say, "Of course I can't do it. I didn't even try."

I have found it very difficult to convince Kari that she should try something once she has made up her mind against it. Therefore, the less attention I can give to this behavior the better. I am trying not to reinforce it. Instead I go ahead and play with Kim, who is game for anything, and then on the side I try to help Kari build the skills necessary to meet success in the task.

I know it works, since a few months ago she wouldn't even attempt to write letters, and now she is writing letters all over the house. I remember when she almost seemed to have a mental block about the alphabet. Now she is eager to tackle a dot-to-dot alphabet book. I sincerely hope that this "don't even want to try" attitude doesn't become her characteristic way of meeting tasks in school. But I realize that I must accept this in her, at this time, while helping her in every way I can to build the skills she needs to tackle difficult tasks. What I am trying to emphasize with all of the children, but especially for Kari's sake, is that the most important thing is to try. It doesn't matter whether you win or lose, pass or fail, swim or sink. What is important is that you are in there trying and trying hard. But as I write this I realize that it is much easier said than accomplished.

The first task on the school entrance exam was to balance on one foot for ten to twenty seconds. The girls had no difficulty. Kevin even shouted, "I can do that, too." He crossed his arms, lifted one foot, placed it in front of his knee, and then leaned up against the coffee table. I don't think he ever did catch on that the idea was to do it without the coffee table.

The second task was to copy these lines and forms:

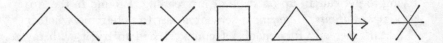

Kari had no trouble until she got to the intersecting arrows, and she couldn't put them together.

The third task was to detect the difference between words that sound similar. I repeated two words, such as ban . . . pan, or ten . . . ten. The girls were supposed to tell me if they were the same word or different words. Kari wouldn't even listen; Kim had no difficulty.

For the fourth task, I made a number of cards with some shapes on them:

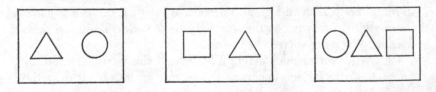

I gave some separate cards to Kim with identical shapes. I showed her a card with a series of shapes, then covered it and asked her to put down the shapes she had on cards in the same order as was shown on my card. Kim had no trouble with her visual memory. Kari wouldn't try.

The fifth task was repeating numbers, which tests auditory memory and concentration. Kim repeated four digits, but the fifth gave her some difficulty.

What did this test prove? Nothing, really. Kim is doing fine and really doesn't need the remedial activities that the article went on to outline. But Kari can use all the help she can get to feel self-confident enough at least to try. I have a feeling that if she concentrated on the tasks she also would pass with flying colors.

We spent the rest of the morning playing some of the games the article suggested, such as balancing, rolling, turning somersaults, bouncing a large ball back and forth, arranging toothpicks in different designs, and repeating long sentences.

Thursday, February 6 / Greenhouse Preparations

Jan brought home a trailerload of redwood sawdust today to mix with sand, dirt, and peat moss for the greenhouse we are planning to build. This was a big event for Kevin. He came running into the house and shouted to me, "Mommy, I am going to help Daddy load off the trailer!"

After the sawdust was unloaded, we decided that we ought to get a few loads of sand before returning the rented trailer. It was drizzling rain, which is a rare event in Southern California. In order to prepare for our excursion in the rain, we brought in from the garage the box of overboots. Inside two of them, we were surprised to find a pair of shoes that had been missing for a year. Of course, they are too small to fit anyone now, but at least the mystery of the missing shoes was solved. Finally dressed in boots, raincoats, and hats and holding umbrellas, we drove out to a "dry" riverbed to get the sand.

We got enough sand to refill the sandbox, which made it so attractive to Kevin that he sat out in the rain for the next hour playing with his buckets, shovels, and cars. The rest of us sat around the cozy fireplace looking through seed catalogs and reading gardening books, dreaming of the rich harvest that would soon be ours from that greenhouse the principal had promised to build for us.

Friday, February 7 / Curiosity and Language

There are two things I consider essential for a child's learning potential: The first is curiosity, and the second is language.

When a problem is posed, even a very bright child won't get very far if he has no intellectual curiosity that will urge him on to seek the answer. All children are born with a healthy amount of curiosity. Just watch a nine-month-old creeper exploring every inch of floor space. And the toddler—well, there is very little that is safe from his curious little hands. But what happens to this inborn curiosity by school age? Too often we box it in. It becomes a nuisance to the rest of the family. "Mommy, Kevin just got into my crayons and broke them all to pieces." "Kevin pulled all the tissues out of the box again." "Who sprinkled baby powder all over the floor? KEVIN, was that you?" "What are we going to do with Kevin?"

All too often the answer is to put him in a playpen, confine him to only one room in the house, fence off a tiny place in the backyard, keep him entertained in front of the TV set, or give him a steady diet of no-nos. And thus over the years we inhibit his curiosity; we subtly tell him that to be curious is to be bad. It gets him into trouble. This course will result in not only diminished curiosity, but also diminished learning skills.

Instead we need to channel his curiosity into constructive paths. We need to find toys (indestructible ones) that are made to be pulled apart, put together, and experimented with. We need to carve out a large living space where the toddler can be free to explore safely without fearing the wrath of an angry parent because some valuable has been accidentally destroyed. A preschooler's curiosity needs to be cultivated and further developed by parents who are willing to ask children questions, and tempt them to find the answers.

"Look, Mommy, what we are finding in the pine cones. They are delicious," exclaimed Kari when I walked in. Kim was sitting with a hammer in one hand, a large Jeffrey pine cone in the other, and a wastebasket between her knees catching the scraps as she pounded on the cone. And sure enough, near the center of the cone she was finding large pine nuts—free; the same nuts that would destroy my food budget if purchased.

We had picked up the cones on a trip to the San Bernardino Mountains. I thought they would make good kindling for the fire, never realizing the treasure they held. I'm just glad the girls found the cones before I burned them. I asked how they had known the seeds were there. Kim said her church schoolteacher had told her that God had placed special treasure in each cone, which the squirrels usually find. But if she would look maybe she would be lucky. That was all it took—just a suggestion.

Now, I knew pine nuts were inside pine cones, but I had never taken the time to look for them. I'm glad the children's curiosity is stronger than mine. It's one thing to know something, and another thing to do something with that knowledge.

After eating my fill of "delicious nuts," I commented, "I'll bet if you plant these seeds they will grow."

"Yippy," said Kari. "We'll grow pine-cone trees."

Now I'm curious. Could we really grow a pine tree? We'll never know unless we try! That's what curiosity is all about.

The second major factor that will determine a child's learning capacity is his language skills. In fact, one of the best tests of one's intelligence quotient (IQ) as well as potential achievement in school is just a simple vocabulary test.

The preschool years are the formative years for language development, and the very best way to enhance a child's language skills is to converse with the child. *That means an investment of parental time.* Sure, the TV set can pound in chain learning, such as counting from one to ten or reeling off the ABCs, but the TV set inhibits the expression of language rather than stimulating it. In front of the TV set, the child becomes passive. Language development requires active participation. Being willing to talk with a child, using a good vocabulary that is slightly above his own level is the very best way to promote language skills.

What about articulation? Usually by the age of six, the difficult-to-pronounce consonants and consonant blends like *k* (often pronounced *tay*), *th* (often pronounced *d*), and *l* (often omitted or pronounced *wah*) are rapidly disappearing. If a child of four or five speaks with such poor articulation that neither adults nor children can understand him, then it is important to seek the professional help of a speech therapist. Otherwise, practice (saying the difficult sounds in a playlike manner) and hearing a good language model will be all the child needs.

Last night I took time to listen to Kevin—even though I had other things to do! I carefully recorded a conversation I had with him, noting specifically his pronunciation of sounds. I was surprised at how many sounds he had difficulty with. Hearing his words so often, my mind hears what he is saying, and I haven't really noticed that his articulation skills are still developing. I found the whole experience rewarding. Here is how it happened:

"Mommy, what's dat?"

"Hum?" I asked absent-mindedly, trying to concentrate on my writing.

"Mommy, what's dat?" Kevin asked again, pointing to the picture on the wall. "Sailboat?"

"Yes, that's a sailboat."

"Mommy, where ducks? Where water ducks?"

"There aren't any ducks in the picture," I replied.

"Dar aren't any ducks?" Then he let out a big yawn and continued, "I'm not tired, I'm seepy. I'm not seepy and tired." (Shaking head) "I don't feel bery good. Yes, I feel bery good. I want to see what you're doing." (Yawn) "Now I'm tired." Noticing a plaque above my desk that was given to me at his birth, he continued, "Dat's a little baby kneeling down saying, 'Dear Jesus, have a good meal.' Dat's his bed? Dat's baby's bed. Who painted dat picture? Mommy, who painted dat picture? Lady did?"

"Yes," I answered, "a lady painted the picture."

"Mommy, what's dat for?"

"What?" I asked.

"Mommy, what's dat for?"

"What?"

"Mommy, what's dat for?"

Finally I realized he didn't know the name for the "what" so I asked him to point to it and then I replied, "That's a paper punch."

"Dat's a paper punch? Can I hold it? Dat's a paper punch. Punch! Punch! Punch! I will punch it. Punch it. Mommy, I can't punch it."

"That's not the way," I instructed. "Turn it around."

"It need you do dis. It's hard." As I started to show him how to use it, he said, "I'll show you how. I know how. Hold my hand like dat." (I was still trying to concentrate on my writing.) "Please hold my hand. Punch! Punch! Punch!" Then he yawned again.

Using his last yawn as a cue, I said, "Kevin, say, 'Good night, paper punch.'

"I love you, Kevin," I said as I carried him off to bed.

"I lub you, too," he said as he grabbed the corner of his blanket, and stuck his thumb in his mouth.

Finally I was back at my desk wondering where my evening had gone.

I wrote the following:

> It is he who keeps you from your work
> With his constant chitter-chatter.
> But when he says, "I lub you, Mommy,"
> Time wasted doesn't matter.

In fact, the time "wasted" talking to a child may be the very best way to help him develop his language skills, which are so crucial to his overall learning ability.

It's not easy to keep track of the language of a talkative two-year-old, but it has given me specific sounds to listen for, such as his substitution of d for th and the b for v.

Analyzing my language model, I would give myself a passing score on parroting the mispronounced sounds back correctly. However, if I would have really been trying to promote Kevin's language, I would have formed more sentences instead of one-word answers and I would have used a few more challenging vocabulary words.

I'd like to suggest that the two magic words teacher-mothers need to remember for the development of their child's learning potential are "curiosity" and "language."

Monday, February 10 / Concept Clarification

It is exciting for me to observe my two-year-old struggle to try to clarify his understanding of the concepts we think are so easy to learn. For example, after a full and happy morning of play with Greg, and a good nap, Kevin came up to me while I was typing and leaned heavily against me. I stopped typing and picked him up. He snuggled up and we just sat for a while. Finally he said, "He bothers me."

"Oh," I said.

"He doesn't like me. I like Kimi. He is not a good-bad boy. Yes, he's not a big boy [shaking his head]. I don't like Greg. I want Kimi."

After a pause, I responded, "You like to play with Kimi, don't you?"

"Yes," he said, as he bounced off my lap to search for her.

I really don't know what caused all of this talk. He and Greg had had a wonderful morning together. I think a child must feel free to sort out all of his thoughts and feelings, without feeling that adults think his feelings are wrong. I know how he loves to play with Greg, but there are probably times when Kevin feels, "He bothers me," just as Greg probably feels the same way.

What is interesting to me is the number of concepts Kevin was trying to sort out in just this short conversation with me, such as "bother," "like," "don't like," "good," "bad," and "big."

Tuesday, February 11 / Stitchery

I always seem to be surprised at how quickly my first child is able to develop new skills. The other children always do these things at a similar age, but since the first was first, I'm not surprised at the next.

Weaving is a skill that most preschoolers enjoy, but I didn't realize they could make anything until we discovered "loopers." Kim, and now Kari, have found success in making pot holders from the loops on a special looper frame.

Embroidery is fun even for the youngest preschool child. A child can push a needle into and out of any piece of material fastened in an embroidery ring. The most difficult task for Kevin is to realize that you don't put the needle into the material from the top each time, but must first go through the top and then the bottom, or the yarn gets wound around the ring. If I draw a design on a plain piece of material, Kim now enjoys stitching around the design with a simple in-and-out weaving stitch.

Needlepoint was the next skill that Kim conquered. She uses the simple continental stitch (diagonal stitch) on the large plasticized canvas. I just draw a simple design such as a letter or geometric shape and she does the rest by using a double strand of thick yarn and a large needle.

Last month the skill was crocheting. A friend of mine showed Kim how to make the chain stitch. When Kim came home and said that she could crochet, I smiled as if I believed her, even though I didn't. With persistent urging Kim persuaded me to buy her the necessary equipment (crochet thread and hook), and to my amazement she crocheted me a long chain. This really was impressive, since I had no idea even how to begin to crochet. Now my six-year-old was teaching me.

It was then that I began to wonder if she might also be able to knit (I knew how to do that). So today as we passed the yarn counter, I remembered and purchased needles and yarn. I cast on a number of stitches and showed Kim how to do the basic knitting stitch. Her fingers were clumsy as she tried to hold the needles and the yarn and co-ordinate the two, but she was determined to master the skill. By evening she had progressed to an inch of knitting and was encouraged by seeing her own progress. Her determination to knit was so strong that tonight as Jan and I were out building the greenhouse by artificial light, Kim was right beside us, sitting on a rock, bundled in her heavy coat, knitting. Her knitting is not mistake-free, but it is growing and hanging together. Once this skill is mastered, she should be able to tackle more easily other skills that require finger co-ordination.

I think the next project will be to make a small latch-hook rug. I have a feeling that Kim, and maybe even Kari, will be interested in accepting that challenge.

Wednesday, February 12 / Lincoln's Birthday

Today's preparation for preschool took me to the encyclopedia to read up on the famous President whose birthday we are celebrating. Then I posed this question to the children: "There are only two Presidents whose birthdays we celebrate. George Washington, the very first President of the United States, and Abraham Lincoln, the sixteenth President. Now, I understand why we celebrate Washington's birthday. He was the first. But why do you think we celebrate Lincoln's birthday? He wasn't even the second President—he was the sixteenth."

The children took a few wild guesses before I continued, "Maybe it is because he was named after the biblical Abraham and his sister's name was Sarah? Maybe it was because he was born in a log cabin? I know: It was because his father was a carpenter and farmer and had never gone to school a day of his life. Is that why?"

"No, no, no," the children answered.

"Then it must be because the total time Lincoln attended school was less than a year? Or because the school he did attend was a 'blab' school where all the children read out loud so the teacher could make sure each child was studying? Maybe it was because his mother died when he was nine and his stepmother had three other children? I know: It must have been because he could do so many things—he farmed, he built a flatboat, he clerked at a store, he was a postmaster, a surveyor, and finally a lawyer. In addition, he was the best wrestler in town, was known as an excellent rail splitter with his ax, and was a great storyteller. Maybe that's why?"

"No, no, no," the children kept saying.

"Then it must have been because he was a circuit-riding lawyer who followed the judge around the country representing people who needed his help."

I received a faint "yes" from that one before I continued, "Or maybe it was because he did not let failure discourage him. He wanted to be a part of the Illinois state legislature, but lost the first time he ran. Then two years later he won and was re-elected three times. When he ran for Congress, he lost, but three years later was successful. He didn't give up when he was defeated for Vice-President and was finally successful in becoming President of the United States."

By this time the children were clamoring for the correct answer. "Mommy, you tell us; please tell us."

This was my answer: "I'm not sure, but I think people celebrate Lincoln's birthday because he was such a good man. He hated slavery. And he risked his career as President to rid the nation of this terrible practice. He was also very honest. People even called him 'Honest Abe.' People could trust Lincoln. They knew he stood for what was right, even though it was not the popular thing to do. This is what makes a man a great man. And therefore, so people would never forget the principles that Lincoln stood for, we celebrate his birthday each year."

I continued to tell them the story about when Lincoln walked a number of miles to return a few pennies of change that were due to one of his customers at the store where he was a clerk. No wonder he was remembered for his honesty. I then asked each of the girls to draw a picture of Abraham Lincoln doing something, so they could remember what this great man stood for.

At sharing time during supper the girls proudly showed their pictures and told their daddy all about why we celebrate Lincoln's birthday. I think Lincoln has become a family hero!

Thursday, February 13 / Money

Grandpa and Grandma sent the children three dollars to spend for a Valentine present. It took a little thought, but the girls finally figured out that if there were three children in the family and they had three dollars, then each child should get one dollar.

I feel that it is very important to begin early in training the children how to use their money wisely. So in the Kuzma house, the children give 10 per cent to Jesus (tithe), 10 per cent to others (offering), and 10 per cent to the bank (savings). Then they are free to use the rest of the money as they want or need. Translating this for the children, it comes out: For every dollar you have, you give ten pennies to Jesus and ten pennies to others and save ten pennies in the bank. If you don't need the rest right now, save that, too.

Today the children opened their banks and decided to count their money to see how much they had accumulated. I decided that I might as well take advantage of their interest in money and start teaching them how much a penny, a nickel, a dime, and a quarter are worth.

Kim sat for an hour figuring out problems such as:

If I give you a quarter and ask for change, what would you give me?

Here are ten pennies. Give me one coin back that is worth the same.

Here are two dimes and a nickel. Give me one coin back that is worth the same.

Then I would write down on a sheet of paper something like $.37, or $1.14, and ask Kim to give me this amount of money. She did a pretty good job. Her interest in money is a large motivating factor.

With Kari, I asked, "What is this coin called?"

"If I give you this coin, how many pennies should you give me?"

"If I hold this coin in one hand, put enough pennies in the other hand so that they will be the same." With Kari we worked on pennies, nickels, and dimes.

As I was working with the girls, I recalled the first day of preschool, when the girls made their lists of what they wanted to learn. They had listed, "I want to learn about money." It has taken me over five months finally to get it into the curriculum. How could I have been so negligent?

Friday, February 14 / Valentine Cards

Valentine's Day—a day to share unique expressions of love. We chose to print our own Valentine cards. I selected a few potatoes, sliced off one end, and fashioned hearts of different sizes on the cut end. I also sliced an orange and a lime, which would give different printed effects. The children selected the colors of tempera paint they wanted for their cards and poured the paint into shallow containers.

Then they put the potato heart or orange or lime in the paint and pressed the painted surface on the construction paper. Once they learned the printing process they began searching through the house for other shapes and materials that would make a unique print. They found that a spool, a small box, a block, the end of a cut piece of celery, and even their own hands made excellent prints.

Next we tried our skills with a little rhyming. We started out with the familiar, "Roses are red, violets are blue . . ." and came up with such things as,

"You are my daddy and I love you."

"So I'll give you a hug or kiss or two—xxoo."

"Here is a pink card especially for you."

"You're my good friend and I like you."

After the Valentines dried, the children wrote the simple messages on the cards and signed their names. (I did most of the writing.)

We could have purchased Valentines, but these were far more meaningful to the children and to the lucky recipients as well.

Monday, February 17 / "Knowledge Inventory Game": Information

Time for a knowledge inventory to see what the children know and what they don't know. This will help me to plan more appropriately for preschool in the future.

There is so much to learn and so little time to learn it that I have decided to take advantage of the time we spend riding in the car to play what I call the "Knowledge Inventory Game."

I have selected five areas of knowledge in which it is important for the children to be competent before school, and that also would be easy to assess in the car. The areas are (1) information, (2) concepts, (3) letters, (4) math, and (5) memory. The sixth category is for miscellaneous out-of-the-car use. I purchased six different colors of four-by-six cards, one for each category. I will write down a different knowledge game on each card. When one of the children knows the information on the card I can put his name on the card, and in this way keep track of the level of knowledge the children gain. On many of the cards the questions will be only an example and I will continue to make up new questions as we drive along. This knowledge inventory can continue growing with the children, by simply adding new cards. The children can select the card (game) they want and I'll ask the questions, giving each a turn and making the questions for Kevin relatively easy compared to the questions for the girls.

This game should make car travel much more enjoyable and a good learning experience, too.

It will probably take me all week to complete the entire project. Here is how I arranged the cards for the information section:

INFORMATION

Personal
    1. What is your first name?
    2. What is your last name?

3. What are your father's and mother's first names?
4. How old are you?
5. When is your birthday?
6. Where do you live? What city? What state?
7. What is your street address?
8. What is your telephone number?
9. Where were you born?
10. Where does your daddy (mommy) work?
11. What does your daddy do at work?
12. What are your grandparents' names? Where do they live?
13. What are the names of your uncles and aunts and cousins?

Occupations
What does each person do?

1. Doctor	7. Mother
2. Policeman	8. Plumber
3. Teacher	9. Gardener
4. Dentist	10. Grocer
5. Father	11. Astronaut
6. Nurse	

Use of objects
What are these objects for?

1. Chairs	6. Soap
2. Glasses	7. House
3. Cars	8. Stove
4. Mittens	9. Refrigerator
5. Trees	10. Roots

Body parts

1. Ears	5. Tongue
2. Hands	6. Feet
3. Teeth	7. Eyelashes
4. Nose	

"What" questions

1. What swims in the water?	5. What sleeps in a barn?
2. What flies in the air?	6. What hurts you?
3. What eats?	7. What can burn you?
4. What bites?	8. What feels good?

9. What feels cold?
10. What do you do when you're hungry?
11. What boils?
12. What scratches?
13. What barks?
14. What growls?
15. What meows?
16. What sings?

Parts of animals
Name the parts of an animal.
Point out parts.
What are these for?
1. Muzzle
2. Paws
3. Whiskers
4. Claws
5. Hooves
6. Mane
7. Tail
8. Fins
9. Gills

Riddles
Guess what I see.
1. It's brown and green and grows. (a tree)
2. It's yellow and has four wheels. (a car)
    etc.

Tomorrow I will work on the concept cards for the "Knowledge Inventory Game."

Tuesday, February 18 / "Knowledge Inventory Game": Concepts

These are the concept cards I have made for the "Knowledge Inventory Game":

CONCEPTS

Alike or different
How are they alike?
How are they different?
1. Bird and dog
2. Flower and tree
3. Orange and apple
4. Water and ice

5. Lake and ocean
6. House and store
7. Boy and girl
8. Carrot and grape
9. Clock and watch
10. Wood and glass

Opposites
1. You sleep at night; you play during the (*day*).
2. A rock is dull; a knife is (*sharp*).
3. A mountain is high; a valley is (*low*).
4. A bird flies; a fish (*swims*).
5. I stand up; you sit (*down*).
6. In the day you see the sun; at night you see the (*moon*).
7. Daddy is a man; Mommy is a (*woman*).
8. Kim is a girl; Robert is a (*boy*).

Give the opposite of
1. White (black)
2. Big (little)
3. Fast (slow)
4. Laugh (cry)
5. Loud (soft)
6. Open (shut)
7. Sad (happy)
8. Awake (asleep)
9. Dead (alive)
10. Top (bottom)
11. Wet (dry)
12. Cold (hot)
13. Soft (hard)
14. Rough (smooth)
15. Heavy (light)

Relational concepts
Ask the child to put an object, or his hand, in the following positions in relation to a box.
1. Below
2. Above
3. Inside
4. Outside
5. On
6. Under
7. Beside
8. Between
9. In front of
10. In back of
11. Higher than
12. Lower than

Which is . . .
1. Which is longer, a pencil or a yardstick?
2. Which is thinner, a fat person or a skinny person?
3. Which is louder, a kitten or a roaring tiger?
4. Which is thicker . . .
5. Which is smaller . . .

General concepts
1. Does the child understand up, down, loud, soft, far, near, nearest, close, closest, cold, warm, hot, hard, soft, rough, smooth?
2. Ask questions such as:
   1. Is the street hard or soft?
   2. Who is the one sitting closest to Kim?
   3. When I turn on the heater will it make the car colder or hotter?
   4. Is sandpaper smooth or rough?

Wednesday, February 19 / "Knowledge Inventory Game": Letters

Letters are sometimes rather abstract for preschoolers, but the more experience a child has with letters in a wide variety of situations the more meaningful they will become. I hope to make learning letter names and sounds a fun experience with the following questions and activities:

LETTERS

Identification
1. What letter does your name start with?
2. What letter does that sign start with?
3. Find a sign that starts with the letter *b*, etc.
4. Spell the word "stop." (Wait for a sign so the child can read it.)

Letter sounds
1. Give the letter sounds and ask what letter it is for.
2. Give the letter and ask what the sound of the letter is.
3. What letter does the sign "Mobil" start with?

Thursday, February 20 / "Knowledge Inventory Game": Math

Too often we think of math for preschoolers as the recognition of numerals, counting, and simple addition and subtraction. Math, however, can be much more, as these activity cards suggest.

MATH

Money
1. What is a penny?
2. What is a nickel?
3. What is a dime?
4. What is a quarter?

Number concepts
How many . . .
1. How many ——— do you have? (eyes, ears, heads, toes, thumbs, noses, broken arms, etc.)
2. How many numbers are on a clock?
3. How many letters are in the word "stop"? etc.
4. How many things are in a dozen?
5. How many feet are in a yard?
6. How many inches are in a foot? a yard?
7. How many pounds do you weigh?
8. How many cars do we have?
9. How many wheels are on the car?

What shape is it?   Different shapes to select:
1. What shape is the ball?   circle   hexagon
2. What shape is that sign?   square   octagon
3. What shape is an envelope?   rectangle
4. What shape is the stop sign?   oval
5. What shape is a door?   triangle
6. What shape is a yield sign?

Addition and subtraction
 1. If a boy had 5 fingers and put 1 ring on each finger, how
    many rings would he need?
 2. What are 2 and 5?
 3. If Mary had 3 apples and ate 2, how many would be left?

Time
 1. What time do you go to bed?
 2. What time do you eat lunch?
 3. What time does Daddy come home?

Friday, February 21 / "Knowledge Inventory Game": Memory and Miscellaneous

So far this week the children have enjoyed answering the questions
and doing the activities in the "Knowledge Inventory Game." In
addition to increasing their knowledge about information, concepts,
letters, and math, I want to increase their ability to remember, and
their visual-motor skills. The following activities should be helpful:

MEMORY

Follow directions
 1. Two directions
    Put pencil on floor and bring me the can.
 2. Three directions

Repeat
 1. Digits: 2, 5, 1
 2. Nursery rhymes
 3. Sentences

MISCELLANEOUS (outside-car activities)

1. Finish drawing the picture of a boy:

2. Draw:

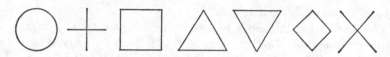

3. Copy block structures: (Use real blocks)

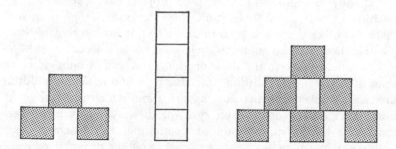

4. Put pieces together to make shape:

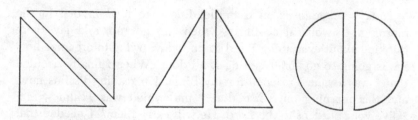

Monday, February 24 / President's Day: Gone to the Beach!

Tuesday, February 25 / Finding Time

I like the idea that if you really, yes, really want to do something you will find the time to do it. I've thought about this a lot in working with my children this year.

At first I tried to keep a regular schedule of 9:00 A.M. to 11:00 A.M. for preschool, but now I have decided that preschool is more meaningful if I am not rigid about the time schedule. I still use this time frame as a guide, but sometimes by nine o'clock the children are already so engrossed in their own projects that it seems an imposition to pull them away from these tasks for "my" preschool tasks. On other days, 9:00 A.M. to 11:00 A.M. is far too short a time. The children want to continue their preschool projects.

I have now come to the decision that preschool at home is more than a full-time job. Quitting time doesn't come until the children are finally tucked into bed for the last time, which is six or eight hours after other paid teachers quit for the day. Being a teacher-mother is having an attitude of commitment to teaching your children, when they are ready to learn, whether or not it conveniently fits into a nine-to-eleven or even an eight-thirty-to-two-thirty schedule.

Today's schedule is an example. I love to read in bed in the morning. I awoke at six-thirty, when Jan got up, and lay there thinking about everything I had to do today, trying to organize how I was going to go about getting it all done. When I finally decided that I was awake I reached for my Bible. I'm reading Psalms now, and this morning the verse that I underlined was Psalm 55:22: "Give your burdens to the Lord. He will carry them." I needed that promise. My "Things to Do" list has become so long that each item has become a burden that I just can't seem to find the time to remove. I need the Lord's help in carrying them.

Then comes the decision: do I get up or not? I listened. The house was still quiet. That meant that I could spend a few minutes just reading for pleasure. By seven-thirty I could hear the girls shuffling things in the hallway, and Kevin calling from his bedroom, "Mommy, I'm awake." By seven-fifty, with the girls' help in setting the table, we were ready for breakfast (cooked cereal, nuts, canned cherries and peaches, cut fresh oranges, toast and cream cheese, milk, and a vitamin pill in case we missed something).

Preschool time now formally starts in our house with Jan's breakfast story. Since the character trait we are emphasizing this week is "happiness," Jan's story this morning was about Jesus in the Garden of Gethsemane when his enemies were coming to take him. One of the men with Jesus took his sword and cut off the ear of the high priest's servant. (I listened intently, always wondering how Jan is going to illustrate the virtue. I really didn't see how happiness fit into this story.) He continued, "But Jesus wanted even his enemy to be happy, so he picked up his ear and put it back on his head. Jesus said that if we live by the sword we will die by the sword. That means that the way we treat others will determine how they will treat us. So if we are happy and make others happy, they will be happy and do things that will make us happy."

By eight-thirty I had been left alone with the children and the dirty dishes and the clothes that needed to be washed and my "Things to Do" list.

Trying to decide what I should tackle first, I noticed that Kevin was still in his pajamas and would probably stay that way all day unless I did something about it. As I dressed him I realized that his hair needed to be cut very badly. Cutting Kevin's hair is a major task. I turned on the UHF channel to see if there was anything on TV that would capture his interest long enough for me to get his hair cut. To my pleasant surprise, I found my friend Mr. Rogers. The girls were amazed at my discovery, thinking he appeared only at 5:00 P.M. They immediately sat down to watch, too.

By nine o'clock Kevin's hair was cut and Mr. Rogers was singing, "Tomorrow, tomorrow, we'll start the day tomorrow with a smile or two. . . ." This reminded me that I wanted to take some pictures of Kevin for a children's book I had just finished writing. If I would take the pictures in the morning Kevin's clothes would still be relatively clean, which would make a better picture. I finally took some shots of the children playing on the swing and the teeter-totter outside. They decided that they wanted to stay there, so by 11:00 A.M. they had their own games going. I started on the dishes.

After lunch I asked the children if they wanted to help me plant the rest of the flowers we had purchased yesterday. They helped as best they could, mostly by watching Sarnoff and yelling every time he tried to pick up a half-planted flower and carry it around the yard.

At one-thirty the children remembered their daddy's last words as he left for work: "Girls, you will make me very happy if you will take all of your dolls and playhouse materials off of the Ping-Pong table." So they started on that task.

By 2:00 P.M. someone wanted to paint. Since it was a beautiful, sunny day (after three weeks of rain), I suggested that they paint outside. We made a makeshift easel by turning the rectangular picnic table on end and taping a large sheet of paper to that. I kept watching them from the kitchen window as I started the lunch dishes and the rest of the housework. Three weeks before, when I had prepared the easel and paints, they weren't interested. But today they painted picture after picture, until the lawn was covered with pictures drying in the sun. By 3:00 P.M. it was clean-up time; 4:00 P.M. was transfer time, when Jan takes care of the children while I go to teach a class.

By 6:30 P.M., when I returned home, Jan had the children fed and had already made a trip to the grocery store. The big news was, "Daddy bought us ice cream!" Since Jan is much stronger than I am on not eating candy, cake, ice cream, and other sugar-sweet foods, the children were just as shocked as I was about their daddy's purchase. I think we can record this as a first.

Jan made some comment about arithmetic, which reminded Kari that we hadn't done any arithmetic all day. She got out her workbook while I sat down beside her to eat my supper. Kevin joined us with his own pencil and paper and meticulously made little circles. At one point, out of the top of one of the little circles he made a long line and announced, "That's smoke coming out." Later I asked him what his picture was, and he said, "It's a drawing." It serves me right. I know you are not supposed to ask young children what they are drawing. It is the process that counts, not the product.

I finally called to Kim and asked her if she wanted to join us for math, but she was busy hiding eggs (large plastic pegs) for Kari to find in the living room. When it was Kari's turn to look for the "eggs," Kim sat down and whipped through seven pages of her workbook. It is almost a waste of paper, it is so easy for her.

By seven-thirty I was reading Kevin his good-night story. If he had his way, I would read to him all night. But I knew everyone was tired.

By the time I tucked Kevin in and went to check on Kari, I found her already asleep. Kim couldn't believe it. "Kari was just up one minute ago," she said. After she checked for herself, she begged, "Now, Mommy, you can read just to me." I told her I had a better suggestion: "You read to me." And so she read me a book and a half. I think it is important that, whatever you do, you do it quickly and get on to something else. So I began timing how fast she could read each little story in the book. She loved it. By eight fifty-five she knelt down and prayed and then happily climbed into bed.

Just recalling today, I'm convinced that a person really can find the time to do what he really wants to do. The children certainly do. And they will have richer lives if we as parents really want to do what they want to do. Even in our busy lives, we must somehow find the time to be effective teachers.

Wednesday, February 26 / Sex Education

I was washing dishes and enjoying the children's merry chatter outside the kitchen window when it happened. In the midst of their play, I could hear Kim instructing Lisa, "First your daddy put an egg in your mommy, and then it grew and it grew and it grew and you came out and now you are here."

"Ya," replied Lisa, who appeared not the least bit interested. Then they began talking of other things.

I've always believed that sex education should not be any different than any other type of education. When the teachable moment comes, when a child asks a question, you respond with the correct answer in as simple a way as possible so that they can understand.

But how far does a parent let this go? A few days ago, in all earnestness, Kari, observing me squeezing the soft plastic honey container and seeing the yellow honey coming out the long pointed spout, commented, "That honey coming out looks just like a penis going potty." The natural response is either to laugh or to reprimand a child severely for such "dirty" talk, commenting perhaps that we are never supposed to talk about that at the table.

But I happen to believe that the more emphasis a parent puts upon innocent comments, the more a child realizes that talk about these subjects is emotion-producing. This gives a child a weapon he can use to get back at parents and grown-ups when he wants to, because it is very hard to control children's talking. It then becomes the thing to do with much laughter and silliness. And so with all calmness I responded, "Yes, it does," and we went on talking about other things.

For the past few days we have been aware that Classy, our female Doberman, may be coming into heat. We have made a valiant attempt to keep Sarnoff, our male, separated from her. The children have been very interested in this and have asked a number of questions about why it is so important to keep them separated.

Each reason has a valuable object lesson for the children to learn concerning sex:

1. The dogs are brother and sister. How do you teach a child about genetics? This would be a starting point.

2. Classy is too young, just barely one year old. Moral: Don't get pregnant too early. It is not good for either the mother or the children!

3. When the right time comes, we will let Classy mate with a dog that is a champion Doberman, so that she will have the very best puppies possible. Moral: Marry the right man, the type of husband you want to be the father of your children.

I knew the children were concerned about helping us keep the dogs apart. But I never considered that they would ask for further help. But to a child, nothing is impossible for Jesus. So at the breakfast table Jan and I were shocked to hear Kari pray, "Dear Jesus, help Sarnoff not to stick his penis into Classy's thing so she won't get pregnant. And bless this food. Amen." It was almost more than Jan and I could do to mask our smiles, and we both hastily started to eat.

Never underestimate the faith of a little child. Later I did tell Kari that the word she could use was "impregnate." And she went on with her play, saying to herself again and again, "Impreg-a-nate. Impreg-a-nate. Impreg-a-nate."

Thursday, February 27 / Sprouts

My children love alfalfa sprouts. If I had to buy them as they come in the supermarkets, grown and ready to eat, our food budget would have to be increased. But they are easy to grow, if you can find where to buy the seeds. I found them at a health-food store. I used to think they grew all sprouts in the ground and always wondered how long it took them to get all of the dirt off. I'm embarrassed to think how long it took me to figure out that sprouts aren't grown in soil.

We use a large peanut-butter jar and make a few small holes in the lid for air. I pour approximately a tablespoonful of seeds into the jar and let them soak in water overnight. The next day I pour off all the water, using a strainer to catch any seeds that try to escape. Then with only wet seeds (no water) I put on the lid and put the jar on a warm windowsill. Seeds do best when kept between seventy-five and eighty-five degrees, out of direct heat, sunlight, or drafts. The last day before eating, I place them in the sunlight to aid in the manufacture of chlorophyll. I like bright green sprouts. Each day, morning and evening, I wash the seeds and pour off all the water. (Larger seeds, like peas, may need a midday rinse.) The sprouts do best when they have room to grow. In three to four days, depending on how warm they have been kept, they are ready to eat. I start a new jar every other day so that we always have some on hand. Otherwise, I find that the children can't wait and eat the half-grown ones.

We use alfalfa sprouts plain as a salad, or in sandwiches instead of lettuce, or mixed up in a tossed salad. They always add a special flavor zest that makes company ask, "What are these little plants in the salad?"

Today for preschool we started sprouting lentils, ming beans, and soybeans. I understand that pea, buckwheat, and radish seeds also make good-eating sprouts.

The girls now handle the planting of and caring for our sprout garden. Even Kevin enjoys watching the little seeds break open and the sprouts begin to grow. With the tiny alfalfa seeds the children needed a magnifying glass to get a good look. But now with these larger seeds the whole miraculous process should be even more apparent.

Friday, February 28 / Independence

It is nice to tiptoe through the house and find every child busily engaged in his own play. Kevin is in his room balancing blocks, and he didn't even notice as I went by. Kari is in her bedroom arranging furniture in her dollhouse, and Kim is in my bedroom trying on (with my permission) some of my clothes and shoes from my closet.

I think it is important for children to learn to work independently; to plan what they want to do, get out their own materials, and persist until they accomplish what they set out to do. I also feel it is important for children to learn to work and play together, but I don't like children always to feel that they have to have someone to play with, or else have their mother or teacher spend every minute with them.

Saying all of this is fine and good, but what do you do to encourage a child to be happy playing alone some of the time and at other times be happy playing with others?

Learning theories would say you should reward a child for doing what you want him to do. So when the child plays quietly alone, you reward him. You start out rewarding him for only a few minutes of play and then, as he increases the time he plays alone, you increase the number of minutes before you reward him. If you want the child to play with other children, you have to make the

experience rewarding. I believe in this theory, but I also believe
there is much more to it:

1. Children follow the parents' example. Do I always feel that I
have to be constantly with others really to enjoy life, or does my
child see me happy and content with my own individual projects?

2. Children need interesting things to do while alone. If the
house is always spotless (which mine never is), and things are always put out of reach, then the motherly message is: Don't touch.
The chances are the child will never feel really free to do things on
his own. But if parents provide a lot of stimulating materials—
paper, glue, paint, crayons, scissors, dolls, puzzles, boats, dress-up
clothes, etc.—then the general motherly message is: Touch, experiment, create, plan, and play. It will happen with or without other
playmates.

3. Children need time to do things by themselves. Some mothers
I know are always going places with their children, providing
planned learning experiences such as lessons in swimming, piano,
French, tumbling, dancing, and nursery school. When children get
used to this rich diet, just staying home doing something by oneself
can seem a little dull.

4. To play independently, children need to learn enough skills to
feel capable of putting them all together. For example, if a child
doesn't know how to dress himself or tie his shoes, it is difficult to
play dress-up alone. If he doesn't know how to cut or paste, then he
always has to do it with someone who can help him.

5. The most important thing, I believe, is to live in an atmosphere where independence is valued. I don't believe it is ever good
to be completely independent. We all need to be able to depend on
certain people for certain things. I wouldn't want to live with a husband who felt so independent that he could get along without me!
But at the same time, if something happened to me, I would want
him to be able to get along without me. Does that make sense?
Well, that is the kind of independence I want for my children.

Days of MARCH, march on
Down preschool paths only once
This year — then are past

Monday, March 3 / Imaginative Toys

Children need raw materials that will bend with their imaginations. The dining-room chairs make an excellent train when placed in a line across the living room. Each chair is a special compartment for a child or a doll. Boxes and wagons and tricycles and boards, put together and placed just so, make an excellent airplane, which flies just as well as a playground model that looks far more real but is not nearly so conducive to airplane play.

Because we as adults have so often lost our childhood imaginations, we purchase toys for children that look just as real as possible. Often these toys, such as dolls, do so many things that it leaves very little for the child to imagine in their play with the toy. It is also true that some of these toys are so expensive that parents are constantly instructing their children to play with it correctly so that it will not break. Or the child actually will play with the toy very little because he knows it *was* expensive and his parents will be upset if he breaks it. So the safest thing is just to set it on the shelf.

Giving children boxes and boards, nails and hammers, and sometimes an idea to get started are of far more value in stimulating a child's imagination and creativity than expensive, elaborate toys.

Tuesday, March 4 / Counting

Have you ever wondered . . .
How many clocks are in the house?
How many doors are in the house?
How many pictures are hanging in the hall?
How many windows are in the house?
How many holes there are on the dial of the telephone?
How many lights are in the living room?
How many teeth are in Kevin's mouth?
How many dolls you have?
How many cans of olives are in the pantry?

These were the activity cards for preschool today. The girls did not always get the same answer written on the cards, but they did get a lot of practice in counting.

Wednesday, March 5 / Making Every Minute Count

Every encounter with a child can be an important opportunity to strengthen the positive parent-child relationship and to teach the child. Today I have changed Kevin's pants twice, but there was a qualitative difference in these encounters. Here is how the first time went.

It had been a busy morning, but at last the children were entertaining themselves. I had a deadline to meet on an article I was writing, so I closed the study door and began typing. Just as I finished part of a page, Kari and Kevin opened the door and Kari said, "Kevin needs his pants changed."

"OK," I responded, still lost in thought. I finished my sentence and automatically got up and carried Kevin to the bathroom. I followed the established routine of taking off the wet diaper and quickly pinned on the dry one. I pulled up his pants and off he ran. Without a word I did what needed to be done while I planned what I was going to say next in my article.

Later, as I was finishing the article, Kevin's pants needed changing again. This time I realized that I hadn't spent much time with him in the past few hours, so as I picked him up, I said, "Kevin, you are getting heavier every day. One of these days you are going to be so big you will be carrying me." He smiled at what seemed to him an impossibility. I continued, "I wonder how much you weigh now? Do you think it is twenty pounds, thirty pounds, or forty pounds?"

"Forty," he said as he nodded his head.

Before changing him I stood him on the bathroom scale. "Kevin, look at the numbers on the scale. It says you weigh twenty-nine pounds. You are getting to be a big boy."

I stood Kevin by the bathroom mirror as I got out the clean diaper. He made a face in the mirror and stuck his tongue in and out. "You look like a hungry frog trying to catch flies. When a frog is hungry he sticks his tongue out and catches a fly with the end of it, and brings the fly right back to his mouth and swallows it."

"Ughhh," he replied.

"You wouldn't want to eat a fly, would you? You think flies taste terrible. But frogs think flies are delicious. They would rather have a fly than an ice-cream cone."

He smiled at what to him sounded absurd, as I finished pinning on the diaper; then he ran off.

"Have a good dinner of flies, Mr. Frog," I called after him.

In both situations the diaper needed to be changed, which took me a certain amount of time. Why not take advantage of the time I *have* to spend with my children to make this time with them a learning time as well?

Thursday, March 6 / A Salad Supreme

Today we had company, and the girls fixed a salad that our guest will be talking about for a long time.

They started out with a little lettuce and got carried away grating carrots, radishes, and Jerusalem artichokes. Next, they added lots of alfalfa sprouts and finished up with a spoonful of capers (they come in a small bottle in the relish section of the market). Kim made the dressing of mayonnaise and lemon juice, with a little salt, a teaspoonful of sugar, and Schilling's Salad Supreme sprinkled in. It was unique and delicious and worth trying again.

Friday, March 7 / Why?

It is usually our children who are stumping us with the "why" questions. "Why do magnets pull things toward them?" "Why isn't it ever yesterday again?" "Why can't we see our angels?" etc.

Today it was Jan's turn to ask some "why" questions, and we were surprised with the answers.

"Kevin, why do we put food in the refrigerator?"

"Because dat's da place for it."

"Why is it the place for it?"

"Because we put da food in it?"

"Why do we put the food in it?"

"Because . . . Daddy, don't be silly."

Then Jan turned to Kari and asked, "Kari, why do you think we put the food in the refrigerator?"

"To keep it cold."

"Why do we need to keep it cold?"

Kari shrugged her shoulders.

"Why do we keep ice cream in the refrigerator?"

"So it won't melt?"

"Why do we keep milk or cottage cheese in the refrigerator?"

"So it won't get the green stuff."

"You mean mold?"

"Ya."

"Kari, why do we put food in the oven?"

"To make it warm?"

"Where do we cook things?"

"On the stove."

"What about in the oven?"

"No, you bake in there."

We do so many things routinely each day—things with which our children are familiar—that we feel they surely understand why these things are done. But now I wonder: Do they? Perhaps if I asked more why questions, I would have a better idea about what I should be teaching the children, rather than making assumptions about their knowledge.

Monday, March 10 / Picture "Photographs"

The children often see me going about my tasks with my 35mm camera around my neck, as I try to photograph the children participating in their preschool activities.

Today, Kim surprised me by saying, "Mommy, I want to take a picture of you." She had put one of my purses with a shoulder strap around her neck and was aiming the purse right at me. Without giving it much thought, I posed for her by sticking out my tongue to the side, and she snapped the picture.

I was *really* surprised when a few minutes later she brought me a drawing of a person and said, "Here is the picture I took of you." And sure enough, there I was, complete with my tongue sticking out to the side. Next time I will smile!

She took a picture of Kari standing by a measuring stick, and then of Kevin sitting down (which was more difficult to portray on paper), and of Jan.

I kept the "photographs," because we will never again have such unique pictures taken of our family, at least not by a purse! But she did give me a good idea. What about suggesting picture "photographs" for a preschool activity? This might be an excellent way for the children to become more observant of their surroundings as they try to capture them with pencil and paper.

Tuesday, March 11 / The Real Things

Jan cleaned out the garage last Sunday and placed an ad in the paper to sell the old baby furniture and equipment that we will no longer be needing. In preparation for the ad, which will appear tomorrow, I started scrubbing and cleaning the dust off the items so that they would look just as good as possible. Kim and Kari helped me. After we finished they asked if they could use the high chair in their playhouse for their dolls and also the stroller, since their doll baby buggies had broken last year. The real stroller has turned out to be much more fun than the small doll buggy, since all ten dolls can ride in it and there is still room on the footguard for the dolls' belongings. And the real high chair doesn't tip over like the doll high chair, and even their biggest doll fits in the real high chair.

"Mommy, it's too bad we have to sell these things. We could sure use them," Kim suggested.

"Well, I could sell them to you and Kari, if you really want them."

"Yes, yes, we do," they shouted.

"What do you think they are worth? What are you going to offer me for them?" I bartered.

"We'll make our beds and clean our room and set the table and brush our teeth after every meal," they volunteered.

"Sold!" I agreed, as I silently wondered how many other items I had put away only to purchase breakable-toy replicas for the children's play, when they could have been using the real things!

Wednesday, March 12 / Rudeness

Our field trip today was well planned. We had role-played the entire sequence and I was quite sure the children were ready to make their first purchase without me. We decided that an ice-cream cone was the thing they wanted most. Grandma sometimes sends them dimes and nickels for ice-cream cones, since she knows how much the children enjoy them and Jan's and my reluctance to buy sweets for them.

So the children have had experience selecting the kinds of ice cream they want, and they have watched me pay for the cones. Now they felt they could do this by themselves. Before leaving home the children carefully counted out forty-five cents, enough money for each child to have a double-decker.

As I drove up to the store, I could see a line at the ice-cream counter, so my last instruction to Kim was just to wait in line for their turn and then speak loudly when the clerk volunteered to help them.

Confidently they piled out of the car and entered the store, with Kim clutching the money in her fist. I parked the car and waited for a few minutes. But then my curiosity got the best of me and I watched through the open door.

The children moved up with the line, but when their turn came, the clerk overlooked them and went on to the adult standing in back of them. I felt the mistake was understandable, and I waited. The children waited until the order was filled and then Kim said quite loudly, "I want an ice-cream cone with strawberry cheese-cake and rainbow."

The clerk completely ignored her, asked the children to move away, and went on to the next customers. My anger was rising and the children were beginning to become frustrated, but they waited.

While the clerk was helping the older customers, I could see Kim and Kari talking together, as if making plans, but I couldn't tell what they said. I quietly moved inside the store since I sensed they might need some help. As soon as the other people had been helped, Kim spoke up quite loudly, "Please, we would like to have some ice-cream cones."

The clerk looked at them as if they were a nuisance and glanced at the line of adults, making a face to indicate her disgust.

She asked in a haughty manner, "Do you have any money?"

"Yes," said Kim, somewhat taken aback, since our role playing had not included this interrogation, and I am quite sure she had never heard anyone ask that of me.

Reluctantly the clerk reached for a cone and in a very rude voice said, "OK, what do you want?"

Kim gave the order.

The clerk put down the cone and asked angrily, "Do you have enough money?"

I could take it no longer and I spoke up, loud and clear, "Yes," in a very matter-of-fact voice.

The clerk looked in my direction, obviously surprised that she was being observed. Without any further words she filled the order, and Kim handed her the money. At that point I could resist no longer. I walked over to the counter, took three napkins from the container (something I had neglected to tell the children to do), and said in a rather cold manner, "Thank you." I wanted to say more, but I didn't want my children to hear what I wanted to say, so we left.

As the children licked their hard-earned ice-cream cones, I tried to explain to them why grown-ups are sometimes so rude to children. I told them that the lady probably had never had any children so young purchase ice cream by themselves, but that she had probably seen other children who stood around the counter and wanted ice cream but had no money. So she mistakenly thought they were like the other children. But, I thought, there is really no excuse for rudeness.

Thursday, March 13 / Thinking Processes

I saw an interesting license plate today, which made me think. It simply said, THIMK. Are Jan and I teaching our children to think? What are the processes involved in thinking? We certainly say to them often enough, "Think," or even more coarsely, "Use your head." But have we given them practice in this skill? After doing a little "thinking" about the subject, here are a dozen processes that seem to be important in stimulating clear thinking:

1. *Observing:* Children need to use all of their senses when mak-

ing observations. They need to learn to listen, to smell, to taste, and to feel as well as just to look.

2. *Reporting:* Children need the opportunity to report what they are observing. This not only helps them with verbal skills, but also they can check their perceptions (their observations) with others to see if they are similar. We like to ask the children at suppertime to report what they did or saw during the day. If children have an audience, reports can be fun at this age. Given the opportunity to practice now, perhaps they will be relieved of some of the trial involved in making reports later in their school lives.

3. *Comparing:* Few things are exactly alike in this world. The children went out the other day looking for two leaves just alike, and by comparing them very closely, they found no two to be identical. Children need to compare and contrast things and ideas in order to discover what is true, or what is of value to them.

4. *Summarizing:* This important skill is often neglected during the preschool years. I do a lot of summarizing for the children, but I'm afraid I haven't given them much practice. The next time one of us tells them a story, I think it would be a good idea to ask them to summarize it for the rest of us. The question, "How would you summarize what was just said?" may lead to a different response from every child, but it would be a way for Jan and myself to know what each one actually got out of the story.

5. *Interpreting:* Parents receive a lot of practice in interpreting what their children are saying to others, and vice versa. But do children get an opportunity to practice the same skill? I have heard Kim say to Kevin, "Mommy is getting angry," as she interprets to him my brisk actions. But I think children should be given more opportunities to explain the meaning of other people's actions or words. "What do you think he meant when he said that?" may be a good question not only to stimulate thinking but also to help children clarify what they heard, and it gives Jan and me a chance to know how much they have understood.

6. *Discovering:* Children need the opportunity to search out answers for themselves. They need to be encouraged to experiment, rather than always blindly accepting someone else's answer. How can you find out if water is always wet? if every leaf is green? if you can find a new way to make paste?

7. *Imagining:* Imagining sounds similar to idle daydreaming, where one's imagination runs wild. But discoveries such as electricity, or the radio may never have been made without imagination. It takes time to imagine. Preschoolers have great imaginations, but too often they are discouraged in this activity by their practical parents. Imaginations can be productive if they are put to work in solving real problems. What would happen if . . . ? If you were all alone on an island, how would you stay alive? If you were a grown-up, how would you spend your time with your children? If you had a hundred dollars, what would you do with it?

8. *Problem-solving:* Children solve problems every day in their work and play. (How can I get the pencils down from the shelf?) Many times I become the easy solution for the problem by helping the child immediately when he asks, rather than pointing out different ways he could solve the problem by himself. (If you get a chair, you could reach the pencils yourself.)

9. *Classifying:* "Sorting" is the word that my children would use to describe this behavior. (Put the blue ones here and the red ones over here. Put all the little ones in one pile. Bring all the forks to me.) Classifying to me is like advanced sorting, where the children actually arrange items into groups according to some system they have worked out, rather than an adult imposing the system on them. A higher level of thinking must take place to work out the system than is used when merely sorting out that which is similar or different.

10. *Planning and executing:* The reward of planning is actually being able to execute the plan. What are some of the things that preschoolers can plan and carry out by themselves? The girls enjoy planning what they will do during the preschool time and finding the materials to work with and then reporting on their plans. Children can plan a simple menu and then set the table and put the items on the table (such as nuts and fruit). Children can plan a garden and plant the seeds and . . . Too often I encourage the children to plan, and then I get busy and forget to follow up on the project. When this happens the project often gets forgotten and lost out in space. It takes time to help them bring their plans to a successful conclusion, but it's worth it. And it will lead to further plans and executions.

11. Criticizing: Children should not always accept things on face value, but should be taught to look at them critically and determine the real value of the statement or thing. Critiques can be positive and constructive rather than negative and destructive. Practicing during these years should be helpful. Questions to stimulate critical thinking might be: How useful is this object? Do we really need it? In what ways could you improve this object so it would be more useful?

12. Analyzing: Analyzing is an advanced thinking process, since it involves separating the whole into different parts in order to find out their nature, proportion, function, or relationship. But preschool children can be helped in this process by pointing out to them the different parts of an object (such as a clock) and showing them what the functions of each part may be, and how it relates to the other parts in order to make the whole object function properly.

Following these steps, I hope to produce thinkers, not thimkers!

Friday, March 14 / Finger Plays

Just now, at 2½ years of age, Kevin is able to use his hands well enough to enjoy finger plays. I was never very good at memorizing long finger plays about squirrels and other animals, but I have memorized a few of the most clever. I find that finger plays are things I'm not very good at if I constantly have to be looking at a book that tells me what to say and do next. But if I have them by memory, then I can use them on the spur of the moment—for instance, when we are riding in the car and Kevin wants something the girls have, and there are only two things (this happened a few minutes ago); or when we are waiting at a doctor's office and I have been foolish enough not to bring along any toys or books to amuse Kevin.

Here are my favorites, and the ones Kevin enjoyed today as we drove to and from the shopping center. Some of the finger plays even have tunes that go with them.

Open, Shut Them
Open, shut them, open, shut them;
Give a little clap.
Open, shut them, open, shut them;
Lay them in your lap.
Creepy crawl them, creepy crawl them,
Right up to your chin.
Open up your little mouth,
But do not let them in.
Open, shut them, open, shut them;
To your shoulders fly.
Then like little birdies
Let them flutter in the sky.
Falling, falling, falling, falling
Almost to the ground.
Quickly pick them up again,
And turn them round and round.
Faster, faster, faster, faster,
Slower, slower, slower, slower.
Clap!

Dickey Birds
Two little dickey birds, sitting on a hill [use thumbs as birds];
One named Jack and one named Jill.
Fly away, Jack. Fly away, Jill [wiggle thumbs and make them fly away].
Come back, Jack. Come back, Jill [one by one bring them back].

Church
Here is the church; here is the steeple [fold hands with fingers inside]
Open the doors and here are the people.

Monday, March 17 / Making Granola

Granola is a breakfast favorite at our house, and we just ate the last of our supply this morning. So for preschool I set out the large pan, measuring cups, and all of the ingredients. The children measured and poured them in as fast as I could mix. Here is our recipe:

Homemade Granola

1 cup oil	3 cups whole-wheat flour
2 cups honey	5 cups rolled oats
1 cup hot water	5 cups rolled wheat
(4 cups liquid ingredients)	1 cup sesame seeds
	2 cups coconut flakes
	2 cups sunflower seeds
	1 cup date sugar
	1 tablespoon salt
	(19 cups dry ingredients)*

* Optional: 3 or 4 cups variety of nuts.

Mix liquid and dry ingredients together. Mixture should be dry enough to rub with hands into tiny pieces or flakes that aren't sticky. Spread in 3 or 4 large baking pans. Bake slowly in oven at 250 degrees until cereal is golden brown. Watch carefully and stir frequently so the cereal doesn't burn. Store in zip-lock bags or covered containers. Use approximately 19 cups of dry ingredients. The essential ingredients are at least 3 cups of flour and at least 5 cups of rolled oats or wheat. The rest of the ingredients can be made up of a combination of different flours (buckwheat, barley, millet, rice, bran, cornmeal, soy, rye or wheat germ), nuts, coconut, etc., instead of what I suggest. This is one recipe that you can use creatively with products on hand rather than making a trip to the store for a cup of something you don't happen to have in your pantry.

Tuesday, March 18 / Maternal Attention

My "Things to Do" list today was a mile long. It was obvious when I started listing items that I'd be lucky to finish half of the things on the list. If I skimped on preschool, I would have a little extra time, and no one would really know the difference. Who would the children report to—the principal? What really would be the harm? My children would be the losers, but does a few hours really matter?

Things were going well, the children seemed to be involved in their play outside, and I was making progress on crossing off my things when Kari came to me and said, "Isn't it time for preschool?"

"Yes, it is," I replied honestly, wondering how I was going to get out of it now. "Do you want to have preschool, or would you rather play?"

"I want to have preschool," she replied.

Now I was caught. After all, I had given her the choice.

"OK," I replied. "I'll write down the things that you would like to do for preschool," thinking that she would mention some things that didn't take much, if any, of my supervision.

So she started naming the things she wanted to do:

Play reading records with Mommy
Do tricks with Mommy
Play the card game
Paint
Play preschool with Mommy
Play house

I quickly realized then that the only thing on her list that fit the description of needing little or no supervision was the last item. So I said, "Why don't you start out by playing house?"

"No," she replied, "let's start at the top of the list." I put my list of needs away and fulfilled her need for maternal attention. I'm happy she helped me clarify my primary responsibility as a teacher-mother.

Wednesday, March 19 / Helping

Kevin often doesn't get much of a chance to experiment to find correct solutions. He has too many bigger people always directing, answering, and showing him just what to do.

Today Kevin opened a new puzzle I got for him at an after-Christmas sale. A puzzle ought to be just what it is called, a puzzle. And yet Kim and Kari, who could easily see where each piece went, immediately started directing him.

"Here, Kevin, pick up this piece."

"Put it here."

"Turn it around."

"Turn it around some more."

"Good. Now pick up this piece."

I like the children to be helpful, but this is going a little far. I asked the girls not to say anything and just watch how Kevin figured out where the pieces were supposed to go. Then I stood and watched and found that my request was almost impossible to abide by. Before I knew it, I said, "No, Kevin, turn the piece around."

I know you should give children helpful hints on the principles of putting puzzles together, such as looking at the picture of the puzzle, and the colors, and shapes of the pieces, and then thinking about where each piece should go. But beyond this type of help, I think a child should be able to discover answers and solutions to problems on his own, if the task is not too difficult. I don't mean we should never help a child. There are times, when frustration is mounting, when a parent needs to step in and help the child over the hurdle. But I think far too many of us hastily give our children the "right" answers without the child having to do any thinking. I'm as much at fault as anyone else.

A few years ago Jan and I purchased the Britannica Junior Encyclopaedia so that it would be there when the children needed it. As a bonus, we received the Britannica's Pre-school Library, a set of thirteen books on different concepts, such as size, shape, color, signs, words, etc. My favorite book in the set is *The Thinking Book*. The first page of the book shows a turtle, horse, dog, spider, and mouse going toward a pond; a barn with a mousehole; a dog house; and a spider-webbed fence. The instructions say, "Find a home for each of these animals."

When Kim was three years old and I asked her to point to the house for each animal, she pointed to the barn each time. The "correct" answer was obvious to me, and knowing Kim had at least average mentality, I thought the correct answer should be obvious to her also. So I said, "No, spiders live in spider webs, dogs in dog houses, horses in barns, turtles in ponds, and mice in the mouse-holes." She never missed that page again. She learned the "correct" answer without having to use her brain to think, which was what the book was all about!

Anyone can memorize if they are reinforced for the correct answer often enough. This kind of conditioning is a very low-level mental process used in teaching dogs, cats, and chimpanzees. I don't know why we can't trust our children's reasoning powers by letting them come up with their "correct" answers. Afterward, I wished I had asked Kim why she chose the barn for every animal. She probably would have had a good reason, based on her own experience. For example, we have an old shed out back, which we call the "barn." We keep tools in it and the hay for the horses. There are many spiders in it. I've never seen a mouse or a mousehole in the barn, but I'm glad I haven't, since I know they are probably there when I'm not. The horses don't live in the "barn." They stay outside. As for turtles, I've seen many ponds in my lifetime and not a single turtle in them. The turtles I know are either in a dish of water or on land. Finally, I've never seen a dog in a dog house. Our dogs sleep in the laundry room next to the garage. Every family I know who has a dog and a dog house claims that their dog rarely if ever goes inside.

So after all this, what is the correct answer? My reasoning has led me to conclude that Kim's answer of the barn for every animal is just about as correct as my answer. The only difference is that she probably did a lot more reasoning to come up with her answer than I did to come up with mine. I was just parroting back all of the old clichés I've learned all my life. It just makes me wonder how many of the "correct" answers that we give children are really only half truths that children have to relearn for themselves later in life.

This reminds me of a story I once heard about Jean Piaget, the outstanding Swiss developmental psychologist, whose theory of cognitive development has stood not only the test of time, but also the onslaught of thousands of psychologists determined to prove him wrong. He says that in order to help a child develop his cognitive skills (thinking, reasoning, problem-solving), we need to stop answering questions and start asking them.

One day when Piaget's daughter was four or five years of age, she was preoccupied with the principles of air and wind. She turned around and around until she was quite dizzy and then asked her father, "Is everything turning around for you as it is for me?"

For most of us this would be the teachable moment, the time to start telling our children about the mechanism inside our heads that helps us keep our balance, and about how twirling affects it and how even though the air appears to be moving, it really isn't, etc. Well, not wise Piaget. All he did was to ask her what she thought. She made no further comment until the next day when she said, "I know why it doesn't turn for you and it turns for me. When I turn it makes a breeze and the breeze blows everything around me. But you are big; you are above the air I am turning, so the breeze doesn't turn up where you are." This may not have been the "correct" answer, but Piaget's question stimulated a whole day's thinking on the subject, which would have been lost if he had answered her question immediately. I often think the word "teacher" is not the best description of the role parents and "teachers" should be taking with their children. A "guide" or a "facilitator" may be more appropriate. What we really need to do is set up situations where learning and thinking can take place and not just regurgitation of "correct" answers.

Thursday, March 20 / Scientific Experiments

Last night I had just tucked the girls into bed when I discovered what seemed to be an unusual amount of static electricity in the load of clothing I removed from the dryer. "Should I, or should I not, show the children?" I pondered. "Oh why not?"

In case the girls were already asleep, I tiptoed into their room with the basket of laundry and was greeted with, "Hi, Mommy."

"Girls," I said, "I have a surprise for you." I turned off the night light and proceeded to pull garment after garment out of the basket —each producing crackles and sparks.

"Wow, how did you do that, Mommy?" Kim and Kari asked with wonder written all over their faces.

"Easy," I said. "The sparks are made by electricity. Remember when you walked on the new carpet and then shocked each other when you touched? It's the same thing."

After the girls were tucked into bed for the second time, I began thinking: "Why not introduce the children to the mysteries and marvels of this world through some planned scientific experiments?"

Today I lit a candle and had the children place a jar over it, and before long the flame flickered and died. I explained how oxygen was essential to life—and even a fire needed oxygen to burn. But I was also quick to bring out the spiritual lesson of our constant need for Jesus to fill our lives so we can shine brightly for him.

Then I sent the children searching for all the pennies they could find. When they returned I had prepared three containers of water. I had Kari add vinegar to one. Kevin added salt to another, and Kim put both salt and vinegar in the third. Then I asked them to drop their pennies into the different containers and observe what happened. It didn't take them long to see that nothing happened when the pennies were dropped into the salt or the vinegar solutions. But those pennies dropped into the salt-and-vinegar solution turned bright and shiny. Chemical reactions are fascinating, but I had another objective. "Children," I said, "this is like a family. Sometimes we get nothing done when we work alone, but when we work together like the vinegar and salt worked together, then we can accomplish a great deal."

By this time the children were fascinated. "Mommy, what other 'magic' tricks do you know?"

"Well, I know how to tell if an egg is boiled or not without cracking it open. Just watch," I said, as I took two eggs out of the refrigerator and placed them on the table. Everyone agreed they looked and felt just the same. "Spin them around," I instructed the children. "Do you see any difference?"

"Yes, one spins and the other doesn't," they replied.

"That's right," I said. "Boiled eggs spin; raw eggs do not." Then they proceeded to spin the eggs. After selecting the boiled one they cracked it open to see if I was right.

"Enough for now," I said. "Let's make these boiled eggs into egg-salad sandwiches . . . and maybe tomorrow we'll experiment with a magnet and a magnifying glass."

Friday, March 21 / Telephoning Daddy

"Kari, will you call Daddy for me?"

"I can't."

"Why can't you?"

"I don't know how. I don't know the number."

"I'll tell you how. First, write down this number. [I say it slowly as she writes.] Then underneath write '3721.' That's Daddy's extension. When the operator answers and says 'Loma Linda University,' you say, '3721.' Then when the next person answers and says 'Biostatistics and Epidemiology,' you say, 'Jan Kuzma, please.'

"Now pick up the receiver and listen for the dial tone."

"What's that?"

"The receiver is the thing you talk into." (I realized that we usually say, "Pick up the telephone.") "The dial tone is the buzz that tells you no one is using the telephone and it is ready for you to dial."

It took her three tries finally to dial correctly. I kept asking her if it was ringing, and she kept shaking her head "no." I took the receiver and listened. There was silence on the other end.

"You must have dialed too quickly. Slow down and dial again."

This time it started ringing, and I coached Kari to say, "3721." The operator answered and Kari said, "3721," and then I coached her to say, "Jan Kuzma, please."

She did as I asked when the next person answered the phone, but then ended up saying, emphatically, "Is my daddy there? Mommy wants to talk to him." Finally Kari shrugged her shoulders and handed me the receiver. It took a minute, but I finally realized the operator had rung extension 2721 and that office had no idea who Jan Kuzma or Daddy was. I apologized for the mistake, hung up, and explained to Kari what had happened. Then I said, "OK, try again."

"No," was her reply. "I don't want to talk to Daddy anyway. If you want to talk to him, you call him yourself."

I hadn't really realized until then how very complicated a telephone call can be for a small child without the proper readiness steps:

Step 1. Practice dialing for me, when I am listening to the buzzes that tell if she has done it correctly or not.

Step 2. Let her listen for the dial tone and dial.

Step 3. Role-play a simple call where she immediately gets the right party, so she learns the correct way to respond, in a clear, strong voice, "Hello, this is Kari. May I speak to Lisa?"

Step 4. Role-play getting the wrong number, so she knows what to say. "I'm sorry. I must have dialed the wrong number."

Step 5. Let her make a simple call to a friend completely by herself.

Step 6. Role-play calling the university with the operator and the departmental secretary answering.

Step 7. Let Kari listen on the extension phone as I call Jan.

Step 8. Call Daddy again.

Monday, March 24 / Swimming

I enrolled the girls in the YMCA water-safety program, which is a special week of swimming lessons during spring vacation to prepare children for a summer of swimming and water safety. The girls took swimming lessons last summer, and in just two weeks were swimming the entire length of the pool.

I believe that swimming is one of the most important skills that a child can acquire. This skill can save his life if he accidentally falls into water. It allows him to enjoy a variety of water sports such as water skiing and snorkeling. Swimming is a skill that one can use his entire life and not have to depend upon a team or even a partner in order to participate. It is an excellent means of keeping physically fit.

I recommend that every teacher-mother add swimming to a child's preschool curriculum. It's a great way to spend vacation time. See you next week—after my spring vacation!

Monday, March 31 / Character-development Review

Now that the first thirteen weeks of emphasis on our character curriculum are over and we are ready to begin again, I feel that this next quarter's activities should be a review rather than a branching out into new memory texts and hymns. I have difficulty remembering words and texts I learned thirteen weeks ago, so I know the children could benefit from a review.

Here are the memory texts and hymns for the various character traits that we emphasized last quarter:

Week 1. Faithfulness: "He that is faithful in that which is least is faithful also in much." (Lk. 16:10) (Kevin said, "If you are faithful in little things you'll be faithful in big things.") Hymn: "Faith of Our Fathers"

Week 2. Orderliness: "Let all things be done decently and in order." (1 Co. 14:40) Hymn: "This Is My Father's World"

Week 3. Self-discipline: "Let your moderation be known unto all men." (Ph. 4:5) Hymn: "Dare to Be a Daniel"

Week 4. Happiness: "A merry heart does good like a medicine." (Pr. 17:22; adapted) Hymn: "Lift Up the Trumpet"

Week 5. Perseverance: "With God all things are possible." (Mt. 19:26) Hymn: "I'm Pressing on the Upward Way"

Week 6. Honesty: "Even a child is known by his doings, whether his work be pure, and whether it be right." (Pr. 20:11) Hymn: "I Would Be True"

Week 7. Thoughtfulness: "Treat others as you would like to be treated." (Mt. 7:12; adapted) Hymn: "My Task"

Week 8. Efficiency: "Whatever your hand finds to do, do it with all your might." (Eccles. 9:10; adapted) Hymn: "Work, for the Night Is Coming"

Week 9. Responsibility: "Be obedient in all things." (2 Co. 2:9) Hymn: "Trust and Obey"

Week 10. Respect: "For man looketh on the outward appearance, but the Lord looketh on the heart." (1 S. 16:7) Hymn: "I'm a Child of the King"

Week 11. Enthusiasm: "[Be] fervent in spirit; serving the Lord." (Rm. 12:11) Hymn: "Holy, Holy, Holy"

Week 12. Humility: "He that humbles himself shall be exalted." (Lk. 18:14; adapted) Hymn: "Not I, but Christ"

Week 13. Peacefulness: "Blessed are the peacemakers, for they shall be called the children of God." (Mt. 5:9) Hymn: "Peace, Perfect Peace"

Preschoolers enjoy repetition. In the zeal to teach something new, teacher-mothers should not hesitate to review the familiar. Most of the things we continue to remember are those things that are continually reviewed and reinforced. It will be the same with the teaching of various character traits.

APRIL's birth of spring
Children and flowers and songs
Bring joy to cold hearts

Tuesday, April 1 / April Fool

It's April Fools' Day, and I feel like a fool. I have tried everything today to get Kim to practice the piano. I even lowered myself to go so far as to tempt her analytical mind with the following proposal:

"Kim, every time you play through a song, I'll give you a nickel." After she dawdled a few minutes, I decided that what she needed was motivation to do as much as she could in the shortest amount of time so that she could move on to other things, rather than sitting at the piano all day. So I went a step farther. "Kim, I will give you a nickel for every five minutes you practice. For every minute you play a song, I'll give you a penny more, but if you let a minute go by that you are not playing, then I will take a penny away. Now is your chance to earn a lot of money for ice-cream cones."

She listened to all of this and said, "I don't want to practice," and got up and walked away.

I finally decided that in this one area, I'm a failure. I just can't seem to motivate the girls to practice the piano.

Tonight I received a call from one of my old musical friends. The conversation led to piano lessons and she started raving about her seven-year-old son's fantastic piano teacher and how well the son is doing. I haven't quite decided, but I think that on this one task—teaching piano—I could use a little help from an outside teacher.

Wednesday, April 2 / Piano Lessons

I called Mrs. Andrews, the piano teacher. Early this morning the girls had their first lesson. What a delightful time the children had and how eager they seem to be to learn something for Mrs. Andrews. Her warm personality just enveloped the children and they felt comfortable and secure with their new teacher at the first meeting. As we walked to the car after the lesson, the girls both said, "Mommy, she is just like Grandma. She calls us 'sweetheart' and 'honey.' Can we come back tomorrow?"

Thursday, April 3 / Doll Clothes

I always thought doll dresses were difficult to make. And they are if you are a perfectionist, but Kim made some "beautiful" clothes today, almost entirely by herself.

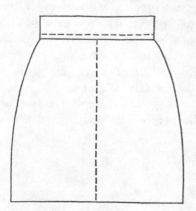
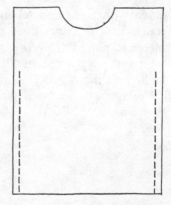

First she made a skirt by cutting a rectangular piece of cloth and sewing the ends together with my machine. Then I showed her how to fold over a half inch of material at the top and stitch it down. Finally she threaded elastic through the top, tied it, and her skirt was complete.

The blouse was almost as simple. She cut another rectangular piece of material. I showed her how to fold it in half and cut a head hole. Then she stitched up the sides, leaving an inch opening at the top for the arms to go through. Her blouse was complete.

This outfit may not look to others like elegant clothing, but beauty is in the eyes of the beholder, and to Kim—it's beautiful.

Friday, April 4 / Timing Device

I have found a secret to getting the girls to practice the piano on their own. I bought them a fancy timer. After two days of use, I'm convinced this purchase was worth it. The children delight in going by themselves to the piano and setting the timer for ten minutes and then busily practicing before it rings.

Ten minutes is just the right amount of time for my beginners to practice. They are just getting started and interested when the timer goes off, so it always leaves them with a good feeling about practicing rather than playing until they are bored.

I really didn't think the girls could practice without my sitting down with them and telling them every move to make: how to count, how to curve their fingers, what the notes are, and what pieces to play. But even Kari now goes to the piano and practices over and over again her five-note scale and plays the game of finding all the A's on the piano and then the B's, etc.

Today the timer is my gimmick for getting the children to practice. I wonder how long it will be before I'll need to find a new one?

Monday, April 7 / Grandparents Move In

Jan and I have been trying to teach the children to be respectful, to share, and to be thoughtful, caring, and flexible. Today I saw it in action. Unexpectedly, Jan's parents moved in with us.

About a month ago, Jan's mother, who is seventy-two years of age, fell and hit her head very badly. This led to a slight stroke, which left the right side of her body partially paralyzed. She had lost control of her left hand twelve years ago when she suffered a stroke, but continued her active life, using her right hand for everything.

Now to lose the use of her right hand and leg was a crushing blow. But she has a strong will. She remained in the hospital until today.

When the decision was made that she would be leaving the hospital, we thought she should go to a convalescent hospital, since she could move very little of her body by herself. We thought we had everything arranged. Then, at the urging of Jan's sister, we again contacted the doctor and asked what would be the benefits of being in a convalescent hospital over being in one of our homes. He couldn't think of any. We had just naturally assumed that the continual care and physical-therapy treatments of the trained hospital staff would be superior to our untrained endeavors. When the doctor suggested that the constant stimulation and hourly physical therapy that a family could give would be better for her, the decision was made. If "Oma" were to live with us, then "Opa," Jan's eighty-year-old father, would have to move in, too, to help take care of his wife.

Our home is not large. It has only three bedrooms. One for us, one for the girls to share, and one for Kevin. In order to have a room for the grandparents, it was decided that Kevin would move in with the girls.

Such excitement. It was almost like Christmas. While the children enjoyed the novelty of the entire situation, I started the process of emptying some of the girls' drawers to make room for Kevin's clothing. I put away some of Kevin's toys, and others I put into the "children's room." By the time Oma and Opa arrived, Kevin's room was clean and nearly empty. But my work had just begun in the children's room. I would still be working on it now, if bedtime hadn't come for tired children needing to sleep. I will just have to finish organizing that room tomorrow.

From the moment the grandparents arrived this afternoon, the children have been little angels of mercy. They helped carry in all of the suitcases and boxes; they fluffed pillows; they covered Oma up; they held the water so she could drink; they rubbed her back; they exercised her arm and fingers; they filled her hot-water bottle; and they carried messages. Finally, when everything was arranged and Opa and Oma lay down for a rest, the girls rested beside them.

A number of times throughout the afternoon, Kari came to me and said, "I love Oma so much." Being a teacher-mother, I couldn't let the opportunity pass without pointing out an important lesson, perhaps the most important the children can ever learn for their own happiness: The more you do for someone, the more your love for them will grow.

I know that the novelty of having grandparents in our home will pass during the next weeks, but I pray that the lessons learned through this experience will last the children a lifetime.

Tuesday, April 8 / Frustration

How can I be so far behind? Yesterday I resolved that I would accomplish something this week, or else. Now I am beginning to feel that it will be the "or else," because my accomplishments so far have added up to zero!

I started out by making a list of everything I needed to do. In reality the list was not new. It turned out to be everything I had recorded on last Wednesday's list that had not been checked off. That means I am at least six days behind. This wouldn't make me feel so bad if I knew that last Wednesday I had started with a new list. But last Wednesday's list contained everything that I had failed to do the week before!

Jan keeps telling me not to start new projects. Just try to finish the old ones. But I can't seem to operate that way. My minds keeps jumping ahead of my hands and I become wholeheartedly inspired with something new that just has to be done immediately or the opportunity will be lost. Everything else gets set aside.

What does this have to do with being a teacher-mother? I am convinced that having the distraction of always being behind makes my efficiency as a teacher-mother reach a very low level. I always seem to have my mind half on what the children need and half on all of those unfinished projects.

Another thing that really distracts me from my job is the telephone. I haven't quite gotten to the point of ignoring the ring, but I have been tempted. Since the word has spread that I am only working part time and "just staying home" with the children, everybody thinks, "Oh Kay's a perfect one to do this or that. Let's give her a call." And I often end up doing "this" or "that" rather than doing something extra for my children in our home preschool.

But it is not just the requests that bother me; it is also the constant ringing of the phone. We can't afford an extension in every room. So I keep one at the desk, a must if I am to get any work done (if ever I sit down to do it), and one in the kitchen, where I end up spending half of my time. It seems as if, just as I am beginning to work with my children and have two of them concentrating on a task and am explaining the instructions to the third one, the phone rings. I usually sigh and hesitate, trying to decide whether it is really worth it to get up and run all the way to the kitchen to answer. Kim, however, catches my hesitation and jumps up to answer it, interrupting her task. In a few minutes she is back saying, "Mother, it is for you." I'm not a bit surprised, since 99.9 per cent of the daytime calls are for me. My preschoolers just don't get that many telephone calls yet. (Thank goodness!) By the time I get back to my children, the orderly activities of preschool have vanished. Kevin has thrown the puzzle pieces all over the floor, Kari has knocked down Kevin's building, and Kim is chasing both of them, trying to get them to put things back in order before I return and the explosion occurs.

Talking about lists, maybe tomorrow I'll add to my list not to answer the phone between 9:00 A.M. and 11:00 A.M. Maybe tomorrow I can get something done. . . .

Wednesday, April 9 / Picture "Twenty Questions"

Today we played "Twenty Questions"—picture style. The object of
the game was to see how quickly I could guess the Bible story por-
trayed in the drawings that Kim and Kari had made. They were
happy if I could guess immediately. They drew pictures of the following scenes:

The manger scene with Mary and Joseph and the Christ child
Noah going into the ark with a rabbit
Shadrach, Meshach, and Abednego in the fiery furnace
The children of Israel going between the waters of the Red Sea
The manna around the tents of the children of Israel
The ravens feeding Elijah near the Brook Cherith
Joseph in the pit with his brothers standing around
The tower of Babel
Daniel in the lions' den

Thursday, April 10 / Chasing Butterflies

For the past few days butterflies have been invading our yard, traveling from east to west in a type of migration pattern. Seeing so
many butterflies, the children have had an irresistible urge to chase
them. So far success has evaded the children. They have not even
gotten close enough really to observe the butterflies' wings. So
today I made them a butterfly net.

I bent an old wire hanger into a circle and straightened the
hanging hook part, then taped it with heavy tape onto an old
broom handle. I cut a rectangular piece of netting that was long
enough to go around the wire circle and sewed it on with large
stitches. I gathered up and tied a string around the other end of the
netting.

The children still haven't caught any butterflies, but it has made the activity more challenging, and they have gotten a lot of exercise in the process. If they should be successful, we have made a pact that they will release the butterfly after they observe it for a short time in captivity. If they set it free someone else can enjoy its beauty and it can lay its eggs so we will have more beautiful butterflies to chase next year.

Friday, April 11 / In Love with Cauliflower. . .

My greenhouse garden is growing. It is really the first I have ever had. I wish that I could say it was the children's garden, but even though they have put in a few seeds and have been excited at some sprouts and have helped me transplant a few plants, I have done the vast majority of the work. And it is work and it takes a lot of time.

While I have spent hours planting, pulling, pruning, and watering, I have often thought of two sayings. The first is, "Anything worth doing is worth doing well." This thought keeps me in the greenhouse a few minutes more. Then I think of the saying, "You always have time for what you really want to do." I really need to be doing so many other things that I'm afraid I sometimes end the day complaining. I guess that I will just have to quit complaining and admit, "I'm in love with my cauliflower, tomatoes, and beans, and I do have time for what I really want to do!" And I'll not feel guilty as long as I continue to involve the children in the project, even though their help is infinitesimal!

Monday, April 14 / A Letter to Grandparents

Every two weeks I write a family letter and send duplicate copies to all of the relatives. I try to encourage the children to include a picture they have drawn or a letter they have written. Today's preschool activity was to write a letter to Grandma and Grandpa. Kim's letter said, "Dear Grandma and Grandpa, I love you. How are you? You need to send us some gum. Love, Kim." Kari managed to say, "Dear Grandma and Grandpa, Love, Kari." And Kevin got an X and an O on the page along with some special scribbles. Children need a lot of practice when they begin writing. Why not make this activity a practical one by writing a letter that will actually be sent to someone who will appreciate it?

Tuesday, April 15 / Preschool Ping-Pong

Our Ping-Pong table, which usually stands in the garage hidden beneath a mountainous pile of odds and ends that accumulate over the years, was discovered afresh this last weekend, as guests came and challenged Jan to a game. Our children were fascinated with the "new" game, but their eagerness to play soon led to frustration when their attempts at hitting the ball failed. Tonight, however, when Jan asked the children what they wanted to learn, they all voted for Ping-Pong. Since it was rather chilly in the unheated garage, Jan brought the paddles and the ball inside and transformed the kitchen table into a Ping-Pong table by placing a medium-sized can on each side of the table in the middle and balancing a yardstick on top of the cans. With the net "barrier" gone, the object of the game was to roll the ball between the cans and under the yardstick, rather than trying to bounce the ball over the top. By narrowing the playing space from the five-foot width of the regular Ping-Pong table to the three-foot width of the kitchen table, the children were able to get to where the ball was rolling toward them and hit it back to their opponent. Success was instantaneous, and preschool Ping-Pong is destined to become a Kuzma favorite.

Wednesday, April 16 / Orderliness

I failed in my January attempt to establish order by listing all of the duties the children were supposed to do and then having them place stars beside the job when it was complete (see January 13). There were just too many items to remember.

So starting in April, when we again emphasized the character trait of orderliness, I simplified the list and organized it around early-morning duties and then duties that centered around meals, so that after each meal we could take an accounting of whether the children had done their jobs or not. Now after only a few weeks on this routine, I can see a great improvement in the children's ability to remember what is required of them. Once this routine is firmly established, I can add more things to the list. It is far better to require little and make sure it is done, than to require a lot and neglect to follow through on anything.

The New Memory List
Before breakfast:
    Make bed
    Get dressed
Breakfast activities:
    Set table, clear table, brush teeth, practice piano
Lunch activities:
    Set table, clear table, brush teeth, practice piano
Before supper:
    Clean up inside and outside
Supper activities:
    Set table, clear table, brush teeth, practice piano
Bedtime activities:
    Bath
    Straighten up room

Thursday, April 17 / The Fifth Birthday

Five years have flown by so quickly, and it is now time to sing "Happy Birthday" to my precious Kari. The most formative years of her life are over. What have I done really to shape her into the kind of individual I want her to be? Those first few years of Kari's life were such busy years, with two tiny girls less than sixteen months apart. I recall the diapers, the bottles, the baths, the feedings . . . in a way it was almost like having twins. Yet Kim, being older, had the advantage of having Jan and me all to herself for almost sixteen months before Kari arrived. Kari always has had to share our attention.

I am glad there is a special day each year when each child is honored. Kari deeply enjoyed her party and her four little guests. Without hesitation she participated in the musical-chair game, when only three months ago at Kim's birthday, she chose not to participate because she was afraid she would lose.

I really don't believe in all the hoopdedo that many parents plan for young children's birthday parties. Children don't need clowns, jugglers, magicians, elaborate games, decorations, and fancy cakes in order to enjoy a birthday. Instead of purchasing a fancy cake, I mixed up a chiffon cake mix with Kari's help and then let her decorate it with imitation whipped cream. I put a cup in the hole in the middle of the cake, and Kari filled it with a bouquet of spring flowers. It was an easy way to decorate a birthday cake! Kari put in her own candles, and no one even commented (or probably noticed) that they were not evenly spaced. A scoop of ice cream and a sliver of cake satisfied her friends. Not one child asked for nut cups or balloons or any of the other fancy trimmings that are so often associated with birthday parties.

After we played musical chairs and sang a few songs around the piano, the children all ran outside to play. I had plenty of time to clean up the paper plates and the wrappings. I also had time to clean out the car while the children were all happily entertaining themselves. They probably had more fun by themselves than if I were to intrude. It was by far the easiest party I have ever given. And it was probably one that the children enjoyed as much as or more than any. Perhaps the secret of a happy birthday party for little children is to keep it small and simple.

Now Kari is five years old. Five has always seemed to be a critical age. It means leaving babyhood behind and stepping out of the home to that new adventure of school. It means learning to write, read, and do all those other "big" things that "big" kids do. In a way, it is sad to think I have lost a little girl. But as I watched her today at her birthday party, I was pleased.

Friday, April 18 / Cutting Weeds

"Kevin, do you want to come to help me pull weeds out of the lawn?"

"No," he replies, busily cutting away on a scrap of paper.

"Are you sure you don't want to go out with me? It's a beautiful day."

"No."

"I've got to go out to pull the weeds or pretty soon there will be more weeds than grass. I don't want to leave you inside all alone. Why don't you come out with me to help me?"

"No."

"Maybe you could cut the weeds off with your scissors."

"Mommy, could I?" he looks up, surprised at my suggestion. "Dat's a good idea." He takes my hand and leads me toward the door.

I think, "How did I happen to strike such a responsive key? I wonder how long it will last?"

I show him how to cut the leaves off the weeds and put them in the wheelbarrow. I'm sure he has no idea that I will have to come back to every weed he cuts off to make sure the root is out.

For two hours he stays with me, chattering the whole time, "Boy, am I working hard. See dis big weed I cut off, Mommy? I'm really helping you, huh? I'm a big boy to be a helper. Dis is hard work.

Kim and Kari aren't big helpers? I got it—I cut it off! See, Mommy? See what I can do? Boy, am I workin' hard."

And so he is.

Monday, April 21 / A Bird's-eye View

A few weeks ago Mother and Father Wren built a nest in the climbing jasmine bush outside our kitchen window. When the activity first became noticeable the children placed a ladder next to the house and near enough to the nest so they could get a bird's-eye view without disturbing the wrens. Now an age-old drama is being acted out. Each day I receive a new report.

"Mommy, there is an egg in the nest."

"Now there are three eggs."

"Today I saw four whitish-brown speckled eggs."

"We can't see any eggs 'cause the mommy won't get up off of them."

Then today the excited word came. "The eggs have hatched, the eggs have hatched. I see four tiny birdies."

We all took turns climbing up the ladder and peering into the nest to view the four tiny skin-pink birds with their huge mouths wide open.

It is one thing to read about birds in a book or to look at them in a museum, but quite another to have them live close enough so preschoolers can have a firsthand experience watching them raise a family. I couldn't have planned a better preschool activity!

Tuesday, April 22 / Family Lessons

Mrs. Andrews has a fantastic arrangement for teaching children piano. In the same room where the lessons are going on, she has special chairs for the parents or other children who may need to

wait. She encourages two children of the same family to come together so that many of the things she says, such as comments about
theory, do not need to be said twice. She has two pianos so that
both children can try the new finger exercises at the same time.
What really amazes me is that she doesn't mind if I bring Kevin.
She even has a special basket of blocks and pull toys that he can
play with. She has color books, paper, and a desk that a waiting
child can use. It is a small but friendly room, and the children love
exploring all the little knickknacks that she has on the shelves for
their enjoyment.

I can remember when I took piano lessons. I had to wait in a separate room with nothing to do but worry about whether I knew my
lesson as well as I should. Now I love to go to the children's lessons
because I really feel welcome. By listening to the girls' lessons I
know what to stress at home when they practice. Mrs. Andrews
teaches me how to be a better teacher-mother at home, without any
extra cost.

When I started the girls in "formal" piano lessons, I felt sorry
that I was giving up my responsibility as a teacher in this area. I
don't feel that way anymore. I am teaching more music to the girls
now that they are taking lessons from someone else for one hour a
week than I would ever have done without this added motivation.
When I know I am paying for a lesson, I'm highly motivated to
work with them during the week so that they will progress as they
should.

Wednesday, April 23 / Cuttings

Kari loves flowers. Today she brought me a book to read to her
about growing plants, like geraniums, by taking a piece of the stem
and putting it in water. I asked Kari if she wanted to try to start a
plant from a cutting. She was excited as we went outside to gather
various cuttings to see which might root. We found geraniums, ivy,
oleander, roses, and a variety of other plants, many of which I
doubt will grow from a cutting. Some we put in water and some in
a mixture of sand, soil, and water. This will be Kari's scientific ex-

periment to discover the different plants in our yard that will grow from a cutting. I think I will learn something, too!

Thursday, April 24 / Riddles

The activity cards for today were homemade riddles. I wrote each one on a card and gave it to the girls. They walked around the house looking for all the answers. Here are some of my riddles:

What gets red when on and black when off? (electric bathroom heater, or stove burners)
What has four green legs and two red covers? (the girls' green bunkbed)
What rings without anyone setting it? (the telephone)
What tells you what time it is without talking to you? (clock)
What has four corners and hangs? (a picture on the wall)
What burns shorter? (a candle)
What has an eye but can't see? (a needle or a potato)
What has legs and black and white keys? (the piano)
What do you chew all day but never swallow? (gum)

In the library, I found *Bennett Cerf's Book of Riddles* and his second book, *More Riddles,* which are for beginning readers. The books are still too advanced for Kim to read, but the riddles are just right for preschoolers. Kari delights in asking Jan, "When can three fat ladies go out with only a small umbrella and not get wet?" The answer is, "When it is not raining!"

Do riddles serve a place in a child's education? Yes, riddles are word puzzles. To solve a riddle, a child must think beyond the logical answer to take into account the hidden facts of the riddle, or be able to delete the irrelevant. At times a child can come up with the correct answer almost easier than an adult can. Take, for example, the riddle, "If the cat is in the house and you turn out the lights, where will the cat be?" Without hesitation Kevin replied, "In the dark!"

Friday, April 25 / A Camping Place

We had a delightful family day today. After lunch the principal joined us and we drove out to "the desert," a lonely spot of earth off the main highway. A narrow road winds up through a canyon where a tiny stream flows over a rocky bed. Here and there a clump of wildflowers brightens the land. It is not a scenic wonder that you would drive for miles in order to explore. It is just a little special "camping place" where we can spend the day away from bustling humanity and pretend we are camping without having to pack our gear for half a week before the trip. We drove to our favorite spot where the road crosses the stream, parked the car, and "set up camp" for the day. The children, equipped with buckets and shovels, immediately organized their play at the water's edge, while Jan and I, equipped with beach chairs and magazines that we hadn't read for the past three months, found a place to read.

I was surprised at how comfortable it was lying on the rocky ground, and I slept for over an hour while Jan watched the children over the rim of the magazine he was reading.

At one point Jan suggested that the children build an altar like the one Abraham and Jacob built in the Bible stories. The idea was a challenge, and they tugged and pulled and pushed to get just the right size rock in the right place.

The edge of the stream was littered with an occasional soda-pop can. We collected all of the aluminum cans and sailed a few of the others down the stream, trying to keep up with them until they floated around the bend. As they became wedged among the rocks in the stream the children threw rock after rock, trying to see who would be successful in dislodging them.

After a very uncomplicated picnic supper (leftovers from lunch), we hiked down the stream and back and then piled into the car for our short journey home.

The sun was setting as we neared home, and we were all commenting on how red it was as it set behind the black mountains in the distance. Kevin sat quietly watching. Finally I said, "Kevin, see how the sun is setting behind the mountain."

He nodded his head. "It is a broken sun."

I looked again. If I hadn't had thirty-some years to learn about horizons and sunsets, my perceptions would have told me the same thing. Sometimes it takes a little child's innocence to make us look at the common things in a fresh, new light.

Monday, April 28 / Calendar

So often I spend money to buy "educational" materials to use with my children, when if I would just use my creativity instead of my money, I could use household items to teach the same principles. The calendar is an excellent teaching tool, and yet before I discovered its true potential, I discarded the extra ones I accumulated yearly. Never again. They are such valuable teaching tools that I'm surprised there are so many free ones around.

Here are some of the things that can be taught from a calendar:

1. *How to write the numbers.* My girls (Kevin isn't to this stage yet) are constantly asking me, "How do you write a 3?" "Does the 7 go this way or that way?" Usually I take my time to show them, but since I found my March calendar filled with a child's practice numbers written beside the calendar numbers, I got the idea that I could send them to the calendar to check their own work, instead of their always having to depend on me. Most calendars are large enough for the child to practice writing his numbers directly on the calendar.

2. *The sequence of numbers.* What comes after 10? or 12? Next time I get a question like that, I'm going to say, "Check the calendar."

3. *Reading from left to right.* To read the sequence of the numbers, children are forced to read from left to right (at least for the majority of calendars). This could be considered a prereading skill.

4. *Reading names of months and days.* If the days are abbreviated, this could lead to a discussion of the reasons for abbreviating

words, and the child could look for the most common, such as Mr., Mrs., St., Ave., etc., once they are acquainted with Mon., Tues., or Jan., Feb., etc.

5. *Weekly, monthly, and yearly cycles.* Seven days make a week; approximately four weeks make a month; twelve months make a year. Every year has a number. The birth of Christ is the beginning of the numbering system to determine the number of the year. (It may be too difficult to get into the backward numbering system of the B.C. years.)

Learning the number of days in a month is confusing. To help, I have taught my children the jingle, "Thirty days hath September, April, June, and November. All the rest have thirty-one, except February, with twenty-eight, and every four, you add one more."

6. *The origination of the weekly cycle at creation.* God created the world in six days, and on the seventh day He rested.

7. *The importance of the moon in establishing the monthly cycle.* The moon is actually pictured on many calendars. My children plot each month when the moon will be in its different stages, and they observe the moon, and it has never failed them yet (except when it's hidden in the clouds).

8. *Arithmetic.* How many days are in the month? If it is the fourth day of the month, and on the seventh we get to go to a party, how many days do we have to wait before the party? It is the eighteenth, and I lost a dime two days ago. What was the date of the day I lost a dime? If it is ten days before your birthday, what is the date of today? Two weeks is how many days?

9. *How to read a calendar.* Today is Tuesday. What is the date? What day of the week will Christmas be on this year? What date will it be next Sunday?

So, whatever the day, it's a great day to take a new look at the calendar!

Tuesday, April 29 / Big or Small—Old or New

A hand-me-down pair of slacks from Kevin's friend Greg led into the following conversation:

"Come, Kevin, let me help you put on Greg's old pants," I said, holding out the pants.

"Mommy, dose Greg's pants?"

"They used to be, but they are too small for him now, so he gave them to you."

"Greg's small. I'm big?"

"No, Greg is bigger, so his pants are too small for him. You are smaller, so he gave the pants to you so you could wear them," I tried to explain.

"I'm bigger than Greg, no. Yes, I am bigger than Missy and Sherry."

"No, you are smaller than Missy and Sherry."

"I'm big boy."

"Yes, you are a big boy, but you are smaller than Greg."

"Dose Greg's old pants?" he continued.

"Yes, these are Greg's old pants, but they are new pants for you, since you have never worn them before."

"Mommy, dese old pants, or dese new pants?"

"These are Greg's old pants. But look, they just fit you, so they can be your pants now."

"I'm a big boy? Yes, I'm a big boy. I'm bigger than Greg. I got Greg's big pants."

"No, you are smaller than Greg."

"Yes, Greg not smaller than me, no," said Kevin emphatically.

"I think that's right. . . ." I said, as I finished zipping up the pants.

It was all getting rather complicated at that point and the pants were on, so I dropped the conversation. Kevin wandered away with his hands stuffed in the pockets of the old-new pants that were at the same time too small and just right, depending upon whether you were big or little. About an hour later he commented to me, "Mommy, I'm bigger than Kari, no?"

I then realized that he had probably spent a good hour thinking about the concepts. The important thing in his little world is to be big. And all the people that he had so far compared himself with were bigger than he. So I helped him out and told him that lots of people were bigger than he, but lots of people were smaller than he. For example, "You are bigger than Timmy, and you are bigger than baby John."

Finally, he seemed satisfied and said, "Mommy, dat's a good idea."

All of these concepts seem so easy for us to understand, but for young children it takes many, many examples to get our whole confusing world sorted out.

Wednesday, April 30 / No More Tears

My girls used to hate having me shampoo their hair (Kevin still hates to have me shampoo his hair). So I told them I wouldn't do it anymore if they would do it themselves. The transformation was dramatic. Now shampooing their hair is a big event. They work to make enough bubbles to make soap boats in the water. Sometimes they make their hair stiff with shampoo so that they can shape it into different hairdos (sometimes sticking straight up). Shampoo time has become so much fun that if I didn't limit it to once a week, they would do it daily.

Today was shampooing day. To my surprise, Kevin allowed the girls to shampoo his hair, including a good rinse, without even a whimper. I really enjoy seeing the children able to do these things for themselves. For some reason they are more willing to do something when I allow them to do it without my help. It becomes a challenge, and it brings them a good feeling of accomplishment. The added benefit is that I have a few more minutes for myself, and no more tears.

MAY's rainbow o'erhead
Reminds of commitments made
On fall days long past

Thursday, May 1 / May Day

It is a beautiful May Day today. It makes me want to hang a flower-bedecked basket on an unsuspecting someone's door, ring the doorbell, and hide, the way I used to do when a child.

Whatever happened to that lovely May Day tradition? It has been years since I have heard of anyone delivering May baskets. I can remember just as clearly as if it were yesterday delivering May baskets when I was in second grade. It must have taken my mother hours to help me make the baskets. I can remember cutting a circle out of construction paper, pasting a doily on top, then cutting from one side to the center to make it into a cone shape (see illustration). After the cone basket was stapled I'd use pipe cleaners for handles, and ribbons for decorations. The last step was to fill every basket carefully with pansies, violets, and mints.

I wrote down everyone to whom a basket was to be delivered, while Mom checked the addresses in the phone book. Then Mom would drive me all over town in that big old DeSoto and wait as I went through the routine. I can't remember ever getting caught and kissed, but there was always the risk.

I had almost forgotten the May Day ritual until Kim made a basket while visiting the classroom she will probably attend next year. I told her how I used to deliver May baskets when I was her age. The idea intrigued her, so she tried to play the game with Kari and Kevin, both of whom, after they had opened the door and found no one there, closed it, saying, "It must have been the dogs ringing the bell again."

What a disappointment for Kim, hiding around the corner waiting to yell, "Surprise!" as they discovered the basket hanging on the door handle.

I quickly coached Kari and Kevin and they opened the door again, found the basket, caught Kim, and smothered her with kisses. Then everyone wanted to make a May basket. At the end of the day we had quite a collection. Here is how we made them:

1. *Flower basket.* Cut a circle from construction paper. Bring the two sides of the circle together, staple, and add a handle.

2. *Fruit-carton basket.* Take a plastic basket for tomatoes or strawberries and weave colorful ribbons in and out. Add a pipe-cleaner handle or a ribbon handle.

Or for a variation, cut out a design (such as a bunny or a flower) and paste the designs on both sides of the carton. Add a paper handle. The basket should look something like this:

3. *Paper-cup basket.* Decorate paper cups with tissue paper and glue, or paint the cups with bright tempera colors (if the cups have not been waxed). Add a pipe-cleaner handle.

4. *Box basket.* Make a box from a square piece of paper by following this pattern. Cut on the solid lines and fold on the dotted ones. Staple or paste the ends in place. Add a paper handle.

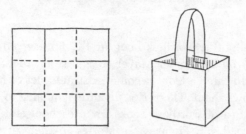

Friday, May 2 / Three Little Kittens

The children discovered that the three little kittens born about a month ago in the barn had been left by themselves. Their wild mother has given birth to numerous litters in the barn, but the babies always grow up wild and disappear. Since Mommy Cat was not around, the children picked up the babies, and, of course, it was love at first sight.

"Mommy, please, can we have them for our very own? Please, please," they begged.

I almost said "no," but I couldn't think of any good reason to counter the whys I knew I would be deluged with if I gave a negative reply.

So, since the kittens were old enough to leave their mother, I gave my permission for the children to raise them. What squeals of delight I heard as Kari (my most expressive one) hugged and kissed me. The kittens spent the afternoon being carried around in doll blankets and riding in the stroller and licking milk off of the children's fingers. Never were babies more loved. How could I deprive the children of something so soft and cuddly and free, even though I knew two dogs and a cat were really enough pets for one family?

Monday, May 5 / Sequence Pictures

I found a delightful wordless book at the library today: *A Boy, a Dog, and a Frog* by Mercer Mayer. It is a story about a boy and a dog who try to catch a frog, become frustrated, leave for home, and the frog follows them. There is a definite sequence to the story.

I like the idea of wordless books for preschool children who are not able to read yet. Pictures are stories in themselves and when placed in a sequence can tell a story to preschoolers while the words are only meaningless scribbles on the page. Sequencing is an important concept for preschool children to learn. I sometimes draw little stick figures doing something in a sequence, then mix the cards and let the children try to put them in order. An easy sequence to draw is about getting dressed. My cards look like this:

Other sequence-picture stories that are easy enough for me to draw are:

Blowing up a balloon:

Eating dinner:

I am now trying to encourage the children to draw their own word-less sequence stories for me to try to put in sequence.

Tuesday, May 6 / Making Bible Stories Meaningful

Jan believes that the Bible stories are sometimes more meaningful to children when they are made practical with some relationship to the world that the children experience daily. This is best illustrated in the Jonah story Jan told during breakfasttime this morning.

"A long, long time ago God said, 'Jonah, go to Nineveh and tell the people that they need to obey me. Tell them to change their bad habits. Tell them that they shouldn't eat between meals. Tell them to brush their teeth. Tell them not to eat too much candy. Tell them to get to bed on time and to eat good food and to get plenty of exercise. . . .'"

Someday our children are going to be asked by a teacher, "Now children, what did God tell Jonah to tell the people living in Nineveh?"

Our children will be the first to raise their hands and they will innocently reply,

> Not to eat between meals
> To brush their teeth
> Not to eat candy
> To go to bed on time [etc.]

The shocked teacher will ask, "Who told you that?"
And they will proudly say, "Our daddy!"

Wednesday, May 7 / Collections

Children love to collect things: shells they find on the beach, bits of broken glass, rocks of all shapes and sizes, bottle caps, bubble-gum wrappers, trading cards. You name it and some kid is probably collecting it.

Today I took advantage of the children's natural desire to collect and suggested they start a plant collection. I gave them each a paper bag and challenged them to see how many different plants they could find in our yard. Kim would concentrate on tree leaves, Kari on flowers, and Kevin on weeds.

When they returned from their "treasure" hunt, I asked the girls to identify the different tree leaves and flowers. I asked Kevin just to count the number of different weeds he found. Then I brought out three old catalogs and showed the children how to press their plant collection.

In a couple weeks we will transfer their dried collections into photo albums with adhesive pages. Then as they find new leaves, flowers, or even weeds, they can add these to their books. In this way they can have concrete evidence of the new plants they are learning about. In addition, each will have a unique collection.

Thursday, May 8 / Educational Magic

A field trip to Lion Country Safari with a group of mothers from the Family Education Center was one of my rewards for teaching the weekly parent-education class at the center. For me it was like a vacation on Thursday—an almost unheard-of occurrence for a teacher-mother! Two large commercial buses transported us, and the center furnished all of the food. I had nothing to do but enjoy watching the animals and my children.

Today was filled with many firsts. First of all, my children had never ridden on a bus before. It was such a common thing when I was a child, and yet somehow circumstances during their lives have been such that they had been deprived of this educational experience until today. Second, the children had never been to Lion Country Safari before and had never seen wild animals, especially the lions, as close to the car as this, in what appeared like their natural habitat. Third, the children had never seen a magic show. Kim had learned a few clever tricks that seemed like magic, and so when I saw a magic show advertised I thought it might be fun to show the children what magicians do.

I was shocked when the magician chose Kari for one of the stunts. She is usually hesitant, but she marched right up on the stage and *believed* everything he said to her.

The idea of the stunt was to have her lie down on a platform, and then remove the supports to make it look as though she were suspended in air. This would have been fine, but he told her he was going to hypnotize her and started speaking in a low, eerie voice. He told her to lie down and close her eyes. To make it even worse, he said that electrical currents were now going through her body. I was petrified for her. She lay perfectly still. I overheard a number of comments from the audience such as, "Wow, is that little girl brave." She was fine until they removed one support. The platform became wobbly, and he kept telling her to close her eyes. She had had enough and so had I. She sat up, started to cry, and said, "I want my mommy." She then watched the stunt done with an older child so that she could see that nothing would have happened to her. But I realized that magic shows are far too advanced for young children, who have complete trust in adults and still believe every word they say. To them it is real. Even though I know it is sleight-of-hand, to them it is mysterious. The little tricks that a child can perform are interesting, but to bring in supernatural, scary things like electrical currents and hypnotism are entirely unnecessary. I would like to see educational magic shows where after every trick the magician would show the children how he did it and tell them how long he had to practice to be able to do things so quickly. But, of course, this would no longer be "magic."

I know that nursery schools try to take field trips regularly. I think I will try to work field trips into my schedule, too. Perhaps monthly I could take off on a weekday, pack a lunch, and just leave my "Things to Do" list behind. The children would not only gain valuable experiences, but also this would be a real break for a teacher-mother, too.

Friday, May 9 / Listening to God

I have been reading a lovely little book my neighbor gave me called *He Touched Me: Women Who Found God,** edited by Ted Miller. All of the stories have been interesting, but one in particular was a real help to me as a teacher-mother.

Every morning I pray for the Lord's guidance in helping me teach what I should to my children, so that they will grow up to have good characters and happy personalities, and find success in school. But it was not until I read the little story by Barbara Bekkering called "While I Listened in Prayer" that I realized I was doing all of the talking and asking of God, without taking much time really to listen to His answer.

I think the two texts presented with the story are especially good promises for every teacher-mother to claim of the Lord.

The first is found in Psalm 32:8 (NEB): "I will teach you, and guide you in the way you should go." The second is James 1:5 (RSV): "If any of you lacks wisdom, let him ask God who gives to all men generously and without reproaching, and it will be given him."

I know the Lord speaks to me in many ways, sometimes so directly that it seems almost as if I have heard a voice. At other times, it is in just a thought or an idea. But if my mind is constantly crowded with what to do next and how to get that done, and the program on TV and the children's quarreling and the dinner cooking, it must be difficult to interrupt. In fact, I think I have made it hard on the Lord to answer my prayers for wisdom in how and what to teach the children. The author of the story said that she took a blank sheet of paper and wrote down "I Asked God" on one side of the paper. Then on the opposite side, she wrote "God Asked

* Irvine, Calif.: Harvest House Publishers, 1975.

Me." She said that it wasn't hard to fill up immediately the things that she had asked God for, but she had a difficult time thinking about what the Lord had asked of her. She mentioned that she had fallen into the trap of expecting all of the privileges of Christianity while accepting very few of the responsibilities. After waiting in an attitude of prayer for these answers, a few simple ideas started coming to her mind like, "Call Mrs. Flintoff; write to Mark; clean busy corner." Then she says, "It became apparent that God had no great tasks for me. Instead, he wanted to become lovingly involved in my life, to bring harmony and order to my marriage, to bring my children to Himself."

As I read, I thought that what God asks me to do may seem like a little task, but co-operating with God in bringing harmony and order to our family life and leading my children to God should be my primary tasks. And when harmony and order come into my life, perhaps there will be more time to do the special activities that are so important to the children.

I have decided to start my own list of things that God has asked me to do, alongside my requests to God. It will take real determination and dedication to do this before I start my own daily "Things to Do" list. But I'm convinced it is a key to being a truly successful teacher-mother. I want to claim the promises as found in Psalm 32:8 and James 1:5.

Monday, May 12 / Meaningful and Messy

The idea of providing finger-painting experiences is not very appealing to most parents. Immediately the picture that comes to mind is messy paint, smeared from head to toe and from kitchen table to bathroom sink. And clay—ushy, gooshy clay. Is it really worth the bother and the clean-up?

Yes, both finger painting and clay are valuable sensory-motor experiences for preschoolers. Not only do children enjoy the cool, slimy, malleable consistency of these products, but also working with them promotes hand co-ordination and small-muscle development. For example, with finger painting, children can experience the freedom of large arm, hand, and finger movements and practice control without a lasting imprint of what they have done. One more swipe of the hand and the whole picture changes.

The manipulation of clay and other similar products (play dough) has been found to be one of the best ways to develop hand co-ordination and control. It's an excellent prewriting task! In addition, using these products does not have to be a messy experience. Here are some guidelines:

1. Work outside where you don't have to worry about spills and splatters.

2. If it is warm, let the child wear the minimum amount of clothing, and then just hose him off when he is finished. (Kevin's outside now in a pair of old underpants.) If it is cooler, have the child wear a plastic apron. If you don't have one, a large man's shirt with a piece of plastic tied underneath should work well. Be sure to button the shirt down the back for maximum coverage.

3. Spread a plastic dropcloth or old tablecloth over the area where the child will be working.

4. Have the child work in a defined area. A large cookie sheet or tray works well. Finger painting can be done directly on this surface. If you want a copy of the painting, a print can be taken by pressing the paper onto the painted surface. In fact, numerous prints can be taken during one finger-painting session.

5. When clean-up time comes, provide the child with warm, soapy water and a large sponge. I think Kevin enjoys clean-up time more than finger painting or clay modeling! He's been cleaning up for thirty minutes now!

A variety of products can be used for finger painting. Rather than purchasing expensive finger paint, I like to whip Ivory flakes into a whipped-cream consistency and add a little food coloring. Liquid starch colored with some tempera paint also works well. Most infants and toddlers get their first experience with finger painting by just getting their hands into the pudding!

Clay must be purchased at an art-supply store. To be effective it has to be the right consistency. If it is too dry, it is difficult to mold; if too wet, it is sloppy. When the clay gets dry, as it will if it sets out in the air too long, I have the children roll it into 2½-inch-diameter balls, make a thumb-size hole in the center part way down, and fill the hole with water. Place the clay balls in an air-tight container for 4 or 5 hours, or until you are ready to use them again.

If the children make a particularly nice clay product it is fun to have it fired, and keep it as a special memento. Most college art departments and some high schools have kilns. Often occupational therapy departments in large hospitals are equipped to do this. Or you may just advertise in the local paper. Most artists won't mind placing a few children's products in their kiln. If the products aren't glazed before firing, then afterward the children can paint these with acrylic paint and spray them with clear lacquer.

Now that I think about it, the children haven't worked with clay for some time. "Kim, Kari, and Kevin, get your shoes on and let's go shopping for some clay!"

Tuesday, May 13 / A Rooftop Experience

"Kim, Kari, and Kevin, come quickly," Jan shouted as he came through the door late this evening. "Hurry, I've got a surprise for you."

The children and I came running from the four corners of the house and followed Jan back outside. He led us to the ladder he had placed against the roof of the garage and said, "Quickly, climb the ladder and sit down on the roof."

I climbed up first, wondering what he was up to now. The children followed, equally curious. Then as we were all sitting quietly surrounded by the night sky, Jan pointed, "There; watch over there, and in a minute or two you will see my surprise." We watched and waited, and sure enough within a few minutes a beautiful huge silvery full moon crept up over the horizon and glided into full view.

We had watched the moon many times before—but never from this vantage point. Sitting on the roof with no distractions made it appear as if we could reach out and touch it. Jan had brought the binoculars along and we took turns looking at its mysterious surface. The moon seemed to be traveling so fast. Why? Jan and I tried to explain that what we were really observing was the earth moving. Yes, the moon did travel around the earth—but that took thirty days (one month) and not just twenty-four hours.

Then we turned our attention to the north, where we spotted the Big Dipper with the two pointer stars in the dipper part pointing to the North Star—the star that never moved. We told the children how sailors for thousands of years have used the North Star to direct them over the oceans and how all the other stars move in a yearly cycle. Twelve months would go by before we would see them in just exactly the same place as they were tonight.

"What if we didn't have any moon or stars at night?" Jan asked.

"Wow," said Kari, "it would be black, black."

"God knew his children needed the light of the moon to see at night and the stars to guide them and so he made them for us on the fourth day of creation," I commented.

"I'm glad God created the moon and the stars," said Kim.

"Me too," we all chorused.

After telling God how we felt, we climbed back down to our real world of teeth that needed to be brushed and toys that needed to be put away.

This was truly a preschool experience that could not be duplicated between 9:00 A.M. and 11:00 A.M. It was indeed a high point of the year—a rooftop experience.

Wednesday, May 14 / Look for the Silver Lining

I knew what had happened the minute I drove in the driveway and noticed that the patio and the stucco foundation completely around the house were wet. I dashed from the car, leaving the children behind. As I opened the kitchen door a stream of water gushed out. The floor was flooded with two inches of water, while more water was spurting from a broken pipe under the sink. Without stopping I splashed through the house and raced out the front door to turn off the main water valve. As I was coming back through the soaking house, shaking my head at the disaster, the children were just coming in the back door screaming with delight. "Hey, look at all the water! We've got a swimming pool in the kitchen."

They started splashing, giggling, and running through it as if they had never seen water before in their lives. I immediately told them to stop playing and get to work helping me get the water out. I handed each of them a broom, opened the doors, and told them to start sweeping it out. I thought it was work, but I've never seen them so eager to participate. We worked for over an hour until dry patches began appearing on the vinyl floor.

While I was thinking, "Thank goodness we got home when we did," they were saying, "Too bad there isn't more water." It will probably take me days to get things back in order. But for the children this was something that may not ever happen again (I hope), and they made sure they enjoyed it to the fullest. In fact, it may turn out to be the most memorable day of our preschool year!

Thursday, May 15 / Positive Reinforcement

Today I tried something new. I've been reading about the research findings on the Follow-through early-childhood education programs, which have been following different models of teaching to see how these differences in methods and materials affect the learning of children. One of the findings seemed to indicate that the programs that used positive reinforcement, such as tokens, produced high achievers. I'm all for high achievers, but I have never really been sold on what I considered "bribing" kids to learn. Today, I thought I'd give it a try. That is one of the nice things about being a teacher-mother. You can conduct your own informal research without having to write a grant proposal.

I made cards as usual, but this time I placed a number on the card that indicated how many pennies I would give the children if they completed the task before eleven o'clock. I gave them this time limit so I wouldn't go broke and they wouldn't dawdle. Kim was immediately interested. Kari wanted to play the game but she showed no particular enthusiasm. I read through the cards (I made a similar set for each child). Kim immediately selected those tasks that offered the largest financial reward, such as:

Practice piano for forty-five minutes (forty-five cents)
Learn to tell time (twenty cents)
Read a book (ten cents)

Kari didn't pay any attention to the amount of money she could earn, but selected those things that sounded like the most fun. She started out by choosing "Get dressed, comb hair, brush teeth (five cents)," because that was already partially done, and dressing was necessary before she could do her next task, "Pick roses for the vase (five cents)." She also chose "Listen to books (five cents)."

Some of the tasks that were not chosen were:

Make pictures (five cents)
Learn telephone number (five cents)
Learn address (five cents)
Do three pages of math book (five cents)
Fold clothes and put away (ten cents)
Clean closet (twenty cents)
Type ABC and name (five cents)

As soon as eleven o'clock came, Kim got my purse and wanted to be paid. Kari seemed indifferent. She was just as pleased with my hug as with the fifteen cents I handed her.

I showed Kim how to add up all the numbers, which was a terribly hard concept for her. After we figured out the total, I had her select eighty cents from my purse. Even though a few months ago we had worked with money values, and Kim was making change fairly well, she had forgotten how much quarters are worth and that two quarters make fifty cents and three make seventy-five cents. In order for facts to be meaningful and remembered, they must be used. Immediately Kim suggested that we get down the bank again and make change, as we had done before. She now felt the need for more knowledge about money.

My general feeling about using positive reinforcements to motivate children is that it is a good idea. But I don't believe that the reinforcement must always be a tangible reward such as money or gum. Depending upon the child, the task, and the circumstances, I find that a social reward, such as a smile, a kiss, or a word of praise works just as well.

I do realize that one day's experimentation with a tangible reward doesn't prove much. If I really wanted to teach the children something or to try to change their behavior, the reward would have to be consistently given over a period of time, until they were performing at the level I desired. I would have to select small goals and reward for little bits of achievement rather than choosing a long-range goal and waiting to reward the children when it was accomplished. I also realize that once behavior is changed and the child is doing or learning what he should, then intermittent rewards are better than consistent rewards.

There are a number of excellent books written about behavior modification, but the most practical one for me has been Gerald Patterson's and Elizabeth Gullion's book *Living with Children* (Champaign, Ill.: Research Press, 1973).

I won't continue paying the children for their preschool activities, but it was a pleasant change for today. It certainly proved that not every child will be instantly enchanted with this motivation technique.

Friday, May 16 / STAFF Meetings

Our preschool morning was interrupted when I received a telephone call informing me that an emergency staff meeting was being held at work, and if possible, I should try to attend. As I left the children at the baby-sitter's, Kim asked, "When can we go to staff meeting?"

Kim's question made me ponder. Every organization needs staff meetings in order to function smoothly. What about the family organization? Is this organization any different in this respect? Or is there an even greater need to plan together and talk together in the family organization than in other organizations? It just may be that we would have more smoothly operating families if we would regularly meet together to discuss our needs and plans. Perhaps what every family really needs is a STAFF meeting—that is, S-T-A-F-F, as in Steps To Active Family Fun.

Successful STAFF meetings must not only have everyone present (the whole family), but also they must be fun. And especially for young children, they must be active.

For most families a weekly STAFF meeting would be ideal—one night a week set aside for doing something together as a family when nothing would interfere. Saturday night is our STAFF meeting night. We always plan something special—even if it is just watching old family movies. Since our children are small, there is more active fun than real discussion, so Jan and I have our own supervisors' meeting after our active ones are in bed. We can then concentrate on our discussion without constant interruptions. We usually talk about what happened during the week and how we can plan better for the next. Any decisions are put into effect the following morning with a round-table discussion during breakfast. So far we haven't had any problems so large that they interfere with digestion, and everyone enjoys the stories that Jan tells to introduce the "lesson."

When our children are older and Saturday night becomes the night for their outside social events, we will change our STAFF meeting to another night. If we call our family night a STAFF meeting, it will be easier to say "no" to outsiders who attempt to infringe upon this time with committees and other meetings.

The next time Kim asks me when she can attend a staff meeting I'll say without hesitation, "Next Saturday night is the Kuzmas' STAFF meeting. I'll expect you there for some active family fun."

Monday, May 19 / Rocking

"Rock-a-bye baby in the treetop. . . ." Rocking the children at bedtime is something that I used to look forward to each evening. It was my time to relax from the hard day's work, and the children's time to enjoy the closeness and comfort of cuddling on my lap. And as I rocked I loved to sing the songs I knew as a child. When the girls were small, I would often have them both in my lap. As they got older and their room became overcrowded with toys, the rocking chair was moved to the living room, and bedtime rocking came only sporadically. Kevin was never one for much rocking and singing. He would say, "Mommy, don't sing. Read me a story." So I was surprised last night when Kevin asked me to rock him before going to bed. I said, "But there isn't a rocking chair in this room anymore."

That didn't discourage him. "There is a rocking chair in my old bedroom," he replied.

So I carried him and his blanket to the other room, and rocked him and sang all my old favorites, like, "How Much Is That Doggie in the Window?" "Doe a Deer," "Fox Went Out on a Chilly Night," "Hush Little Baby," and "Jesus Loves Me." We had a delightful time. I'm glad Kevin is not too old to ask me to rock him. I must remember to ask the girls if they wouldn't like a special rocking and singing time again, too. I would like that.

Tuesday, May 20 / Museum in the Making

Children love a surprise. Today on our way home, I thought I saw a few cars around the new county museum. It had been under construction for the past year. Now, seeing the cars in the parking lot, I wondered if the museum had opened and I had missed the announcement. I turned off the freeway, and sure enough their sign on the door read, "Open." That was the invitation we needed.

The museum was not officially opened as yet, so we were able to see all of the large stuffed animals before they were put behind glass. We were also privileged to see the museum workers decorating the scenes in which birds and animals would be placed. It is a rare experience to see a museum in the making. As we looked at all the exhibits, the children delighted in identifying the animals and birds with which they were acquainted. I was surprised how well the children did. It was a good field trip. Today I'll give myself an F for *Flexibility*.

Wednesday, May 21 / Songbooks

Years ago when I taught nursery school, I made some picture "songbooks" for the children so they would be able to tell what came next in the song. I'm glad I kept these "songbooks" because now my own children enjoy them.

"Hush Little Baby" was one song I illustrated. I started out on the first page with a picture of a baby, then continued with each item:

Hush little baby, don't say a word,
Mommy's going to buy you a mockingbird.
If that *mockingbird* won't sing . . .
If that *diamond ring* turns brass . . .
If that *looking glass* gets broke . . .
If that *billy goat* won't pull . . .
If that *cart and bull* fall over . . .
If that *dog* named Rover won't bark . . .
If that *horse and cart* fall down, you'll still be the sweetest *child* in
  town.

Even if the drawings are little stick drawings, or pictures out of a magazine, it makes little difference. The child can still "read" them.

Another song I illustrated was "Do-re-mi," from *The Sound of Music*. I drew the following:

Doe, a *deer*.
Ray, a drop of *sun*.
Me, a picture of a *person*.
Far, a long *road* with *someone running*.
Sew, a *needle*.
La, a *note*.
Tea, a *drink* in a teacup.

The selection of songs that can be illustrated like this is endless. What about "Old MacDonald Had a Farm," or "She'll Be Comin' Round the Mountain"?

Another thing that the children have enjoyed doing is finding and cutting out magazine pictures that remind them of a song they know and putting these together in a book to make their own "songbook." A lamb on page 3 may be for "Mary Had a Little Lamb," while the lamb on page 8 may be for "I Am Jesus' Little Lamb." I may not know the difference, but they do.

As they learn new songs, a record of these songs can be kept by putting the pictures in a three-hole notebook and adding each new picture of the song as it is learned. We keep the secular songs in one book and have a special book for worship songs.

Thursday, May 22 / The Zoo

I had an appointment in Los Angeles today. Why not combine this with a field trip for the children? After all, the appointment wouldn't take all day. I selected a few attractions that I felt would be appropriate and asked the children to vote. The zoo was chosen unanimously.

When we arrived, we took our time and did just what the children wanted to do. "Mommy, please can't we ride on the tram?" was their first request. It went around the perimeter of the zoo, and in our travels the children noticed some swings at one of the stops. They all shouted, "I want to swing." But we continued riding until it was announced that at the next stop we would see a three-week-old African elephant. After watching the tiniest elephant I had ever seen, I asked the children what they wanted to see next. "We want to swing," came the reply. So that's where we headed—even though we have the same attraction in our own backyard!

Later, as we walked through the zoo, I was amazed at how many animals my children knew and how many animals I didn't know. I wish we lived close enough to go back weekly. Then we could feel that we didn't need to see the whole zoo at once, but could concentrate on a few animals and watch them and talk about them and then come home to the library and read about them.

It was the animal family groups that seemed to interest the children the most. The lesser pandas never came out of their hole in the log while we were there because a sign explained that Mommy and Daddy Lesser Panda were expecting a family at any moment. This really intrigued the children. Because of this they spent extra time looking at the lesser pandas' picture and learning about their habits.

There was a family of Egyptian geese that were also interesting. They were in an open pen with the tapirs when we arrived on the scene. (This was apparently the wrong place for the geese to be.) As the seven little goslings were nonchalantly walking and swimming, the goose and the gander were hissing and honking, running to the goslings and then to the edge of the pen. Finally we noticed that two peacocks had just hopped over the fence and were walking up the steep slope of the pen. Every time they stopped and looked around, the parent geese started honking. Then, as the peacocks disappeared behind some of the shrubbery, they would go back to their goslings. They were doing a splendid job of protecting their family. In the middle of all this, the zookeepers came and tried to get the geese to move toward the back of the pen, where they had a box to transport them elsewhere. We watched as they led the geese to where they wanted them to be by dropping a path of lettuce right into the box, rather than by having to force them. Later we saw the family swimming in the large zebra pen—minus zebras and peacocks.

Mother Grizzly Bear and her two cubs reminded me of a human family. One cub was confident and fearless. We came when he was down in the bottom of a steep trough surrounding the pen. He scampered up a ladder to the top and seemed to urge his brother to follow him down. Brave One went down again. His brother, Scared One, went cautiously down one rung, then even more cautiously turned around so as not to fall, and went back up again. He then sat down and just watched his brother, Brave One, run around the bottom. Finally Mother (with Scared One following) started down the steep incline. Scared One took a few steps and then turned back. Mother went on down and grunted to Scared One a few times, but he just sat up on top and cried. As Mother and Brave One ran around the trough of the pen below, Scared One ran along the top, looking down. He made a few attempts at following, but always turned back. Finally Mother came back up the ladder, nudged Scared One, and walked off toward her den. Scared One ran right beside her, never leaving her side. A few minutes later, Brave One scampered up the ladder with no effort at all, ran to the den, immediately ran out again, and started down the ladder. We reluctantly moved on, but I left with a greater appreciation for the way that the mother bear treated her children. She allowed Brave One to do his thing. She saw that Scared One wanted to do it, too. So she showed him how, but she didn't push. And when he still wouldn't come down, she came back and joined him, without a reprimand.

As we were leaving the zoo, I asked the children what they liked best. I was almost afraid the swings would get their vote, but it was the myna bird that talked to them. Any animal that says, "Hi, Walter," "Hello," "How are you?" and can give an ear-catching wolf whistle would be a favorite of all.

The children now have some good really-truly animal stories with which to entertain their daddy and their friends. The children also have some firsthand experiences that should be good subject matter for dictating stories and drawing animal pictures.

Experiencing the zoo through a book, film, or other medium is a good preschool activity, but it can never take the place of the real thing.

Friday, May 23 / Techniques for Practicing

I have tried so many techniques to get the girls to practice the piano that I could write a book on the subject. A few weeks ago I tried a goal device that I thought would teach fractions at the same time that it would motivate the children to practice. I divided their practice sessions into fifteen-minute sessions and explained that for every fifteen minutes they practiced they could color in a quarter of a pie. I drew seven pies on a piece of paper for each day of the week, and one for any extra time the children practiced over the sixty minutes per day (wishful thinking). Kari wasn't impressed with my efforts and said she didn't want to play the game. Kim kept it up for a week, but I constantly had to remind her to practice.

Tuesday	Wednesday	Thursday	Friday
⊕	⊕	⊕	⊕
Saturday	Sunday	Monday	Extra
⊕	⊕	⊕	⊕

For weeks now Kim has been imploring me to buy her a Barbie swimming pool and town house. I think it is silly to waste all of that money on something a child can improvise. So I have said, "NO." A week ago, after a very trying day of saying every few minutes, "You need to practice," I said, "OK, Kim. You win. I am not going to buy these Barbie doll things for you, but you can earn the money yourself to buy them if you really want them badly enough. I will pay you one penny for every minute you practice. But for every minute you don't practice up to sixty minutes a day I will take away one-half penny." (I wanted to take away a whole penny, but I knew she would be in the hole before she ever got started.) I continued, "But you have to practice without my telling you to practice, and your practicing must be done by 7:00 P.M."

"OK," she chirped as she sat down, set the timer, and practiced sixty minutes in one stretch without another word from me. It has been seven days now ($4.20 worth), and Kim has progressed to a point where the notes are coming easier. Practicing is becoming fun as she sees herself able to learn the pieces faster. At this rate I will either be broke in a few weeks or she will realize that practicing can be fun in itself, whether you are paid to do it or not.

With Kari, I'm still searching. Perhaps she is too young. I think in a year or two she will see much more value in practicing. And when she is older, she will be able to learn much more quickly. Then practicing will have its own reward.

A parent cannot continue to pay a child to practice all his life.

The best reward is when it is intrinsic, when the reward is in the satisfaction and fun of learning. But if payments can help establish the habit, then they are well worth it.

Monday, May 26 / Spring Cleaning

These were the preschool activity cards for today (see illustration).

These activities may sound more like a maid's list than preschool, but there are many things a child can learn from practical work experiences. For example:

1. The materials you need to wash windows or polish piano keys.
2. How to dust without spreading the dust around the room.
3. The importance of order when it comes to finding lost library books.
4. Sorting skills, from organizing silverware to socks.

The girls found the greatest challenge in pasting the redemption stamps in the books. First they had to sort the different types of stamps; then determine the value of the stamps; finally run a wet sponge over the stamps and carefully place them on the appropriate page.

As a reward for their labors, I took the children to the redemption center to redeem the stamps. They went through the store selecting items that sold for less than the number of books we had. Finally, after much discussion, they selected a clock radio. They reasoned that if Kim were going to start real school next year she would need an alarm. Kevin thought the dump truck looked much more attractive, but the girls argued, "Why should he get a dump truck when we did most of the work?" I agreed that their reasoning sounded fair, much to Kevin's displeasure, and the purchase of the clock radio was made.

My experience with motivating the children to do household cleaning tasks has taught me the following:

1. The children enjoy tasks with a challenge. For example, past-

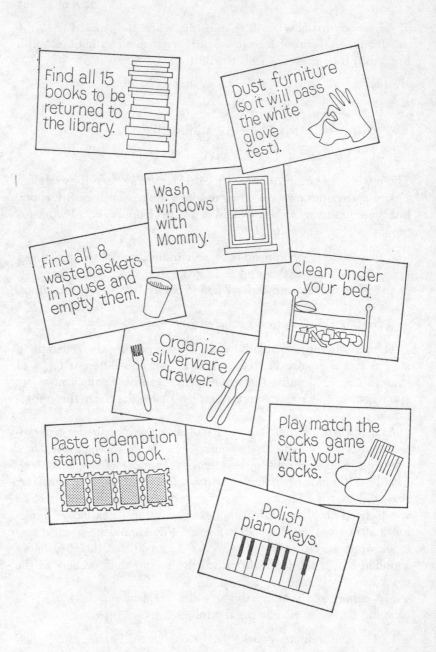

ing in the stamps and washing windows were tasks that were more fun than emptying wastebaskets.

2. Working together with a parent is more enjoyable than working alone. "Mommy, you do it with us," is their constant request.

3. It helps to make a game out of the activity. For example, "You start polishing the piano keys at the bottom and I'll start at the top and let's see where we meet."

4. An occasional reward for their labors serves as an effective incentive. The clock radio would still be in the store if they had not helped me organize the stamps.

Spring cleaning can be an important part of preschool. The challenge of a teacher-mother is to build a challenge into the common tasks and to find the not-so-common tasks with a built-in challenge. In this way the children will enjoy learning how to apply their skills to useful labor.

Tuesday, May 27 / Oma and Opa Go Home

Oma has been steadily improving during these past few weeks, and can now get around fairly easily in her wheelchair. So after a family council it was decided that she was ready to move back to her own house.

It has been a couple days now since they have gone. The house seems strangely empty. No longer are the children entertained by Opa's harmonica or Oma's stories about when their daddy was a little boy.

For preschool today we decided to bake cookies, wrap them in a pretty package, and go visit Oma and Opa. The children were greeted with open arms. As Opa was hugging Kari, he said, "How's my little sweetheart?"

Kevin immediately came running up to him and said, "Here is your other little sweetheart."

I'm glad grandparents have an abundance of time and love for their grandchildren. Kim, Kari, and Kevin never seem to tire of receiving their attention.

Although Oma and Opa didn't take part in the organized pre-school program for the children, their stay in our home was an important part of our children's education. It was an extracurricular activity that allowed them to practice such character traits as responsibility, kindness, and tolerance.

The rewards of having Oma and Opa in our home far outweighed the inconvenience.

Wednesday, May 28 / Harvest Time

It's harvest time. MMMMMmmmmmmmm—fresh peas right out of our garden . . . and lettuce, radishes, turnips, baby beets, and more. What a treat for the children to pick the fruits (vegetables) of their labor, wash them off with the hose, and eat them only minutes from picking time.

Raw peas are a delicacy, but so are the pods (even the type where the pod is not meant to be eaten). Just bend the half piece of pod back until it cracks. Peal off the thin layer of skin and take a bite. It's delicious. The children even enjoy raw beets and turnips more than cooked ones.

Planting a greenhouse garden has been a good learning activity for the children. But I'll be the first to admit that I was probably the one who learned the most.

With preschool days almost over for this year, I'm looking forward to a special harvest of memories in the years to come as I think back on the days when I was a teacher-mother.

Thursday, May 29 / Evaluation

Our preschool year is almost over, and now that the end has come I feel as unprepared as I felt at the beginning.

Was being a teacher-mother in our home preschool worth it?

What did I learn?

Have I accomplished what I wanted to accomplish with the children this year?

"Yes, lots, and no," would have to be my answers to these questions.

First of all, *yes*, it was worthwhile spending the year being a teacher-mother to my children in our home preschool. The children not only gained from the experiences that we enjoyed together, but also it was a learning experience for Jan and myself. Here are some of the reasons why I would recommend this project to other parents:

1. It's fun. By looking at my motherly role as a teaching job, I didn't feel that it was a waste of time to be playing with the children, or taking care of them, or cleaning up after them. I didn't have any guilt feelings when I was (what some would call) wasting my time with them. In fact, I have found that spending time with the children when they are happy and interested in learning is one of the most enjoyable things I have done. And being close to them is one of the main ingredients for keeping them happy and interested in learning.

2. It's a once-in-a-lifetime treat. The children are only preschoolers once. Often I hear grandparents lamenting over the fact that they wished they would have had as much fun with their own children as they have with their grandchildren. This doesn't have to be the case if parents start now to think of this aspect of their lives as a once-in-a-lifetime opportunity. Being parents of preschoolers is a busy task, but why not enjoy it while it is happening?

3. The children loved it. The children enjoy having anyone spend time with them, but I have found that they enjoy Jan and me most of all. They looked forward to the daily preschool activities and complained when I neglected to plan something for them. I even enjoyed their occasional reminder, "Mommy, you haven't played with us all day," because I know it was their way of saying that they enjoyed spending time with me.

4. The children were given a variety of experiences that they would not have had otherwise. And because of these experiences they learned more than they would have ordinarily learned.

5. The children learned. I could see a daily improvement in them. Since I knew what I was teaching them, I could follow up on these experiences as we traveled in the car, or wherever we were, taking advantage of situations that otherwise may have passed without comment.

6. *I took advantage of every situation to teach,* since teaching was my primary responsibility.

7. *The children came first.* I found that I screened my appointments and outside commitments very closely so that as much as possible those responsibilities that I did accept could complement my job as teacher-mother. By putting the children first, I found it easier to either say "no" to others, or to include the children in my other activities.

8. *The house was better organized for children's activities.* It was their classroom, rather than my showpiece!

9. *Preschool brought our family closer together.* We planned together as well as played together.

10. *Evaluation became a part of our everyday life.* I evaluated myself more often as a mother, and as a teacher, than I ordinarily would do. Jan and I evaluated the program we were offering the children, as well as evaluating the children's performance. This evaluation, even though informal, was important in determining the activities planned for the children, and our methods of teaching.

What did I learn? If I were asked on a final examination to list what I learned this year about children and about parents, these are the items my lists would contain.

What did I learn about *children?*

1. *Each child is a unique individual.* I must accept my children as they are and work with each one's strengths and interests. Strong attempts to change a child only meet with resistance.

2. *Children have their own developmental timetables.* Spurts of development may be sparked by preschool experiences, but development and learning can't be forced.

3. *Children need and want direction.* They want to learn how to do new things: how to put the Tinker Toys together; how to knit; how to tie their shoes. Without parental guidance the children are handicapped and often feel neglected.

4. *Children need and want free time.* They need time to practice by themselves what they have learned about the world. A constant

round of planned activities is really detrimental to their development.

5. *Children enjoy spending time alone with a parent.* Bedtime talks and stories are examples of quality time together—even though they don't cost anything but time.

6. *Children need to be appreciated.* They are eager to please and to help when they are rewarded with appreciation.

7. *Children need encouragement.* They need to know that their parents have faith in them. Encouraging a child to do his best gets far better results than reprimanding.

8. *Children need a routine and a break in a routine.* An orderly environment allows a child to feel safe and secure enough to enjoy a change.

9. *Children need consistent standards.* They want to know what is right and wrong, what is good and bad, so they can internalize standards on which they can begin making choices, rather than guessing through life.

10. *Children need practice in making decisions* and experiencing the consequences of those decisions, while parents are still around to counsel and cushion the falls.

11. *Children need association with other children.* But during the preschool years, the more is not the merrier. Associations need to be limited and supervised. Through these associations, children need to learn to respect the rights of others, how to win friends, and how to keep them by learning to get along with them.

12. *Children need our love* most of all, and the best expression of that love is in spending good-quality time together with them. It is through spending time with them that Jan and I can influence them in subtle ways about our values, attitudes, and habits. And if they know that we willingly and joyfully spend our time with them, then they know that they are loved. This knowledge—that they are loved and valued—helps a child feel good about who he is.

What I learned about *parents.*

1. *Parents need more time to be parents.* If we as parents don't make the commitment to be teachers and principals to our children and schedule time to be with our children, it is very easy for other duties and other roles to interfere with the time we should be spending with them.

2. *Parents must make a commitment to spend time daily with their children,* talking, listening, learning, and exploring, or these things often don't get done.

3. *Parents must spend time observing* and getting to know their child, finding reasons for behavior and not just trying to treat symptoms.

4. *Parents need time to be alone . . . with each other.* A yearly "second honeymoon" is in-service education!

5. *Parents need to set goals for their children.* Then the parents need to plan how they are going to achieve those goals, and discuss the results.

6. *Parents need preparation not only for childbirth, but, more importantly, for child-rearing.* No matter how many courses I take, no matter how many books I read, I always learn something new, which helps me to be a better parent.

7. *Parents need to clarify their value systems* to determine what they feel is important to teach children.

8. *Parents need to work together.* Two teachers are better than one—but only if they agree and are supportive of each other.

9. *Parents must have patience*—tons of it.

10. *Parents must be good examples.* Children do what we do, not necessarily what we say.

11. *Parents need to remember how they felt as children* and treat their children accordingly.

12. *Parents need divine guidance.* This task is far too complex and important to try it alone.

As I sort through the children's activity cards, I am impressed with the variety of things they did this year, but my mind is spinning with other things they need to learn. This year was just a beginning. Education is a continuous process throughout life.

In order to evaluate the children's knowledge in a variety of areas, I have been quizzing them informally as we ride in the car or go about our practical duties. I must admit that although I am sometimes surprised at their knowledge, I am more often surprised at their lack of it.

Some of what seems to be a lack of knowledge may actually be the difficulty that preschool children have in finding words to express what they know. Children must be given practice in expressing themselves, and one way this can be done is by asking questions in the form of a story. For example:

"Once upon a time there was a little girl whose name was Kari. She was walking down the street and all at once she realized that she was lost. A policeman came by and he asked the girl if he could help her. What would you say, Kari?"

"Yes, I'm lost," Kari replied.

"What is your name?" I continued. "And your last name? How do you spell that?" Then I continued to ask her for her phone number, her address, and the names of her father and mother.

Evaluations of preschool children do not have to be the pencil-and-paper variety, but can be conducted informally wherever the parent and child are together. Evaluations can be a game.

Tonight after the children are sleeping, I must look over the curriculum outline I wrote down at the beginning of the year (see September 6), the character-development curriculum (January 1 and March 31), and the knowledge inventory (February 17 to 21) to see just how much we did accomplish. And then, based upon this evaluation, I must begin planning the activities for summer school.

Friday, May 30 / Renewing the Commitment

This is the end. Preschool is over for this school year; at least it is over on paper. But as with all graduations, it is really just the beginning.

I prepared "diplomas" the children could hang on their bulletin boards or keep in their scrapbooks to help them always remember our special year together when I said "yes" to their earnest request, "Mommy, you teach us." (See illustration.)

Jan and I presented these to the children at a special graduation (family only) celebration. Each child made a "speech" about what he learned during preschool time, or what he liked best about preschool. The principal said a few words of commendation and then handed them their diplomas tied with a ribbon. We shook hands,

GRADUATION DIPLOMA

_____
(name)

has successfully completed
one year of preschool at the
KUZMA FAMILY SCHOOL

Date: _____
Teacher: _____
Principal: _____

hugged, and kissed, and then to truly celebrate, went out for fresh strawberry pie!

For a teacher-teacher, graduation means saying good-bye to his students and looking forward to a few weeks or perhaps months of vacation before taking on the commitment of another group of students. But for a teacher-mother, the end and the beginning merge. There is no vacation. Each day is an opportunity to open new wonders and insights to one's own children—the most important students in the world. And no one can afford to stop to rest—the product is too valuable.

With JUNE's sun shining
On growing preschool children,
Summer calls — "The End"

———————❖———————

Appendix A

Books for Parents

Every year new books are published that are helpful to parents in better understanding, disciplining, and planning activities for their young children. Often a list of recommended books is no sooner in print than it is out of date. But as I glance through my library, there are some books I feel are a must for parents no matter what the publication date may be. I have been selective, and offer you only my favorites.

To keep up with the latest publications for parents, I would recommend that you periodically browse through the books on the parents' shelf at a large bookstore. This is the way I find out what is new and decide whether I want to invest in it. If the book looks good, but I still can't make up my mind, I call the local library. If they don't have the book, I request that they order it. They are always very willing to do so, and they call me as soon as the book has been received. Then I have a chance to read the book before deciding whether it is worth investing my own money to have the book on my shelf.

So after much sifting and sorting, this is my list.

Books for General Child-rearing

Arnstein, Helene S. *What to Tell Your Child*. Westport, Conn.: Condor Publishing Company, 1978. An excellent guide for answering children's difficult questions about birth, death, illness, divorce, and other family crises.

Baker, Pat A. *Mom, Take Time*. Grand Rapids, Mich.: Baker Book House, 1976. A Bible-based, excellent guide for child-rearing.

Bock, Lois, and Working, Miji. *Happiness Is a Family Time Together*. Old Tappan, N.J.: Fleming H. Revell Company, 1978. Gives ideas on having a special time of family togetherness to help teach self-worth, God's love, growth, family background, the family in the outside world, future plans, etc.

Braga, Joseph and Laurie. *Growing with Children*. Englewood Cliffs, N.J.: Prentice-Hall, 1974. Excellent book for a developmental understanding of infants and preschool children and how to help them develop a good self-concept. Various sections are written by experts in their field. Research based with good referencing.

Briggs, Dorothy Corkville. *Your Child's Self-esteem*. Garden City, N.Y.: Doubleday & Company, Inc., 1975. The author places self-esteem at the center of all growth and behavior. Excellent ideas and well written.

Campbell, Ross. *How to Really Love Your Child*. Wheaton, Ill.: Victor Books, 1977. An excellent book on how to show your child love through eye contact, physical contact, and focused attention. Also how to discipline with love. Easy reading and very practical for Christian families.

Chess, Stella, M.D.; Thomas, Alexander, M.D.; and Birch, Herbert G., M.D., Ph.D. *Your Child Is a Person*. New York: Penguin Books, 1977. A guide for understanding individual differences from birth through first grade.

Dobson, James. *Dare to Discipline*. Wheaton, Ill.: Tyndale House, 1970. Fun reading and practical advice is given on the topic of discipline. The primary thesis is that parents should not be afraid to spank when the child defies parental authority.

———. *Hide or Seek*. Old Tappan, N.J.: Fleming H. Revell Company, 1974. Exposes the false value system of our society and presents ten comprehensive strategies through which parents and teachers can cultivate self-esteem in every child. A must for every parent of a preteen-ager to understand those adolescent years. During the preschool years is not too soon to start!

———. *The Strong-willed Child*. Wheaton, Ill.: Tyndale House, 1978. Excellent guide, but do read the whole book and understand carefully when to apply this method.

Dodson, Fitzhugh. *How to Discipline with Love*. New York: Rawson Associates, 1977. A wide variety of disciplinary methods related to different ages. The most complete book on discipline I've ever read.

———. *How to Father*. New York: Nash Publishing Corporation, 1974. Excellent guide for fathers with children from birth to adolescence. Excellent appendices.

———. *How to Parent*. New York: New American Library, 1973. Excellent age-related guidelines for children from birth to six years of age. Excellent appendix on educational materials.

Dreikurs, Rudolf. *Children: The Challenge*. New York: Hawthorn Books, 1964. Strong on natural and logical consequences. Rudolf Dreikurs's understanding of children and why they behave as they do is outstanding.

Drescher, John M. *If I Were Starting My Family Again.* Nashville, Tenn.: Abingdon Press, 1979. A beautiful Christian view of the ideal parent. A must for enjoyable reading and for setting new ideals.

Fraiberg, Selma H. *The Magic Years.* New York: Charles Scribner's Sons, 1968. A classic book for understanding children's behavior and problems at different ages.

Freed, Alvyn and Margaret. *The New T.A. for Kids.* Sacramento, Calif.: Jalmar Press, 1977. A follow-up book for *T.A. for Tots,* or can be used by itself for late preschoolers and school-age children.

Freed, Alvyn M., Ph.D. *T.A. for Tots and Other Prinzes.* Sacramento, Calif.: Jalmar Press, 1978. Transactional analysis in words and pictures that preschoolers can understand. Clever—beautifully done.

Ginott, Haim G. *Between Parent and Child.* New York: Avon Books, 1973. This is a gem. It is easy reading and gives helpful hints on how parents and children can talk together to solve problems.

Gordon, Dr. Thomas. *P.E.T.: Parent Effectiveness Training.* New York: New American Library, 1975. Explains a no-lose method of discipline for children who verbalize well. A technique every parent should master.

———. *P.E.T. in Action.* New York: Wyden Books, 1976. An excellent follow-up on *P.E.T.*

James, Muriel. *Transactional Analysis for Moms and Dads.* Menlo Park, Calif.: Addison-Wesley, 1975. T.A. principles and how to apply them to specific situations. It gives good suggestions on how to get in touch with your feelings and your children's feelings, ways to give positive strokes, how to change recurring negative behavior, and ways to promote better feelings within families.

Kelly, Marguerite, and Parsons, Elia. *The Mother's Almanac.* Garden City, New York: Doubleday & Company, Inc., 1975. The discriptions on the cover say it well. "The most complete book ever written on loving and living with small children. Everything from discipline and independence to cooking, crafts, and other activities."

Kuzma, Kay. *Understanding Children.* Mountain View, Calif.: Pacific Press, 1978. A guide to understanding children's needs, individual characteristics, emotions, discipline, and self-worth. The book is accompanied by a Bible-based study guide and ten cassette tapes of the Understanding Children seminar.

———. *Child Study Through Observation and Participation.* San Francisco, Calif.: R & E Research Associates, 1978. Developmental psychology (from prenatal development through adolescence) made easy. Includes observation and participation forms and a variety of activities to use for preschool children.

———. *Prime-time Parenting*. New York: Rawson, Wade Publishers, 1980. A book primarily geared to working parents about how they can get more out of the time they spend with their children.

Kuzma, Kay and Jan. *Building Character*. Mountain View, Calif.: Pacific Press, 1979. The importance of and methods that can be used in developing character traits in children. Includes the complete character curriculum the Kuzmas used with their children.

MacDonald, Gordon. *The Effective Father*. Wheaton, Ill.: Tyndale House, 1977. An excellent, Christian approach for fathers (and mothers).

Patterson, Gerald R., and Gullion, M. Elizabeth. *Living with Children*. Champaign, Ill.: Research Press, 1976. This is a programmed instruction booklet on behavior modification. For problem behavior this is excellent.

Rockness, Miriam Huffman. *Keep These Things—Ponder Them in Your Heart*. Garden City, N.Y.: Doubleday & Company, Inc., 1979. A beautiful diary-type book on the joys and difficulties of a Christian mother with three small children.

Satir, Virginia. *Peoplemaking*. Palo Alto, Calif.: Science and Behavior Books, 1972. A well-known family therapist gives her unique philosophy of parenting. Interesting and thought-provoking.

Schaefer, Charles, Ph.D. *How to Influence Children*. New York: Van Nostrand Reinhold Company, 1978. Excellent discussion of three basic areas: discipline, guidance, and building positive relationships. The most complete book on specific suggestions I've seen.

Shedd, Charlie. *You Can Be a Great Parent*. Waco, Tex.: Word Books, 1970. A pastor's humorous, compassionate, retrospective view of the successful rearing of four children. Could be summed up with this quote: "You can do almost anything with a child if you love him enough." Deals in the broad principles of: (1) self-government; (2) lessons in how to love (self, others, and God); and (3) the dignity of work. Contains a good discussion of "plus marks," an interesting alternative to spankings!

Simon, Sidney B., and Olds, Sally Wendkos. *Helping Your Child Learn Right from Wrong*. New York: Simon and Schuster, 1976. A values-clarification approach to use with children. Many excellent strategies.

Strauss, Richard. *Confident Children and How They Grow*. Wheaton, Ill.: Tyndale House, 1975. This book seeks to show parents that the Bible does contain principles that will enable them to rear their children successfully. The reading is very light and the applications that he suggests are practical.

Sutton-Smith, Brian and Shirley. *How to Play with Your Children*. New

York: Hawthorn Books, 1974. Suggestions are offered for ways in which parents can stimulate creative and meaningful play in children who are at various stages of development. Very practical appendix of children's skills and appropriate games.

Books for Preschool Activities

Beck, Joan. *How to Raise a Brighter Child.* New York: Simon and Schuster, 1967.

Braga, Joseph and Laurie. *Children and Adult: Activities for Growing Together.* Englewood Cliffs, N.J.: Prentice-Hall, 1978.

Cahoon, Owen. *A Teacher's Guide to Cognitive Tasks for Preschool.* Provo, Ut.: Brigham Young University Press, 1975. Piagetian tasks with easy directions for parents and teachers.

Croft, Doreen J., and Hess, Robert D. *An Activities Handbook for Teachers of Young Children,* 2nd ed. Boston, Mass.: Houghton Mifflin Company, 1975. Ideas that can be easily adapted to the home.

Engelmann, Siegfried and Therese. *Give Your Child a Superior Mind.* New York: Simon and Schuster, 1966. This program is a little too rigid for me, but I did get some good ideas out of it.

Gordon, Ira J. *Baby Learning Through Baby Play.* New York: St. Martin's Press, 1970. Pictorial guide of play activities for the first two years.

———. *Child Learning Through Child Play.* New York: St. Martin's Press, 1972. Learning activities for the preschooler.

Gregg, Elizabeth M. *What to Do When "There's Nothing to Do."* New York: Dell Publishing Company, 1970. Age-related activities for children.

Marzollo, Jean, and Lloyd, Janice. *Learning Through Play.* New York: Harper & Row, 1972. Excellent.

Matterson, E. M. *Play and Playthings for the Preschool Child.* New York: Penguin Books, 1965. Best inexpensive guide that I have found.

Painter, Genevieve. *Teach Your Baby.* New York: Simon and Schuster, 1971. Activities for children during the first three years.

Prudden, Bonnie. *How to Keep Your Child Fit from Birth to Six.* New York: Harper & Row, 1964. Exercises for children.

Sharp, Evelyn. *Thinking Is Child's Play.* New York: Avon Books, 1970. Activities to stimulate thinking.

Shuttlesworth, Dorothy Edwards. *Exploring Nature with Your Child.*

New York: Harry N. Abrams, 1978. A must for the parent interested in nature.
Taylor, Barbara J. *A Child Goes Forth.* Provo, Ut.: Brigham Young Uni-
versity Press, 1972. Excellent curriculum guide for parents and
teachers of preschool children.
———. *When I Do, I Learn.* Provo, Ut.: Brigham Young University Press,
1974. Simple-to-apply ideas for group or home use.
Walker, Georgiana (ed.). *The Celebration Book.* Glendale, Calif.: Regal
Books div. of G/L Publications, 1977. Fun things to do with your
family all year-round.
Worthington, Robin. *Enjoying Your Preschooler.* Mountain View, Calif.:
Pacific Press, 1973. A lot of ideas for less than a dollar.

Appendix B

Books for Children

This list of books is not a comprehensive list, but it is a list of the books my children have enjoyed the most. The list is divided into two sections. The first section is alphabetized by authors who I think have written a number of excellent books. (Once I have found an author I like, I find I enjoy reading all of his books.) The second section is of books I have listed under different categories. These are books written by an author I am less well acquainted with or who may have written only one or two books.

I have placed an asterisk beside the names of those authors or the titles of those books that are especially good for the youngest preschooler.

My Favorite Authors of Children's Books

Alexander, Martha
Anderson, Clarence Williams
Balian, Lorna
Brown, Margaret Wise*
Burningham, John
Burton, Virginia Lee
Cameron, Polly
Carle, Eric
Carroll, Ruth*
Delton, Judy
Dennis, Wesley
De Paola, Tomie
Flack, Marjorie*
Freeman, Don
Gag, Wanda
Ginsburg, Mirra
Graham, Margaret Bloy
Hoben, Russell
Hutchins, Pat
Keats, Ezra Jack*
Krauss, Ruth*

Lenski, Lois*
Lindman, Maj
Lionni, Leo
Lobel, Arnold
McCloskey, Robert
Marshall, James
Miles, Miska
Palmer, Helen
Peet, Bill
Politi, Leo
Scarry, Richard
Sendak, Maurice
Spier, Peter
Tresselt, Alvin
Viorst, Judith
Wildsmith, Brian*
Wright, Dare
Yashima, Taro
Zion, Gene
Zolotow, Charlotte

Children's Books Listed by Categories

(Books of authors in previous list are not mentioned here)

Animal Stories

Asch, Frank. *Monkey Face.* New York: Parents' Magazine Press, 1977.

Conford, Ellen. *The Impossible Possum.* Boston, Mass.: Little, Brown & Company, 1971.

Dugdale, Vera. *Album of North American Birds.* New York: Random House, 1967 (information for adults to tell children).

Freschet, Berniece. *Bear Mouse.* New York: Charles Scribner's Sons, 1973.

Gackenbach, Dick. *The Pig Who Saw Everything.* New York: Seabury Press, 1978.

Garelick, May. *What's Inside? The Story of An Egg That Hatched.* New York: Scholastic Book Services, 1970.

Gay, Zhenya. *Small One.* New York: Viking Press, 1958.

Grabranski, Janusz. *Grabranski's Birds.* New York: Franklin Watts, 1968.

———. *Grabranski's Cats.* New York: Franklin Watts, 1967.

Hazen, Barbara Shook. *Animal Daddies and My Daddy.* New York: Western Publishing Company, 1976.*

Kwitz, Mary D. *Rabbit's Search for a Little House.* New York: Crown Publishers, 1977.

Newberry, Clare Turlay. *April's Kittens.* New York: Harper & Brothers, 1940.

Preston, Edna. *Squawk to the Moon, Little Goose.* New York: Viking Press, 1974.

Provensen, Alice and Martin. *Our Friends at Maple Hill Farm.* New York: Random House, 1974.

Rabinowitz, Sandy. *The Red Horse and the Bluebird.* New York: Harper & Row, 1975.

Waber, Bernard. *Rich Cat, Poor Cat.* New York: Scholastic Book Services, 1970.

Ward, Lynd. *The Biggest Bear.* Boston, Mass.: Houghton Mifflin Company, 1952.

Williams, Barbara. *Albert's Toothache.* New York: E. P. Dutton, 1974.

Williams, Jay. *Pettifur.* New York: Scholastic Book Services, 1977.

Bible and Character-building Stories

The Children's Bible. New York: Golden Press, 1965.

Degering, Etta B. *My Bible Friends* (ten vols.). Washington, D.C.: Review and Herald Publishing Association, 1964.

Egermeier, Elsie E. *Egermeier's Favorite Bible Stories*. Anderson, Ind.: Warner Press, 1965.

Jahsmann, Allan Hart, and Simon, Martin P. *Little Visits with God*. St. Louis, Mo.: Concordia Publishing House, 1957.

———. *More Little Visits with God*. St. Louis, Mo.: Concordia Publishing House, 1966.

Kuzma, Kay. *The Kim, Kari, and Kevin Storybook*. Mountain View, Calif.: Pacific Press, 1979.

Ladder of Life. Washington, D.C.: Review and Herald Publishing Association, 1977 (eight books of stories for preschoolers on faith, virtue, knowledge, temperance, patience, godliness, brotherly kindness and love, and a teacher's guide).

Maxwell, Arthur. *Uncle Arthur's Bedtime Stories*. Washington, D.C.: Review and Herald Publishing Association, 1964.

Mueller, A. C. *My Good Shepherd Bible Story Book*. St. Louis, Mo.: Concordia Publishing House, 1969.

Taylor, Kenneth N. *Taylor's Bible Story Book*. Wheaton, Ill.: Tyndale House, 1976.

Books Without Words

Mayer, Mercer. *A Boy, a Dog, and a Frog*. New York: Dial Press, 1967.*

———. *Ah-choo*. New York: Dell Publishing Company, 1976.*

———. *Bubble, Bubble*. New York: Parents' Magazine Press, 1973.*

———. *The Great Cat Chase*. New York: Scholastic Book Services, 1975.*

Children and People Stories

Adamson, Gareth. *Harold the Happy Handyman*. New York: Harvey House, 1968.

Allard, Harry. *Miss Nelson Is Missing*. Boston, Mass.: Houghton Mifflin Company, 1977.

Bemelmans, Ludwig. *Madeline*. New York: Penguin Books, 1977 (a series).

Blue, Rose. *I Am Here, Yo Estoy Aquí*. New York: Franklin Watts, 1971.

Brenner, Barbara. *The Five Pennies*. New York: Alfred A. Knopf, 1963.

Cannon, Calvin, and Wickens, Elaine. *Kirt's New House*. New York: Coward, McCann & Geoghegan, 1972.

Carrick, Carol and Donald. *The Dirt Road*. New York: Macmillan Publishing Company, 1970.

Charlip, Remy. *Where Is Everybody?* Reading, Mass.: Addison-Wesley Publishing Company, 1957.

Cook, Bernadine. *Looking for Susie*. Reading, Mass.: Addison-Wesley Publishing Company, 1959.*

Ets, Marie Hall. *Just Me*. New York: Viking Press, 1965.*

Fisher, Aileen. *My Mother and I*. New York: Thomas Y. Crowell Company, 1967.

Francoise. *The Things I Like*. New York: Charles Scribner's Sons, 1960.

Fraser, Kathleen. *Adam's World: San Francisco*. Chicago, Ill.: Albert Whitman & Company, 1971.

Kay, Helen. *Apron on, Apron off*. New York: Scholastic Book Services, 1972.

Miller, Arthur. *Jane's Blanket*. New York: Viking Press, 1972.

Oppenheim, Joanne. *On the Other Side of the River*. New York: Franklin Watts, 1972.

Parish, Peggy. *Amelia Bedelia*. New York: Harper & Row, 1963 (a series).

Schlein, Miriam. *The Way Mothers Are*. Chicago, Ill.: Albert Whitman & Company, 1963 (a "people" story with animal pictures).

Singer, Susan. *Kenny's Monkey*. New York: Scholastic Book Services, 1969.

Slobodkina, Esphyr. *Caps for Sale*. Reading, Mass.: Addison-Wesley Publishing Company, 1947.*

Concept Books

Allen, Robert. *Numbers*. New York: Platt & Munk, 1968.*

Cerf, Bennett. *Bennett Cerf's Book of Riddles*. New York: Random House, 1960.

Chaffin, Lillie D. *Bear Weather*. New York: Macmillan Publishing Company, 1969.

Ernst, Kathryn F. *Danny and His Thumb*. Englewood Cliffs, N.J.: Prentice-Hall, 1975.

Hoban, Tana. *Big Ones, Little Ones*. New York: Greenwillow Books, 1976.

———. *Circles, Triangles, Squares*. New York: Macmillan Publishing Company, 1974.

———. *Count and See*. New York: Macmillan Publishing Company, 1972.

———. *Push, Pull, Empty, Full: A Book of Opposites*. New York: Macmillan Publishing Company, 1972.

Ipcar, Dahlov. *The Song of the Day Birds and the Night Birds*. Garden City, N.Y.: Doubleday & Company, Inc., 1967.

Mizumura, Kazue. *If I Built a Village*. New York: Thomas Y. Crowell Company, 1971.

Tudor, Tasha. *Around the Year*. New York: Henry Z. Walck, 1957.

Easy Reading Books

Bonsall, Crosby N. *The Case of the Hungry Stranger*. New York: Harper
& Row, 1963.
Eastman, Phillip D. *Go Dog Go*. New York: Random House, 1961.
——. *Are You My Mother?* New York: Random House, 1967.
Hillert, Margaret. *Cinderella at the Ball*. Chicago, Ill.: Follett Publishing
Company, 1970.
——. *Funny Baby*. Chicago, Ill.: Follett Publishing Company, 1963.
——. *Magic Beans*. Chicago, Ill.: Follett Publishing Company, 1963.
——. *Three Bears*. Chicago, Ill.: Follett Publishing Company, 1963.
Hoff, Syd. *The Horse in Harry's Room*. New York: Harper & Row,
1970.
——. *Thunderhoof*. New York: Harper & Row, 1970.
——. *When Will It Snow?* New York: Harper & Row, 1971.
Holland, Marion. *A Big Ball of String*. New York: Random House, 1958.